Imagined country

The myths and symbols of spaces reveal how society regards its environment. *Imagined Country* attempts to describe the relationship between society and the physical world through representation. As cultural perception shifts, altered by location and time, so its representations of the physical environment change. Representation, the artistic re-creation of the physical world, reflects interpretation. Analysis of such representation can disclose not only the reasons but also the understanding behind the myths and symbols of the natural world.

John Rennie Short describes the varying images of wilderness, countryside and city as they are expressed in cultural forms. His analysis focuses on American westerns, English novels and Australian landscape painting. The choice of media may reflect national ideology as may the specific representation itself. However, the book's aim is not to compare countries but to explore a physical and metaphorical geography in search of motifs, of archetypes of land and man.

John Rennie Short is Professor of Geography at Syracuse University, New York, and was formerly a Lecturer in Geography at the University of Reading. He has published a number of articles on social and political geography.

Imagined country

Environment, culture and society

John Rennie Short

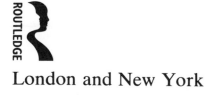

London and New York

First published 1991 by Routledge
11 New Fetter Lane, London EC4P 4EE

Simultaneously published in the USA and Canada
by Routledge
a division of Routledge, Chapman and Hall, Inc.
29 West 35th Street, New York, NY 10001

© 1991 John Rennie Short

Typeset by J&L Composition Ltd, Filey, North Yorkshire
Printed in Great Britain by
Biddles Ltd, Guildford and King's Lynn

British Library Cataloguing in Publication Data
Short, John Rennie
   Imagined country: society, culture and environment.
   1. Environment. Related to culture
   I. Title
   304.2

   ISBN 0–415–03854–5
   ISBN 0–415–05830–9 pbk

Library of Congress Cataloging-in-Publication Data
Short, John Rennie, 1951–
   Imagined country: environment, culture, and society / John Rennie
   Short.
      p.   cm.
   Includes bibliographical references and index.
   ISBN 0–415–03854–5. — ISBN 0–415–05830–9 (pbk.)
   1. Landscape assessment—Great Britain. 2. Landscape assessment—
United States. 3. Landscape assessment— Australia. 4. Western
films. 5. Landscape painting, Australian. 6. Landscape in
literature. I. Title.
GF90.S48   1991
304.2′3—dc20   90–19200
                                                        CIP

For Aunt Nana
With much love and many thanks.

Contents

Figures and tables

FIGURES

TABLES

Acknowledgements

I have benefited from the generosity and help of a number of individuals and institutions. In London, staff at the British Library and British Film Institute were most helpful.

In 1985 I was awarded a British Academy Fellowship to the Huntingdon Library in San Marino, California. The opportunity enabled me to spend three happy months in one of the great libraries of the world. The staff and other Fellows provided a stimulating and gracious environment.

Between 1985 and 1987 I was a visiting Senior Research Fellow in the Research School of Social Sciences at the Australian National University. I was given every opportunity to pursue my research. In Canberra, people at the National Library, National Film Archives and National Gallery met my requests with efficiency and politeness.

The typing of the manuscript was undertaken by Chris Holland. It was retyped by Mandy Jeffries. Both deserve a very special thank you.

This book has been immeasurably improved by my publisher. In particular I wish to thank Tristan Palmer for having faith in the enterprise, Emma Waghorn for great editorial work, Ros Ramage who did an excellent job of copy-editing, and Ann Hall for producing such a fine index.

I have been thinking about this book, on and off, for ten years and writing it, on and off, for six years. During all this time I have been very fortunate. Many people have helped and encouraged me. The book means many things to me but, above all else, it is a way of saying thanks.

She tried to visualize the interior, to which her presence might have lent reality, but which in her continued absence must remain an imagined country, a tangle of indeterminate scrub burning with the tongues of golden teasel.

Patrick White (1976) A Fringe of Leaves

Introduction

Let me begin with a clear recognition of my debts. There are two very important ones. The first began one Friday night in November 1970, at Marischal College, Aberdeen University, when I listened to a lecture by Professor William Kirk. He was a round, plump-faced man. He had come from Belfast to speak to our Geographical Society. He spoke with wit and intelligence and I was impressed. Later that year I read some of his work. His most interesting ideas, for me, were first raised in a 1951 paper entitled 'Historical Geography and the concept of the Behavioural Environment'. This was published in the Silver Jubilee volume of the *Indian Geographical Journal* and did not reach a huge audience. A revised version was published in 1963 under the title 'Problems of Geography' (Kirk 1963). This was the version which I read in 1970. It left a deep impression on me.

Kirk maintained there were two types of environment: the *phenomenal environment*, the one of empirical facts, and the *behavioural environment*, the environment as perceived. Take a simple example. The city exists in total, a phenomenal environment. But as individuals we know only parts of it, selected areas and known routes. Our behavioural environment of the city is much smaller, more circumscribed than the phenomenal environment of the city. We all have our own unique behavioural environments, made up of personal experience, but what interested me was the notion of shared behavioural environments. What do we mean, for example, when we use the term 'city'?

The second debt is my understanding of the work of Raymond Williams. My first acquaintance was through his book, *The Country and The City*, first published in 1973. I found it a fascinating historical account of the way in which the city and country were treated in English literature. This was literary criticism, sharp and socially focused, aware of the power relations in texts and the textual relations of power. Williams introduced me to a critical analysis which was sensitive to the social relations embodied in cultural expression.

From Kirk I took the notion of an environment as a social construct, from Williams the idea that this construct bears the marks of power and contestation. Kirk gave me a subject, Williams provided an angle of vision.

Kirk's behavioural environment is too big a concept to work with; we need to divide it up. A division can be made with reference to scale. At the coarser-grained end, there are the elements of Genesis: light and dark, heaven and earth, seas, plants, stars, creatures of air, sea and land, and other people. At the finer-grained end, there is the world of our daily interaction, the more personal spaces of dwelling, streets and neighbourhoods. I intend to write two other volumes covering these ends of the scale but in this book I shall be concerned with the middle range and, in particular, with the concepts of wilderness, countryside and city; meso-scale ideas which cover a continuum from the 'natural' to built environments, a progression which mirrors the long-term human occupancy of this planet. These three concepts constitute an ensemble, they reference one another; definitions of wilderness relate to the creation of the countryside, attitudes to wilderness implicitly express attitudes to city growth and rustic values have meaning only in comparison with those of the city. Each of the three terms resonates with meaning about the other two, each one helps to define the others. They have meaning only in relation to each other. To distinguish wilderness from countryside and the countryside from the city is to do more than classify different environments; it is to apportion social significance and political meaning.

There are things, there are words for things, and there are ideas-behind-words-for-things. I am concerned with the ideas behind the words for wilderness, countryside and city. To be more precise, I am interested in myths, ideologies and texts.

I shall use the term *myth* to refer to an intellectual construction which embodies beliefs, values and information, and which can influence events, behaviour and perception. Myths are (re)-presentations of reality which resonate across space and over time, which are widely used and reproduced, which are broad enough to encompass diverse experiences yet deep enough to anchor these experiences in a continuous medium of meaning. The term 'myth' does not imply falsehood to be contrasted with reality. An environmental myth can contain both fact and fancy. The important question is not 'is it true?' but 'whose truth is it?'

In Part I I shall examine the environmental myths associated with wilderness, countryside and city. I will focus on archetypal attitudes, those broad positive and negative views of wilderness, country and city which provide the template for more subtle variations.

To handle the specificity of environmental myths which are used in particular contexts, I will use the term *national environmental ideology*; these are myths mobilised in the course of state formation and nation-building. Societies occupy space as well as time, an occupancy which provides a rich source for the production of national legends and social metaphors. Ideologies, as used here, refer to myths of wilderness, countryside and city which are used in the creation of a national identity. National environmental ideologies are myths which reference particular territories and specific societies.

In Part II I shall examine aspects of the national environmental ideologies of the UK, the USA, and Australia. My aim is not to compare and contrast. The exposition is not repeated three times with the same checklist of themes. Rather, the three separate examples give an opportunity to widen the discussion. Thus, more attention is paid to the countryside in the chapter on the UK while there is a longer treatment of the concept of frontier in the USA chapter. This uneven treatment enables the richness of environmental ideologies to be noted.

Part III examines how myths are portrayed in particular ideologies in specific *texts*. Texts may be language, poems, newspapers, plays, paintings, advertising slogans, songs and proverbs. Environmental ideas are widely used in texts. The Russian countryside in Tolstoy's novels, wilderness in the classic western movies and the bleak city scenes of Edward Hopper are just some examples which spring to mind. The relationships can also be more direct, as in the use of the term 'country' and its association with 'freshness' and 'natural' in the marketing of some food products. Environmental terms are also used in the language of everyday social interaction. To call someone a peasant, to dismiss another as a suburban intellectual or to accuse someone else of having a small town mentality is to draw upon a deep reservoir of environmental abuse.

I will consider the environmental ideologies and myths embodied in three 'texts': 'English' novels, the cinema of the US 'western', and Australian landscape painting. My aim is to show how these texts reference general myths and particular ideologies.

Myths, ideologies and texts are not separate sets of ideas but different ways in which ideas are used. Myths are stories which are widely shared. Ideologies have a more limited production and a more selective quality. They record the experiences of some groups and ignore others. Texts are produced for specific audiences yet they make general reference to myths and particular reference to ideologies. The analytical distinction should not hide the connectivity between the three. Creators of texts draw upon ideologies and myths, ideologies use selected texts and myths are generalised ideologies.

There is a threefold structure to the book. Part I examines the myths of wilderness, countryside and city. Part II discusses how these myths are articulated in the national environmental ideologies of the UK, the USA, and Australia. Part III considers some of the environmental themes employed in the texts of English literature, US cinema, and Australian landscape painting. The book can be read in a number of ways. Part I is best read first, as a whole. Those interested in considering the role of wilderness in each of the three countries may take a cut through the first part of each of the chapters in Part II. Those interested in one country can read the relevant chapters of Parts II and III. Those interested in the USA, for example, may want to read Chapter 8 immediately after reading Chapter 5. The text is a series of overlapping themes, parallel arguments and circular narratives. The story is more a mosaic than a straight line.

My aim is simple, to identify and decode the major sets of ideas about the wilderness, country and city in the belief that there is nothing so social as our ideas about the physical environment.

Part I
Myths

Introduction

A myth is, of course, not a fairy story. It is the presentation of facts belonging to one category in the idioms appropriate to another. To explode a myth is accordingly not to deny the facts but to re-allocate them.

Gilbert Ryle (1949) *The Concept of Mind*

By 'myth' I do not mean an idea that is simply false, but rather one that so effectively embodies men's values that it profoundly influences their way of perceiving reality and hence their behaviour. In this sense myths may have varying degrees of fiction or reality.

Richard Hofstadter (1955) *The Age of Reform*

Myths destroy time. They are messages passed through the ages and over the generations, kept fresh by use and reuse. In this section of the book I shall deal with the mythic qualities of wilderness, countryside and city. These are qualities which, although expressed in particular historical configurations, echo down through the centuries. They are of fundamental importance in how all societies 'see' their physical environments. I will focus on the recurring ideas, through the use of oppositional archetypes. The term 'archetype' comes from Greek and originally meant the original patterns from which subsequent copies were made. In the next three chapters I will identify the pro- and anti-archetypes of wilderness, countryside and city.

1 Wilderness

Different minds incline to different objects, one pursues,
The vast alone, the wonderful, the wild,
Another sighs for harmony, and grace
And gentlest beauty.
                    Mark Akenside (1744) *The Pleasures of Imagination*

In hunting and gathering societies there was and is no distinction between wilderness and the rest of the environment. Since there is little or no cultivation or domestication of animals all land is uncultivated, all animals are wild. There is no central dichotomy between cultivated and wilderness. In 1975 the cultural historian Rodney Nash visited South East Asia:

> I had the opportunity to talk, through an interpreter, with a man who hunted and gathered in the jungles of Malaysia. I tried without success to discuss wilderness. When I asked for an equivalent word I heard things like 'green places', 'outdoors', or 'nature'. Finally, in desperation, I asked the interpreter to ask the hunter how he said 'I am lost in the jungle'. An exchange occurred at the conclusion of which the interpreter turned to me and said with a smile that the man had indicated he did not get lost in the jungle. The question made as little sense to him as would asking an American city dweller how he said 'I am lost in my apartment'. Lacking a concept of controlled and uncontrolled nature, the Malaysian had no conception of wilderness.'
>
> (Nash 1982: xiv)

Wilderness is a social definition with origins in the agricultural revolution almost 10,000 years ago. The term 'wilderness' emerges then because it is only with settled agriculture that a distinction is made between cultivated and uncultivated land, savage and settled, domesticated and wild animals. In Hebrew, one definition of wilderness is *unsown land*, in ancient Greek it meant *not cultivated* and, in Latin, *barren waste*. In English, the expression may come from the old English term, *wildeoren*, referring to wild beasts.

Wilderness is a word whose first usage marks the transition from a hunting-gathering economy to an agricultural society. We can identify two archetypal responses to wilderness, which I shall refer to as classical and romantic.

The classical perspective sees most significance in human action and human society. The creation of livable places and usable spaces is a mark of civilization. Human use confers meaning on space. Outside of society, wilderness is something to be feared, an area of waste and desolation. It is human society which gives meaning and social significance to the world. For the romantics, in contrast, untouched spaces have the greatest significance; they have a purity which human contact tends to sully and degrade. Wilderness for the romantics is a place to be revered, a place of deep spiritual significance and a symbol of an earthly paradise.

There is an associated difference in attitudes to time. The classical stance tends to be avowedly progressive. It sees human action in a broad, upward, improving trajectory, a movement from shadow to light, from the darkness of the past to the light of the present, sometimes with a utopian belief in the bright glow of the future. The transition from hunting-gathering to settled agriculture is a success story, part of the emancipatory movement of human society. The romantics are more pessimistic. They tend to have a regressive view of human history. Life in the present is a shadow of the spiritually richer and deeper life of the past. It is a view marked by regret and nostalgia, a story of the decline from a golden age. For the classicists, the conquest of wilderness is a signal of human achievement, a victory over the dark forces and a measure of social progress. For the romantics, it is a measure of the fall from grace. While the classicists fear the wilderness and want to subdue it, the romantics revere it and want to preserve it. These attitudes are not separate entities. Even the words have the same origins; at root, both *fear* and *revere* mean 'to stand in awe'.

My basic premise is that in the Western world the classical position predominated until the last two hundred years when the romantic conception began to gain more ground. It is not a sharp divide, more an uneven progression with outliers on either side of the division.

A PLACE TO FEAR

Fear of the wilderness was one of the strongest elements in European attitudes to wilderness up to the nineteenth century, with the eighteenth century marking a period of transition. It is clearly expressed with regard to those places not yet brought under the plough. The eighth-century epic *Beowulf* is full of references to evil spirits lying beyond the glare of the camp fire: 'That grim spirit was called Grendel, the renowned traverser of the marches, who held the moors, the fen and fortress' (quoted in Burchfield 1985: 59).

The large tracts of forest were seen as wilderness (see Figure 1.1). The term 'wilderness' may also have its root in *weald* or *waeld*, the old English word for forest. The traditional agrarian view saw forests as the home of

Figure 1.1 Fear of the wilderness is expressed in this painting, *A Hunt in the Forest*, by Paolo Uccello (c. 1465). In the Middle Ages, the forests of Europe were places of wild beasts.

evil spirits. European folklore is populated with demons and dangers who dwell in the forest: that was where little Red Riding Hood met the wolf. Forest dwellers were seen by urban and agrarian communities as uncivilized people of the wilderness. The word 'savage' literally means 'pertaining to the woods', coming as it does from the Latin *silva*, meaning 'wood'. This view held sway up to the early modern period:

> 'When Elizabethans spoke of wilderness they meant, not a barren waste, but a dense, uncultivated wood, like Shakespeare's Forest of Arden, 'a desert inaccessible under the shade of melancholy boughs'. A mid-seventeenth century poetical dictionary suggests as appropriate epithets for a forest: 'dreadful', 'gloomy', 'wild', 'desert', 'uncouth', 'melancholy', 'unpeopled' and 'beast-haunted'.
>
> (Thomas 1983: 194)

This environmental attitude was taken across the Atlantic. Many settlers in New England described the forest as 'howling', 'dismal', 'terrible'.

A similar tale can be told of mountains. As the most inaccessible parts of the landscape, mountains often resisted attempts at agrarian subjugation. In folklore and literary traditions, mountains, like forests, became populated with demons and gods. For the ancient Greeks it was from Mount Olympus that Zeus and his unruly clan affected life on earth. In the Middle Ages in Europe this environmental belief was filtered through Christian theology to see mountains as places of witchcraft. It is no accident that the most intense European witch hunts centred on the mountain regions of the Alps, the Jura, the Vosges and the Pyrenees. The witchcraft phase passed but the distaste for mountains lived on throughout the sixteenth and seventeenth centuries, when mountains were regularly referred to as distortions on the surface of the earth.

Fear of the wilderness has three elements. First, it is found in most societies where a sky-centred religion has replaced an earth-bound animism. Yi Fu Tuan (1979) refers to traditional hunting-gathering communities as fearless societies in relation to their environmental attitudes. When gods and spirits are in the earth and on the bough and all around, wilderness as a place to fear cannot exist. But when there is tamed and untamed nature and when gods are shifted from the earth to the sky, as in the replacement of animist religion by Christianity, then uncultivated places become the wilderness beyond human control, a place to fear. The clearest literary image is Daniel Defoe's *Robinson Crusoe*. First published in 1719, this book portrays the sailor's initial fear at being left on a *desert* island. Reflecting a strong current of contemporary opinion, Defoe expresses Crusoe's revulsion, not delight, at being marooned in a lonely, wild spot.

Second, the fear of the wilderness involved and reflected a fear of those living in the 'wilderness'. By definition they were not part of the formal social order. The wilderness was the residence of marginalized elements in society. The myth of Robin Hood and his merry (oppositional) band in Sherwood Forest is one of the most popular tales which romanticize the forest dwellers. But more often forest dwellers and hill peoples were seen as a threat to the people of the towns, villages and isolated farms. The Englishman John Smith could describe New England in the seventeenth century as 'a hideous and desolate wilderness, full of wild beasts and wild men'.

Third, there was a fear of the effects of the wilderness on the individuals exposed to its influence. As a symbol of the wild, the untamed, the wilderness became a symbolic representation of the id. Contact with the wilderness was contact with the wild unconscious. The term 'bewildered' captures this particular effect. Since the agrarian revolution, wilderness has been seen as a dark elemental force, an atavistic element, the Jungian shadow of the individual. This view has been presented in folklore, art and literature. John Bunyan began his *Pilgrim's Progress* (1678) with the phrase: 'As I walked through the wilderness of the world'. It is indicative of a person at a loss, temporarily bewildered, lacking direction. Wilderness was a symbol of spiritual despair. The wilderness as uncivilizing experience persists as a motif in contemporary culture, from William Golding's *Lord of the Flies* (1954) to the movie *Deliverance* (1972). In *Lord of the Flies*, a group of English schoolboys are marooned on a desert island. Dark elemental forces quickly emerge from beneath the cloak of public school respectability. In the movie *Deliverance*, three men from the city make a canoe trip down a river in the remoter parts of Appalachia. Two of them have a fight with 'mountain' men and one of them is subsequently killed. Throughout the movie the brooding presence of the river and forests suggests a wilder environment, and the climax shows a return to savagery. The end of the voyage is a return to civilization. Each of these forms shares an influential belief that civilization is a thin veneer, quickly burned off by contact with the wilderness to reveal the dark underside of the human condition. Wilderness becomes an environmental metaphor for the dark side of the psyche.

There were good, solid reasons for the early fear of wilderness. Huddled around the camp fires, frontier settlements could hear the call of the wild beasts, the sound of the wind in the trees or the thunder storm circling around the mountain tops. These were not reassuring noises to an agrarian population with limited knowledge of nature and even more limited ability to control it. The fear of the wilderness was a rational response. Today we are still frightened of the wilderness. In part it may be a reasonable response to the still obvious dangers of truly wild places. It may also be an element of our collective unconscious; there is a part of us still huddling together round camp fires, keeping our spirits up in the face of the great blackness beyond. It may also be of symbolic importance. The wilderness represents the uncivilized, the untamed. It represents the underside of the individual soul and the collective unconscious.

A PLACE TO REVERE

For the romantics, the wilderness is to be revered, a sacred space to be contrasted with the profanity of human contact. Where the classicists see progress in the defeat and control of the wilderness, the romantics see regression from a golden age. The romantic vision has strengthened because wilderness, as its size lessens, has become a symbol of lost innocence, a source of nostalgia for a golden age and a metaphor for the fall from grace.

For the romantics, contact with the wilderness brought about not a bewilderment but a renewed contact with deeper psychological truths and a more pronounced spiritual awareness. Contact with the untamed meant a rejection of imposed social values and a return to the moral authority of a self closer to god. In the wilderness lay individual redemption and universal truths.

The love of the wilderness implied a very different attitude to the inhabitants. In comparison to the 'savages' of the classicists the romantics saw the noble savage as being closer to a purer, simpler way of life. The life of the primitive other became a poignant contrast with the spiritual impoverishment and crude materialism of the contemporary. Where the classicists saw men no different from beasts, the romantics perceived the people of the golden age and a vision of life before the fall.

With the rise of agriculture, wilderness became an ambiguous concept. On the one hand, its defeat was a marker of human progress. On the other hand, it became a symbol of an earthly paradise, the place of before the fall where people lived in close harmony and deep sympathy with nature. Uncultivated land was something to be revered, part of God's work untouched by human intervention. In the rest of this chapter I shall consider how major discourses in the western traditions contain references to these opposing views; not as separate discrete entities but combined in the tension of shifting ambiguity.

CREATING THE GARDEN

The wilderness is an important metaphor in the Judaeo-Christian traditions. In the land of its birth, a fertile region was hemmed in by the deserts of the Negev and the Sinai in the south and by the desert of the Judaea in the east (see Figures 1.2 and 1.3). The wilderness became symbolic. In the Bible, one of the most sustained narratives of an emerging agricultural community, the role of the wilderness oscillates between two poles. At one extreme it is a place of God's creation, a source of spiritual insight; at the other, a place whose transformation by human actions allows the possibility of redemption. Wilderness is sacred space, God's work to be contrasted with human sin, but human transformation of the wilderness is

Figure 1.2 The desert of Judaea: attitudes to the desert have, through the Bible, influenced western thought

Figure 1.3 Olive tree groves in Galilee: the wilderness of the desert has always been contrasted with the order of settled agriculture

God-guided. There is an ambiguity reflecting the deeper dualism of the fall, yet the possibility of redemption. Wilderness is an environment central to this tension.

Recall the story of Adam and Eve, cast out from the Garden of Eden for eating from the tree of knowledge of good and evil. Thereafter they had to till the ground. In one sense this can be read as deep regret and a sense of loss at the movement from hunting-gathering to a settled agriculture. This particular reading is reinforced when we remember that Adam and Eve had two sons, Abel and Cain. Abel was a shepherd, Cain a tiller of the ground. Cain slew Abel and went on to found the first cities.

George H. Williams, in his analysis of the role of wilderness in the Christian tradition, came to this conclusion:

> We shall find in the positive sense that the wilderness or desert will be interpreted variously as a place of protection, a place of contemplative retreat, again as one's inner nature or ground of being, and at length as the ground itself of the divine being. ... In its negative sense the wilderness will be interpreted as the world of the unredeemed, as the wasteland, and as the realm or phase of punitive or purgative preparation for salvation.

(Williams 1962: 4–5)

These positive and negative attitudes resonate through the Christian world and they have become closely intertwined with the belief systems guiding people–environment relationships. One strand has been the legitimacy of man's domination over nature. Genesis 1.28 captures the theme:

> and God said unto them, Be fruitful, and multiply, and replenish the earth, and subdue it: and have dominion over the fish of the sea, and over the birds of the air, and over every living thing that moves upon the earth.

The sentiment is echoed throughout the Bible and surfaces in Psalms 8.6:

> Thou hast given him dominion over the works of thy hand, thou hast put all things under his feet.

Its most enduring metaphor was the creation of a garden from the wilderness. The garden became the image of human achievement and ethical endeavour and subduing the wilderness contained the possibility of moral redemption. The creation of the garden on earth incorporated spiritual salvation, practical activity and social involvement. This theology was used as a justification for the clearing of the wood, the draining of the fen and the claiming of the heath. It was particularly marked in medieval Europe because the Church was no mere ideological mouthpiece; it was a major landowner with important agrarian interests.

The theology of European Christianity was taken across the ocean by Protestant sects. For the Puritan settlers of the north-eastern seaboard of North America, transforming the wilderness was a sacred act of redemption as well as a secular act of survival. For subsequent settlers, the religious significance of the subjugation of the wilderness has diminished but not vanished. The notion of an elect group of people doing God's work in a 'new' land has a deep hold in the intellectual and political life of the USA. Waves of settlers involved in more profane acts of agrarian settlement and urban expansion could still see the hand and light of God in their work. In few other countries of the world has the possibility of the creation of the garden been so widely accepted. The early Puritan legacy lives on in the belief of a chosen people doing God's work.

Biblical quotes may be seen on the desk of the late David Ben-Gurion. The father of modern Israel lived in a small house in a kibbutz in the Negev desert. On his desk he had quotes from Isaiah:

> I will plant in the wilderness the cedar, the shittah tree, and the myrtle, and the oil tree; I will set in the desert the fir tree, and the pine, and the box tree together (41.19).
>
> For the Lord shall comfort Zion: he will comfort all her waste places; and he will make her wilderness like Eden, and her desert like the garden of the Lord (51.3).

These were no idle words. As a Zionist politician, Ben-Gurion sought to establish a Jewish homeland, to transform the 'wilderness' into cultivation and to make the desert bloom. Outside of his house there is proof positive of these sentiments.

The importance of wilderness as a place to subdue in the Judaeo-Christian rhetoric has led Lynn White, Jr to argue that this theology

> established a dualism of man and nature and insisted that it is God's will that man exploit nature for his proper ends ... made it possible to exploit nature in a mood of indifference to the feelings of natural objects.

> (White, Jr 1967: 1205)

I think it may overstate the case to assume that religious doctrine has been a major and consistent cause of environmental damage. We cannot make too simple a connection between Christian theology and social action. There is plenty of evidence of sound conservation principles being adopted by the Church fathers. For example, in the fifteenth and sixteenth centuries, every Bishop of Bamberg in Germany, on taking office, had to swear to protect the forests under his control. There is also the other Christian message, embodied in the life and work of St Francis (1182–1286), which proposes an alternative conception of wilderness as garden under human stewardship and of redemption lying in our conservation of the natural world. The quote from Psalms 8.6 can be read as a plea for sound stewardship over nature. However, the alternative Christian tradition has generally been one of retreat, of withdrawal and contemplation. It reached its peak in the Desert fathers of the fourth and fifth centuries who saw the zenith of religious life as one of contemplation in the desert. It surfaced again in the hermitic tradition of the Middle Ages. (The term 'hermit' is of Greek origin, meaning 'one who dwells in the desert'). A famous example in England was Julian of Norwich. Julian was an anchorite. She withdrew from the world not by going off to the wilderness but by restricting herself until death to a cell beside the church of St Julian and St Edward. She is famous because, on 8 May 1373, she had what she and others regarded as divine revelations. She wrote of her experience and the *Revelations of Divine Love* has continued to exercise a powerful influence. But, like other mystics, her message is one of withdrawal and contemplation. This rarely helps with the function of living with other people. Sadly, in terms of environmental implications, the withdrawers, those who revered the wilderness, had much less influence than the subduers of wilderness.

Prior to 1500, the garden from wilderness theme was an understandable theology for agrarian populations with only the merest footholds on the earth; it was part hope and part whistling in the dark. The tragedy is that human ingenuity outgrew the belief systems. Human societies now have the capacity to damage the environment irrevocably and yet some still subscribe to the ideology more appropriate to an earlier epoch.

The dominant Judaeo-Christian theme has been the possibility of salvation through making the garden from the wilderness. This has held sway up until the twentieth century. However, with the onset of environmental issues such as pollution and destruction of the ozone layer, and the consequent perceived threat to the natural world, there has been a resuscitation of an alternative reading of the Bible which sees the wilderness as a place of spiritual regeneration. Christian texts have been re-examined for evidence of ecological awareness and St Francis may be seen as one of the first Christian greens. The Judaeo-Christian theology has enough ambiguity to make it susceptible to alternative readings.

THE AESTHETIC IMPULSE

Art is the pursuit of the beautiful. Aesthetic issues revolve around the twin questions of what are worthy subjects of art and what constitutes the beautiful. The depiction of wilderness has been an important part of the answers to these questions. Both Latin and Greek definitions of wilderness refer to desolation, desert, abandonment, solitary lonely places. Wilderness as deserted empty space held little attraction for classicists. For Aristotle, only men in action was a fitting subject for poetry. The Greeks loved nature and built temples on the mountains, in groves and in the hills. The subject of art, however, was the human condition, the human form and the body politic. This is the basis of the aesthetic impulse in the classicist tradition which has echoed down the centuries. It is one where the wilderness had only a marginal position. The poetry of Petrarch (1304–74) is seen by many as an early Renaissance indication of the romantic love of nature. In April 1335, Petrarch climbed Mount Ventoux in what was subsequently seen as the first recorded mountain climb taken for aesthetic reasons. But even here the classical influence resurfaced. 'As I descended', he later wrote, 'I gazed back, and the lofty summit of the mountain seemed to me scarcely a cubit high, compared with the sublime dignity of man' (quoted in Nicholson 1959: 50).

Although the divide is not sharp and clear cut, we can make a distinction in the dominant aesthetic impulse in Europe between the classical period up to the seventeenth century and the modern period, with the late-seventeenth and eighteenth centuries acting as a transition period. The shift is evident in various artistic realms. In 1657, the English poet Andrew Marvell (1621–78) wrote of mountains as ill-designed excrescences that deform the earth and frighten heaven. This was just one example of the profound belief, up to the eighteenth century, that the earth's surface was made flat by God, and it was the great flood that caused the deformities of smooth design. According to the very influential *Sacred Theory of The Earth*, written by Thomas Burnett in 1681, mountains were not part of God's creation but a product of man's sinfulness.

The classical view of mountains continued to find its literary standard terms even through much of the eighteenth century. In 1773 that great classicist Samuel Johnson, accompanied by his acolyte Boswell, ventured on the trip that he later described in *A Journey to the Western Isles of Scotland* (1775). For him the mountains were a

> wide extent of hopeless sterility. The appearance is that of matter, incapable of form or usefulness, dismissed by nature from her care and disinherited of her favours, left in its original elemental state, or quickened only with the sullen power of useless vegetation.

Forty-five years later, in 1818, another English literary figure, the poet P.B. Shelley, in *Prometheus Unbound* described a mountain as

> Fit throne for such a Power, magnificent
> How glorious art thou.

Marjorie Hope Nicholson, in her book *Mountain Gloom and Mountain Glory* (1959), charts in detail this shift in poetic response to the mountains. Up to the eighteenth century, mountains were, in Marvell's words, hook-shouldered excrescences which deformed the earth, a physical reminder of sin and ugliness. By the early nineteenth century, the romantic poets had changed the angle of vision. For Byron, Wordsworth and Shelley, mountains were a symbol of a divine force, a thing of beauty and a point of contact with the infinite. For the romantics, sublime dignity lay in people's contact with and appreciation of the wilderness.

The change can also be seen in paintings. Landscape appears in the canvasses of the Renaissance but always in association with human figures or mythical beings. Even the landscapes of wilderness are given meaning and shape and form with reference to people. The many paintings of St Jerome in the wilderness, for example, show the saint's cave contrasted with the image of a town as if the wilderness on its own is not a fitting subject for a painting; to paint only the wilderness would be to paint a void. By the nineteenth century, scenes of mountain and forest became a major focus of painting. For Caspar David Friedrich in Europe, Thomas Cole in America and Eugen von Guérard in Australia, the pictorial representation of wilderness became a way of presenting the aesthetics of the infinite (see Figure 1.4).

The change also had an effect on the landscape itself (see Chapter 4). In terms of design, the landscape gardens of the seventeenth century were tightly controlled in regular lines, enclosed by walls radiating out in straight-line avenues. By the early to mid-eighteenth century, gardens in England were being created in which the straight was replaced by the irregular, vegetation was allowed to leap over the walls and, in place of avenues, circular paths wound their way through the trees.

Behind all these changes lay a change in attitude not only to wilderness but also to God and the individual. God was no longer seen as a deity who had created the world and then abandoned it to sinfulness. The romantics had a pantheistic vision, a belief that God was everywhere. It was an ability

Figure 1.4 Wilderness as a place to revere is highlighted in this painting, *Mt Kosciusko*, Australia (c. 1864), Eugen von Guérard. Notice how the small figure is gazing in awe and wonder at the natural vista. (Australian National Gallery, Canberra)

To see a World in a Grain of Sand,
And a Heaven in a Wild Flower,
Hold Infinity in the Palm of your hand,
And Eternity in an hour.
(William Blake (1803) *Auguries of Innocence*)

Aesthetic sensitivity was redefined as an ability to appreciate the divine presence of God in nature. It also involved a redefinition of the individual. The self was no longer only a social aggregate but an individual capable of appreciating beauty in a personal experience. Nature provided both a confirmation and an affirmation of individuality.

SCIENCE AND THE WILDERNESS

Attitudes to wilderness, and nature in general, were also part of the development of a culture of science. The period 1500–1700 is generally seen as the period of transition. One popular model sees the scientific method, based on reason and logic, challenging a world based on religious dogma and faith. But there was no such sharp distinction between science and religion. For every Galileo challenging the religious hierarchy there was a Newton who combined scientific rigour with mystical belief. In Newton's *Principia Mathematica* (1687), Old Testament figures keep wandering onto the pages and the words of the prophets intermingle with the codification of calculus. The experience of the astronomer Kepler is also revealing. While trying to establish a sun-centred planetary system between 1615 and 1621, he also had to defend his mother against the charge of witchcraft and fight to save her from being burnt alive. The scientific revolution carried the birthmarks of the old society.

The scientific work of Galileo, Bacon, Descartes, and Newton gave codification to the way in which the world was perceived. The image of the organic unity of Mother Nature was replaced by the notion of the world as a machine with dimensions susceptible to measurement and control. According to Galileo, '*Il libro della natura scritto in lingua mathematica*' (the book of nature is written in the language of mathematics). There was a mechanization of the world picture (Dijksterhuis 1969). Some writers have seen this change as the root cause of our ecological crisis. Carolyn Merchant (1980), for example, equates the development of the mechanized world view with the death of nature and the destruction of wilderness. It is a plausible argument but, to my mind, ultimately untenable because it reads off present crisis from the scientific revolution. It seems more appropriate to see the scientific endeavour as an enterprise subject to diverse influences and capable of changing directions. In the period 1500–1700, it was part of the development of capitalism and the extension of agricultural frontiers. But the concern with reason and measurement can also be used to defend the wilderness. The view of the world as a machine may be spiritually impoverished but it does not of itself lead to the destruction of nature. The notion of a delicate ecological balance, for example, is the language of the machine but applied to a very different purpose. Scientific work has been influential in stopping the use of DDT. Science is a social enterprise and like all human acts is just as capable of good as of evil.

WILDERNESS AND NATIONALISM

For states in the New World, nation-building has been intimately related to conquering the wilderness. Throughout America and in Australia the national histories have consisted of creating a country from the forest and the grasslands. The transformation of the wilderness has a special place in their national identity. Two basic arguments can be identified.

The classicists argue that contact with the wilderness constitutes a leave-taking from civilization, a process of collective bewilderment in which the society loses its culture. This was the predominant response of nineteenth-century Russian intellectuals to the eastern advance of Czarist Russia. For Sergei Soloviev (1820–79), the eastward advance drew off population from the settled areas, kept population low and retarded economic development. Others shared this pessimistic view that the eastward movement encouraged an aimless restlessness. The extension of the frontier was a move away from civilization and a cause of social backwardness.

The alternative position was clearly enunciated in the USA by Frederick Jackson Turner (1861–1932) for whom the westward expansion of the USA in the nineteenth century was cause for celebration (see Chapter 5). It was a move away from contact with an effete Europe. The extension of the frontier involved a battle with the elements from which emerged democracy and self-reliance. It was in contact with the wilderness that a genuinely democratic American society was formed. In the nineteenth century not all shared Turner's enthusiasm. There were Americans who shared the fears of Soloviev and worried that the frontier was brutalizing American society. As a popular belief, however, Turner's views predominated. If the eastward movement in Russia became a sign of cultural regress, the westward drive in the USA became a symbol of progress.

Attitudes never remain fixed. They are always in flux, shifting and changing. In 1865, Walt Whitman could celebrate the defeat of the wilderness in his poem *Pioneers! O pioneers!*

We primeval forests felling,
We the rivers stemming; vexing we and piercing deep the mines within,
We the surface broad surveying, we the virgin soil upheaving,
Pioneers! O pioneers!

The form and the rhythm of the poem are in sympathy. The strong trochaic beat is a marching song in line with the image of a new world army

Worrying About Our Environment Won't Help!

Wilderness everywhere is under threat. Even in Tasmania, where the Franklin River is safe, only half the wilderness has World Heritage protection. The rest, including places like the Gordon Splits, Denison River, Weld River and Lemonthyme Forest, are still threatened by hydroelectric schemes, mining and clearfelling.

And in north Queensland the Daintree tropical wilderness, like so much of the world's tropical rainforests, is at the mercy of bulldozers and chainsaws.

But with swift action, these places **can** be saved. The Wilderness Society, with the experience of Australia's hardest ever conservation campaign behind it, is now fighting for **all** Australian wilderness. It was with the spirited support of a large membership that we saved the Franklin. You can help us now to save Daintree and the rainforests of the wet tropics; the entire western Tasmania wilderness; and places like the Kimberley and Kakadu.

If you are already a member of the Wilderness Society, please stay with us. Membership subscriptions are now due. And if you're not a member, how about joining?

A membership form is on the reverse side.

Joining The Wilderness Society Will.

Figure 1.5 The wilderness as a place to protect: advertising for the Wilderness Society in Australia

conquering the wilderness and establishing a new civilization. If the nineteenth century saw the defeat of the wilderness as a necessary precondition of creating an American landscape, the dominant image of the late-twentieth century saw in wilderness protection the preservation of the truly American landscape. The change reflected a shift in what wilderness represented: it was no longer something to be defeated, but something to be preserved and saved (see Figure 1.5). This was not a world-wide phenomenon. Poorer countries, such as Brazil, were still overwhelmingly dominated by the nationalist notion of the defeat of the forest. Locating the new capital, Brasilia, in the middle of the jungle interior was a statement of hope, a concrete marker in the middle of the wilderness representing nationalist hopes and economic expectations. In the richer countries such sentiments have to compete with those who share the sentiments of Gerald Manley Hopkins:

> What would the world be, once bereft
> Of wet and wilderness? Let them be left
> O let them be left,
> Wildness and wet;
> Long live the weeds and the wilderness yet.
> *(Inversnaid*, 1881)

WILDERNESS AND THE INDIVIDUAL

With the onset of agriculture a distinction could be made between domesticated and wild, tamed and untamed. Theorists of the unconscious make a similar distinction: ego and id (Freud), ego and shadow (Jung). The wilderness became a symbol of the individual unconscious. Two models can be identified. On the one hand, there is the classical perspective which sees the negative element of the wilderness experience – the view that wilderness quite literally bewilders. The wilderness strips away social conventions and sanctions. A recurring theme in pre-romantic literature, shown in such diverse authors as Dante and Bunyan, is of wilderness as a place where people have lost their way. To be stuck in the dark forest is a metaphor for having lost one's bearings. In European folk tales, to be lost in the forest represented a loss of direction, a symbol of being untracked from the course of life. It also figures in modern literature, such as William Golding's *Lord of the Flies* (see Chapter 7), where contact with the wilderness can reveal the dark elemental forces of the human psyche.

The alternative model sees the wilderness as the opportunity for discovering hidden depths and unused talents. This is the wilderness as a place of spiritual regeneration. Stripped of its spiritual significance, the wilderness experience becomes one of individual growth and development. This is the rationale behind all those outward bound courses, wilderness holidays with their mountain climbing, forest trekking, river paddling opportunities. In the wilderness lies greater self-knowledge.

At the heart of these different attitudes is the contrasting symbolism of wilderness for the individual psyche. For the classicists, the wilderness embodied and encouraged atavistic remnants of a more savage order. For the romantics, individual salvation lay in exposing the repressed elements of our mind because there lay the authentic, the positive features of our individuality which could balance out the artificiality of our public lives.

THE PEOPLE OF THE WILDERNESS

The ancient Chinese made a distinction between 'raw' and 'cooked' peoples, according to their degree of contact with Chinese civilization. The 'raw' people lived on the other side of the frontier.

For the progressives, the 'raw' were a couple of notches down the evolutionary ladder, to be described as savages or natives. They were wild, untutored in the ways of civilized society. In 1662, Michael Wigglesworth could describe New England as

> A waste and howling wilderness,
> Where none inhabited
> But hellish fiends, and brutish men.
>   (quoted in Nash 1982: 36)

In the process of expansion from the fifteenth century onwards, the Europeans encountered societies very different from their own. Formal societies, such as the Aztecs or Incas, were delegitimized with reference to their lack of a Christian religion. Elsewhere the hunting-gathering societies were denied the status of society or the existence of culture. The philosopher John Locke could argue for the displacement of Indians in the New World because, since they did not cultivate the ground and simply gathered the fruits of the earth, they had no rights to the land. The very use of the term 'wilderness' in these cases was part of an attack on the inhabitants, their culture and their rights. To describe people as natives, Aborigines and Indians was to dissociate them from civil society and deprive them of dignity and the rights of civilized treatment. Robinson Crusoe on his desert island soon decided that 'my only way to go about an escape was if possible to get a savage into my possession'. Eventually, he acquired one and 'The next day I set him to work... and in a little time Friday was able to do all the work for me.' In Vietnam in the 1960s, areas held by the Vietcong were referred to by US military personnel as 'Indian country'.

The alternative view was of the noble savage, seeing in these 'uncivilized' communities the remnants of a golden age. This was the perspective of the romantics, who saw the advance of civilization as a decline in the quality of life. The native as noble savage has a long history. Lovejoy and Boas (1935) have shown its roots in classical Greece, where a distinction was drawn between the hard primitivism of warlike tribes and the soft primitivism of less aggressive societies. In the modern period, the most influential figure in European ideas was Jean Jacques Rousseau (1712–78), whose distaste of the idea of progress is summed up in the opening sentence of his book, *The Social Contract* (1762): 'Man is born free, and everywhere he is in chains.' In *Discourses* (1754) and *Emile* (1762), Rousseau maintained an attack on civilization and praised the notion of man close to nature, free from constraints of contemporary society and morality. Rousseau gave early intellectual sustenance to the romantic movement.

For the romantics, hunting-gathering groups became a vehicle to criticize their own societies. If Wigglesworth could describe the people of New England as brutish men, another seventeenth-century Puritan, Roger Williams, could turn the argument on its head by making an Indian say:

> We wear no cloaths, have many Gods
> And yet our sinnes are lesse:
> You are Barbarians, Pagan wild,
> Your land's the wilderness.
>   (quoted in Williams 1962: 103)

Whenever Europeans came across other societies, the competing ideas of ignoble and noble savage could always be found (see Figures 1.6 and 1.7). In 1688, William Dampier, along with the rest of the crew of the *Cygnet*, spent some time in north-west Australia. In *A New Voyage Round the World*, published in 1697, he recalled his impressions of the people:

> The Inhabitants of this country are the miserablest People in the World ... who have no Houses and skin Garments, Sheep, Poultry and Fruits of the Earth. ... they differ but little from Brutes.
>   (Dampier 1927: 453)

Almost a hundred years later, James Cook, the skipper of the *Endeavour*, sighted Australia in 1770. He sailed up the east coast of Australia and in his journal he wrote of the people:

> they may appear to some to be the most wretched people upon Earth, but in reality they are far more happier than we Europeans; being wholly unacquainted not only with the superfluous but the necessary convenience so much sought after in Europe, they are happy in not knowing the use of them. They live in a tranquility which is not disturbed by the Inequality of Condition. The Earth and sea of their own accord furnishes them with all things necessary for life, they covet not magnificent Houses, Household stuff etc. .... In short they seem'd to set no value upon any thing we gave them. .... this in my opinion argues that they think themselves provided with all the necessarys of life and that they have no superfluities.
>   (Cook 1955: 399)

From James Cook to Margaret Mead, Laurens van der Post and *Crocodile Dundee*, these comments have echoed down the years. The noble savage theme has been a counterpoint to the industrial order, the tyranny of the clock and the age of consumption with its uncertainties of continued choice and excesses of materialism. The Pacific islanders, the Australian Aborigines, the North American Indians and the Bushmen of the Kalahari

3. Sydney Parkinson: *Two of the Natives of New Holland, Advancing to Combat*, 1773

Figures 1.6 and 1.7 Contrasting views of Australian Aborigines: the noble savage (British Museum) and the ignoble savage (National Library of Australia)

have all been presented as exemplars of a more ecologically sound, spiritually richer, freer, and less alienated society than our own.

Today the dominant view is of the primitive other as noble savage. We no longer have the same belief in progress, and the untarnished confidence in our own civilization, as shown by our Victorian predecessors. The people of the wilderness are a mirror against which we hold our own values and our own society and find them hollow and wanting. The passing of the 'people' of the wilderness is now a source of regret, as if drops of innocence are being squeezed from our world.

T.R.Browne: *Hump-Back'd Maria, a Female Native well known about Sydney,* 1819

THE MODERN WILDERNESS

In 1984 a friend asked me what I was working on. When I said 'attitudes to the wilderness', she asked, 'You mean what people think of places like Brent Cross shopping centre?' She was expressing a popular view that the wilderness as negative space is found in people-made places. The negative attitudes to wilderness and the consequent terms have been transferred to the urban. In *Tropic of Capricorn* (1938), Henry Miller described New York as a 'mad stone forest'. Later, when James Baldwin in *Another*

Figure 1.8 The urban wilderness: stone-built jungles, the places of
modern nightmares (New York)

Country (1962) described New Yorkers as 'citizens of the world's most
bewildered city', he was endorsing a belief that the big cities had become
the modern wilderness (see Figure 1.8). They are concrete jungles where
the weight of numbers and the thick densities of population have created
an alienating environment where we are all strangers, all part of a lonely
crowd. The big city is now the modern equivalent of the medieval forest
populated by demons. Baldwin went on to describe New York as

the most despairingly private of cities. One was continually being jostled, yet longed, at the same time, for the sense of others, for a human touch; and if one was never – it was the general complaint – left alone in New York, one had, still, to fight very hard not to perish of loneliness. This fight, carried on in so many different ways, created the strange climate of the city.

(Baldwin 1962: 178)

The 'left alone' feeling could have come from an ancient folktale of being lost in the forest.

The ultimate man-made wilderness has become a possibility. Since 6 August 1945, when an American aircraft dropped the first atomic bomb over the Japanese city of Hiroshima, killing 78,000 people, the world has had to live with the image and possible reality of species extinction. Today the most fearful space is the one after the nuclear holocaust; the ultimate wilderness where no birds will sing, no plants will grow and all human life will have been extinguished. This vision has waxed and waned, disappearing as we have become used to living with the collective nightmare, reappearing whenever superpower conflict, accidents, technological developments and political failures have thrown up the image in our faces and our dreams. The most desolate wilderness is the one we could create ourselves. There is a real possibility, in the words of the classical poet Andrew Marvell, that

And yonder all before us lie
Deserts of vast eternity.
(*To His Coy Mistress*, undated)

2 The countryside

We must therefore use some illusion to render a Pastoral delightful; and this consists in exposing the best side only of a shepherd's life, and concealing its miseries.

Alexander Pope (1717) *A Discourse on Pastoral Poetry*

The Pastoral is a *mythical* view of the relationship of men in society, at the service of those who control the political, economic and cultural strings of society.

John Barrell and John Bull (eds) (1974) Introduction to
The Penguin Book of English Pastoral Verse

ORIGINS

From ancient times to the present day, attitudes to the countryside have been shaped by a response which we can term the pastoral. The literal meaning of 'pastoral' is 'pertaining to shepherds'. The originator of the western pastoral tradition was Theocritus, a Sicilian born between 300 and 310 BC, whose *Idylls* recalled his youth on the island of Kos. The term 'idyll' is now used to refer to an idealized picture of a country scene but Theocritus was also aware of the hard side of a shepherd's life. The sense of loss and the presence of death which permeates *Idylls* meant that this was no arcadia but in the *Idylls*, as for much subsequent work, the countryside became a symbol for a lost youth, an innocence recaptured by memory and imagination.

Theocritus took the ancient tradition of shepherds' singing contests and transformed it into an intellectual's view of the countryside, a depiction for people who were neither shepherds nor farmers but urban dwellers. The pastoral was a view of the countryside from the town (see Figure 2.1).

The single most important classical influence on the pastoral literary tradition was Virgil, who was born on a farm near Mantua in 70 BC. He read Theocritus and extended the pastoral tradition in the *Eclogues*, written between 42 and 37 BC. There are ten eclogues each of about 100 lines of poetry, alternately dialogue and monologue, in which shepherds

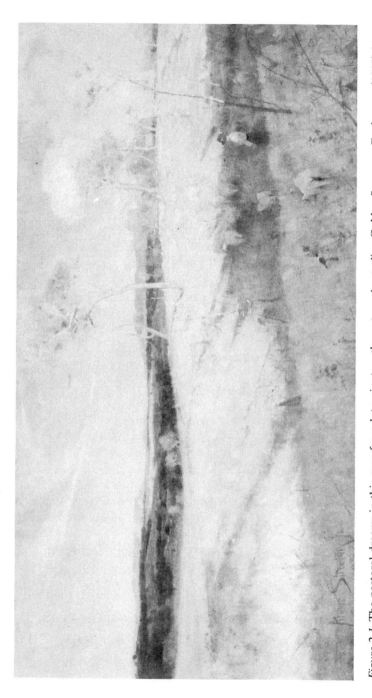

Figure 2.1 The pastoral dream: in this case from late nineteenth-century Australia, *Golden Summer, Eaglemont* (1889) by Arthur Streeton (Private collection)

are either together or alone. It is commonly assumed that the *Eclogues* presents a rosy view of the countryside. That element is there and it is strong, but the *Eclogues* is firmly set in a particular context. In the first eclogue, two shepherds describe the countryside 'all in such turmoil' as one of them has been dispossessed of his land. In 42 BC, after the defeat of Brutus and Caesar, the Caesarian party took land from landowners and gave it to the returning soldiers. Up to one quarter of the land in Italy changed hands at this time. The first eclogue references this contemporary event. The *Eclogues* as text contains both particular references to the existing state of affairs and more generalized representations of country life. But through time the *Eclogues* has been prised from the context to leave just the general picture. When contexts are lost, ideologies become myths.

The Virgilian myth was transmitted through western culture first by the oral tradition of pastoral songs and then by the printing and translation of his work. Virgil was particularly popular in the Middle Ages. It was widely believed that the fourth eclogue prophesied the birth of Christ and in a theocratic age Virgil was acceptable to the Church fathers. An edition of his work first appeared in Italy in 1469 and his work was translated into the major European languages. He influenced poets in the English language from Spenser and Milton to Tennyson. His work was also cited in the discourses on agriculture which began to appear from the sixteenth century (Johnstone 1937). Works such as Conrad Heresbach's *Rei Rusticae Libri Quatuor* (1570), Oliver de Sernes's *Théâtre d'agriculture* (1600) and Walter Blith's *The English Improver Improved* (1649) took as their model the praise of agriculture first found in Theocritus and Virgil.

ELEMENTS OF THE PASTORAL MYTH

The myth which has been repeated through the centuries has a number of elements.

An agricultural life, it is argued, is more wholesome, more spiritually nourishing, more natural. The country dweller is seen, in the myth, as more simple and less compromised by social convention. The dominant image is of the happy swain close to nature, connected to the rhythms of the earth and the seasons of the year. Just as the demarcation of the wilderness comes only with the development of agriculture so the praise of agriculture comes only with the development of urban centres. The praise of agriculture is part of the criticism of urban society. Virgil's countryside is contrasted to what his contemporary, Horace, described as

> The smoke and wealth and noise of Rome
> And all the busy pageantry
> That wise men scorn and fools adore.
> (*Become Impervious to Fortune*, quoted in Grant 1979: 186)

In the Middle Ages the power centres were the royal courts. As a fifteenth-century French poet noted:

> The court is a sea whence come
> Waves of pride, thunderstorms of envy
> Wrath stirs up quarrels and outrages
> Which often cause the ships to sink:
> Treason plays its part there.
> Swim elsewhere for your amusement.
>   (quoted in Huizinga 1954: 134)

In poems and songs, pastoral simplicity was used as a contrast to court life. In the eighteenth century, French court life idealized the rural. In a corner of Versailles, Marie Antoinette had a fake village built where she and her ladies dressed up as milkmaids and shepherdesses. Even in the twentieth century, the British royal family present a number of public images. Contrasting with the formal political and diplomatic duties of Buckingham Palace is the world of Balmoral and Sandringham, a life of rural pursuits, green wellies, fishing and horses.

For the past four hundred years the idealized countryside has been contrasted with the rise of the city and the power of the market. The two are often joined in the contrasting image of the evil city dominated by the love of money, a moral cesspit to be contrasted with the fresh air, moral purity and good life of the country.

As myth, the countryside has always been a counterpoint. Its usage first appeared in English in the sixteenth century with the growth of London. Its 'simple life' has always been praised in contrast with something else: the convention of the court, the brutality of the market or the anonymity of the city. It has become the perfect past to the imperfect present and uncertain future. The myth has increased in potency as urbanization and modernization have continued apace. Whenever social tensions increase, fear of the future heightens, urbanization intensifies and large-scale social changes loom large, then countryside as myth becomes more prevalent. In the contrast with city, court and market the countryside is seen as the last remnant of the golden age. The countryside is the nostalgic past, providing a glimpse of a simpler, purer age.

The countryside as golden age has retained its power over the centuries because it has proved capable of various interpretations. There has been the golden age of the wealthy who ignored the social relations between themselves and agricultural workers and could thus see the products from countryside as nature's bounty. This was the countryside as a place of play. The garden of delight is the icon of this golden age and is represented best in the paintings of Fragonard and Boucher, where silk-clad courtiers disport themselves in manicured arbours. It is a garden without the gardeners. Then there has been the golden age of the small owner-occupiers, a time before the big institutions of government and business.

This is the 'organic' community of the past, to which the hard pressed can look back as a better time when individuals had more influence and a legitimate, more recognized place in society. For the more radical there has been the golden age of primitive communism. A peasant song of England in the Middle Ages had the refrain:

> When Adam delved, and Eve span,
> Who was then a gentleman?

This looks back to a time before the onset of social hierarchies and inequalities, a time of communal landownership. This image has been the basis of a whole series of rural utopian creeds from Shakers to hippies. It is the communizing of the rural idyll.

Capable of various interpretations from aristocratic to communist, from arcadian to utopian, the countryside as the setting for the golden age has continued to exercise the western imagination. It has persisted in the modern period because an idealized countryside has been a point of

Figures 2.2 and 2.3 View of the countryside as a state of mind: contrasting renditions of the French countryside by the same artist, Vincent van Gogh: *The Harvest* (1888) and *Wheatfield With Crows* (1890), his last painting, completed shortly before he committed suicide (Both: Vincent van Gogh Foundation/National Museum of Vincent van Gogh, Amsterdam)

criticism of capitalist social relations and big city life. The countryside as contemporary myth is pictured as a less-hurried lifestyle where people follow the seasons rather than the stock market, where they have more time for one another and exist in a more organic community where people have a place and an authentic role. The countryside has become the refuge from modernity.

The whole shift of world population has been from rural to urban. There has been an urban transformation which, like a car going down a hill, seems to speed up with time. The juggernaut of world urbanization has accelerated in the last two hundred years. The speed of the change means that rural to urban shift is within the range of family biographies and national social histories. Rural to urban migration has been the predominant population redistribution. The countryside figures as the place of our past. Many households can look back to rural roots. It is the location of nostalgia, the setting for the simpler lives of our forebears, a people whose existence seems idyllic because they are unencumbered with the immense task of living in the present.

This nostalgia is also the basis of the role that the countryside plays in national identity. At its simplest, the countryside becomes the image of the country, indeed the term 'country' has the double meaning of 'rural land' and 'native land'. It becomes the scene of national harmony, peace and stability, to be contrasted with the conflict, strife and change of the present; it becomes the container of national identity and the measure of social change. Tom Nairn (1977) describes nationalism as the modern Janus, which looks both backwards and forwards. The backward glance is invariably to the countryside, the 'folk' traditions that are the cultural bond between a people and their territory. These folk traditions are created and re-created to suit various interpretations. In the main they have been used as an ideological filler to hold up the structure of national identity. L.P. Hartley begins his novel *The Go-Between* (1953) with the sentence: 'The past is a foreign country: they do things differently there.' We can legitimately rephrase it to: 'The country is a foreign past, they do things better there.' The countryside as past is often used in contrast with the fears of the present and the dread of the future (see Figures 2.2 and 2.3).

The countryside as myth also has its manifestation in economic debates. Agricultural fundamentalism, which sees agriculture as the prime generator of wealth and cities and urban populations as so many parasites, has a long history. It was codified in the eighteenth century by a group known as the Physiocrats, including François Quesnay, physician to Louis XV. The Physiocrats held that only agriculture produced a surplus; every other activity merely distributed this surplus. Agriculture was the basis of all wealth. Their ideas received formal incorporation into the emerging discourse of economies through the writings of Adam Smith who visited France in 1764–66. Although the ideas of the Physiocrats are no longer part of formal economics, they still provide the currency of economic debates. The economist Kenneth Galbraith notes:

> For a time in my youth I served as research director for the American Farm Bureau Federation, the big conservative farm organization, farm-supply cooperative and farm lobby then at the height of its power. Each December our members met in convention. In the days that followed, the voice of physiocracy – the claims that agriculture is the source of all wealth – rang through the halls. I wrote some of the speeches. And the voice is not yet silent. When politicians campaign for the few farm votes that remain, the message of physiocracy may be heard.
>
> (Galbraith 1977: 78)

This is true not only when vote-buying. In general, in most rich countries, rural voters are overrepresented and oversubsidized in comparison with the people of the cities.

In most countries the countryside has become the embodiment of the nation, idealized as the ideal middle landscape between the rough wilderness of nature and the smooth artificiality of the town, a combination of nature and culture which best represents the nation-state.

THE ANTI-PASTORAL

The very strength of the pastoral tradition has produced the anti-pastoral which seeks to debunk the myths. Where Alexander Pope wanted to expose only the best of a shepherd's life, the anti-pastoralists want to expose only his miseries. I have some sympathy. In the summer of 1973 I worked on an estate in the Highlands of Scotland. Before the deer-shooting season began I worked with the shepherds. I had often seen sheep on the hillside and occasionally seen shepherds at work. From a distance it looked serene. Close up the pastoral experience was different. I was given a sheepdog which was strong and brave, but very stupid. It was the only sheepdog who did not want to chase sheep. The sheep were eventually gathered in pens. The young male sheep had elastic bands placed around their testicles which cut off the blood supply. The band and their balls would eventually drop off. All the lambs had their tails docked. The tail was placed on a wooden platform and was cut off. For a time I had the job of wielding the knife. The lambs flicked their tails and spattered me with blood. At the end of the day I looked more like an extra from a Jacobean tragedy or the *Texas Chain Saw Massacre* than a shepherd in an arcadian idyll.

It would be easy but wrong to say that the anti-pastoral focused on the reality of the countryside whereas the pastoral concentrated on the myth of the countryside (see Figures 2.4 and 2.5). There is a difference between experiencing the countryside, as I did when I slashed at the lamb's tails, and rendering it for consumption, as I did a few lines ago. The anti-pastoral

Figures 2.4 and 2.5 Alternative depictions of the rural condition, from Australia: *My Harvest Home* (1835) by John Glover, a scene infused with a pantheistic light suggesting a harmony between God's bounty and man's work (Tasmanian Museum and Art Gallery, Hobart) and *Man Reading A Newspaper* (1941) by Russell Drysdale, an isolated figure in a bleak, eroded, drought-stricken countryside (University of Sydney)

shares with the pastoral a distance from the actual events, a disjunction between experience and rendition. In Fred Kitchen's *Brother to the Ox* (1939), we have the story of agriculture from the viewpoint of an agricultural labourer, but once it is codified in language, there is a distancing from the experience. The audience for the anti-pastoral may be different from the pastoral but they both are predominantly urban and each is distanced from the countryside. The bottom-up correction that the anti-pastoral makes to the idealized myth of the pastoral is valuable but just as distanced from the events.

There is a strong tradition in the anti-pastoral of giving voice to those who are present in the pastoral only as dumb extras. It focuses, as in the novels of Fred Kitchen, on those denied space in the pastoral, it gives a voice to those made silent by the image of bucolic labour. It seeks to subvert the literacy convention by showing how hard life is. In the French movie *Jean de Florette* (1985), for example, the harsh sunlight and lack of water becomes almost a metaphor for the hard life of the agriculturalist and the unforgiving social relationships between competing families. In the British film *On The Black Hill* (1988), the sullenness of social relations and

the brutalization of farm labour is shown. The anti-pastoral seeks to show the world of work and the lives of the workers.

In one strain of the anti-pastoral tradition the characteristics of the country-dweller are loutish and ill-mannered and rural life is shown to be hemmed in by deference to authority and tradition, a suffocating network of ritual obligations. Rural life, from this perspective, is a restraint on individual growth and a block on social development. For the progressives who see an upward movement in civilization, the countryside is regarded as backward. In the *Manifesto of the Communist Party*, first written in 1848 (printed in English in 1888), Marx and Engels noted:

> The bourgeoisie has subjected the country to the rule of the towns. It has created enormous cities, has greatly increased the urban population as compared with the rural, and has thus rescued a considerable part of the population from the idiocy of rural life.
>
> (Marx and Engels 1968: 39)

For such firm believers in the progressive march of history, urbanization gave workers an experience of their collective strength, allowed them to break away from 'the idiocy of rural life'. For them, and others, the countryside and its inhabitants are a symbol of conservatism, and social backwardness. Where some see stability and tradition in the countryside, the progressives see reaction and the environmental context for anti-progressive forces. The countryside is the past, to be contrasted with hope of the future.

In *Volpone*, a play written in 1606, Ben Jonson satirizes the explicit greed of an embryonic capitalism. The main character says at one point:

> I wound no earth with ploughshares; fat no beasts
> To feed the shambles; have no mills for iron,
> Oil, corn, or men, to grind 'em into powder;
>
> (I.i. 34–6)

The image of the first line is striking – ploughing as wounding of the earth, furrows as scars, as disfigurements of the ground. It is a criticism of agriculture for hurting the earth, a criticism tied to a more general critique of the commercialization of agriculture.

The pastoral tradition has always had a difficulty with agriculture. The idealized view of the countryside which we have termed pastoral originally developed from the depiction of shepherd life, a rural pursuit closer to hunting-gathering and less connected with the back-breaking labour of ploughing, sowing and harvesting. Shepherds can more easily be shown as standing around watching the wool grow on the backs of sheep. Nature does most of the work. It is more difficult to show ploughmen swanning around. Robert Burns (1759–96), the ploughman turned poet, described his working experience as 'the cheerless gloom of a hermit with the unceasing toil of a galley-slave'. Agrarianism is more hard work and more obviously a commercial enterprise. Volpone's remarks are an early example of the dual criticism of agriculture for its ecological damage and its commercialism. Agriculture grinds people as well as corn.

The romantic response of the eighteenth and nineteenth centuries involved a more favourable consideration of wilderness. The percolation of this belief, sometimes shorn of its theological significance into a taken-for-granted set of popular beliefs, ultimately involved a reassessment of the countryside. For some, it became less an ideal landscape, no longer an harmonious balance between nature and the civil, and more a grubby assault on the purity of the wilderness. The popular perception of the tropical rainforest as a wilderness under threat from farmers and loggers is an example of this emerging critique. The whole pastoral myth has been sullied by the use of pesticides and fertilizers and by the emergence of factory-farming systems where cows never feel grass beneath their feet and hens live and die in small cages in sunless rooms lit only by electric light.

Farming is as much a target for the green movement and animal liberationists as chemical works or fur coat manufacturers (see Figure 2.6). Rachel Carson's *Silent Spring* (1962) was an influential ecological tract. Much of her anger and her analysis is against the use by farmers and the agri-business of chemical poisons with such disastrous results. In the final sentence of the book she refers to terrible weapons turned against the

Figure 2.6 The anti-pastoral has focused on the environmental harm done by farmers, such as the stubble burning of this field in Dorset, UK

earth. It is an echo of Ben Jonson's remarks. Where agriculture used to be praised for civilizing nature, it is now criticized. The loss of wilderness, with its importance in an increasingly urbanized, agrarianized world, means that we can no longer see the civilizing of agriculture in quite the optimistic way of the past. Current demands from animal rights groups, biologists and landscape campaigners are for a more 'natural' agriculture. At root (the term is suggestive), it is a criticism of agriculture as a commercial enterprise. Commercial agriculture is about making money and only incidentally about food production, animal rights, landscape preservation or long-term ecological balance. Behind the criticisms lies a disappointment with the failure of agriculture to meet the standards of the pastoral myth. Myths are important. They furnish expectations. Failure to meet these expectations provides the space for creative criticisms.

3 City

The increasing tendency to reside in towns and cities . . . is manifested by the inhabitants of all countries, as they make progress in the arts and refinements of civilization.

Jessup W. Scott (1843) 'Internal Trade of The United States',
Hunt's Merchants' Magazine

The city has become a serious menace to our civilization. . . . Here is heaped the social dynamite: here toughs, gamblers, thieves, robbers, lawless and desperate men of all sorts, congregate: men who are ready on any pretext to raise riots for the purpose of destruction and plunder; here gather foreigners and wage-workers; here skepticism and irreligion abound; here inequality is the greatest and most obvious, and the contrast between opulence and penury the most striking; here is suffering the sorest.

Josiah Strong (1885) *Our Country*

In December 1984 I went to the Museum of Modern Art in Oxford to see an exhibition of fabric and crockery produced in the Soviet Union in the period 1917–30. It proved to be an exhilarating experience. That period saw a flourishing of artistic endeavour, an incandescent flame of creativity between the cold repression of the overthrown Czar and the Stalinist ice-age to come. The colours and design were vibrant and original. They had kept their freshness to such an extent that a casual observer over fifty years later could look on with delight and appreciation. A closer look at the fabric and plates revealed repeated patterns of new buildings, building sites, tractors, concrete mixers, power stations and lightbulbs. These motifs of modernity were a celebration of urbanization and industrialization.

On leaving the exhibition and feeling thirsty, I went to a tea shop. Here the designs on the tablecloths, the wallpaper, the cups and saucers were of flowers and shrubs, cottages and green fields; it was a chintzy portrayal of a pre-industrial, pre-urban Britain. The whole place had the feel and atmosphere of a resolutely non-urban, non-industrial pastoral. I had left an optimistic vision of the future and entered a nostalgic glance at the past. The two places had two very different attitudes. These were not restricted to the particular exhibition or the specific teashop but embodied the archetypal responses to the city.

We can make a distinction between different types of city. At the top are the world cities: London, New York, Tokyo and Paris. These are huge urban agglomerations with a rich variety of neighbourhoods and a cosmopolitan population. The world cities are as much connected to each other as they are to other cities in their own country. They are tied together by the movement of people and ideas and by the circulation of capital. Next are the national cities, still large, sometimes with over a million in population, maybe even a country's capital, but not quite large enough or important enough to belong to the big league. Such is Birmingham or Glasgow in the UK. Below them are the regional cities, capitals of regions rather than whole countries. In the UK, cities such as Bristol, Norwich and Newcastle fit this bill; in the US, Houston and Phoenix. Sliding down the scale we come to towns, small towns and villages. Urban myths vary through the urban hierarchy. Images of the small town, and even sometimes the regional city, merge into the same set of beliefs which underpin the pastoral idyll. The praise of small towns is a celebration of knowing one's place. Criticisms of small towns tend to centre on their supposed small-mindedness, lack of culture and parochial viewpoint. Those who praise the big cities, in constrast, revel in size, heterogeneity and fluidity, while criticisms of big cities are discourses on alienation, rapid social change and cosmopolitan populations (see Figures 3.1 and 3.2). In the rest of this chapter I shall limit my remarks to the big cities of national and international importance.

THE PRO-URBAN

One reason for the celebration of urbanism is hinted at in the quotation on page 40 from Jessup W. Scott: the city as the setting for a civilized life. This has a long history. In the western mind it has its roots in the classical world where city states emerged as the unit of social and political organization. Whenever people applaud the city, as in Samuel Johnson's remark, 'When a man is tired of London, he is tired of life', there is always an element of respect for the achievements of the Greek city states or imperial Rome. At the heart of the 'city as civilization' argument is a belief in the ability of social aggregation to create more possibilities than the sum of the individuals. T.K. Smith, in *Altruria* (1895), a novel depicting an urban utopia, praised the city because 'we are all near neighbours, and enjoy the quickening impulses of an intelligent society'.

The city is a metaphor for social change, an icon of the present at the edge of the transformation of the past into the future. Attitudes about the city reflect attitudes about the future.

The pro-urban view has long been associated with optimistic radicals. If the conservatives look to the countryside for support, then the radicals

Figure 3.1 Cities can be places where people come together: a political gathering in Barcelona

Figure 3.2 Cities can also be places of loneliness: a man sits alone on a park bench in Bristol

look to the emancipatory trajectory of urbanization. In the feudal period there was a German saying, 'city air makes men free'. Cities, and especially big cities, have played an important part in radical iconography. When Marx and Engels said that towns saved people from the idiocy of rural life, they were endorsing the widely accepted correlation between urbanism and emancipation.

The very size and complexity of the big city is for some people part of the attraction. Dr Johnson loved the 'wonderful immensity' of London and for Henry James 'the mere immensity of the place is a large part of its merit'. For James, the appeal of London was that one could 'hear the rumble of the tremendous human mill' (James 1893: 9).

The big city is more cosmopolitan, more connected to world events than are small towns and rural areas. Big cities are more like foreign countries. Cicero (106–43 BC) described the big coastal cities of imperial Rome thus:

> These towns become adulterated with strange languages and habits, and import not only foreign cargoes but foreign morals which inevitably prevent their national tradition. Indeed, the inhabitants themselves do not stay attached to their homes but are forcibly transported far away from them by their ambitions and imaginings.
>
> (quoted in Grant 1979: 32)

A similar view was expressed almost two thousand years later by Tom Wolfe, in describing the visit of the first US astronauts to New York:

> Like most military people, including those in the Brooklyn Navy Yard, they didn't really consider New York part of the United States. It was like a free port, a stateless city, an international protectorate. Danzig in the Polish corridor, Beirut the crossroads of the Middle East, Trieste, Zurich, Macao, Hong Kong. Whatever ideals the military stood for, New York did not. It was a foreign city full of a strange race of curiously tiny malformed gray people.
>
> (Wolfe 1980: 290)

As citizens of a foreign country, the people of the big city are less tied to national traditions, fixed attitudes and set ways. For traditionalists, the big city is a shiftless, feckless, rootless place, unconnected to the stability of the nation. For radicals, it is the hope of the future. Connected to a wider world, it is beyond the narrowing confines of a single national culture, an incubator for creative thought and the breeding ground for radical action.

The size and cosmopolitan quality of cities is thought by some to encourage individualism. For Jonathan Raban, the city is an emporium where individuals can choose their lifestyles. In his book *Soft City* (1974), Raban celebrates the heterogeneity and anonymity of the city. The populations of villages and small towns come down hard on explicit displays of individualism while the big city encourages and allows their expression. But Raban's city is the inner city, the neighbourhoods of transients, the London of Soho and Earls Court, not the London of Bow and Kew. Raban's city is the city of the newcomer, the city of the railway stations, bus depots and air terminals where migrants come with a change of clothes in their suitcases and a change of lifestyle in their imaginations. Only in cities big enough or interesting enough to attract such people can we really speak of the 'soft city'.

The newcomer to the city has long been used as an image of the loss of innocence. The arrival in the bus station or the exit from the airport is so often used as the beginning of a morality play as to constitute a modern myth. The city becomes the scene of the gaining of wisdom and the loss of innocence, a place of tension between naïvety and experience, youth and maturity, dreams and realities.

Even the most nature-loving newcomer can find something of interest in the big city. Between 1799 and 1805, William Wordsworth (1770–1850) wrote an autobiographical poem, *The Prelude*, which was published only after his death. Subtitled *The Growth of a Poet's Mind*, it is divided into fourteen books. Here is the personal history of one of England's greatest romantic poets, whose name is synonymous with Lakeland scenery, daffodils and solitary figures wandering over the hillside. The seventh book is entitled 'Residence in London' and here Wordsworth reconstructs in poetic form his experience of the city. It is a kaleidoscope of impressions:

> This endless stream of men and moving things
> Before me flow the quick dance
> Of colour, lights, and forms; the deafening din;
> The comers and the goers face to face,
> Face after face, the string of dazzling wares,
> Ship after ship with symbols, blazoned names

Above all, this seventh book is a celebration of the urban, the crowds, the strange people, the theatre, the great tide of humanity. There is a tone of criticism of the perpetual whirl, 'Of trivial objects, melted and reduced to one identity', but the main theme is of the sheer excitement and life of London. Even for the arch-romantic, the big city could be admired.

THE ANTI-URBAN

Cities are the terrain of competing interpretations. Where the pro-urbanists see a place for civilized life, individual freedoms and the full flowering of collective endeavour, the anti-urbanists see an unnatural setting for the anonymous interaction of an alienated population. While some celebrate urbanization, others decry the rise of big cities. For every Jessup Scott there are many Josiah Strongs (see page 40).

Consistent criticisms of the city focus on morality, fear of the mob, fear of disease and fear of crime. Cities have always had a bad press. In the Bible, the cities of Sodom and Gomorrah were places of sin and iniquity.

The image has stuck. In 1880 John Ruskin, in a letter to the clergy, could note that the great cities of the earth became 'loathsome centres of fornication and covetousness – the smoke of sin going up into the face of heaven like the furnace of Sodom'. In the late-twentieth century, such language is rarely used, except by evangelical preachers with a penchant for purple prose, but the sentiments are still shared by many. Where the pro-urbanists see opportunities for individual and collective self-expression, the anti-urbanists can perceive only the lack of moral markers and the decline of traditional values. These values have been 'declining' ever since the first city was established.

A major element in the criticism of the city is the fear of the crowd. The crowd has always been an agent in urban social life. In an enormously influential essay, E.P. Thompson (1971) examined the nature of the crowd in eighteenth-century England and, in particular, crowd action related to food riots which occurred every ten years from 1740. He demolishes the argument that the riots were spasms of hunger. They were a 'highly complex form of direct popular action, disciplined and with clear objectives. The people were informed by the belief that they were defending traditional rights of customs . . . supported by the wider consensus of the community.' The actions of the crowd were concerned with redistributing food and setting new prices, moral prices of the community instead of the price of the market. Urban crowds throughout history have been concerned with the moral economy rather than the market economy. As cities grew bigger and classes became more distinct and separated out into the different urban worlds of segregated neighbourhoods, the crowd, which had been an occasional threat to the established order, now posed a permanent point of fear.

Alexander de Tocqueville noted:

> in cities men cannot be prevented from concerting together and awakening a mutual excitement that prompts sudden and passionate resolution. Cities may be looked upon as large assemblies of which all the inhabitants are members; their populace exercise a prodigious influence upon the magistrates and frequently execute their own wishes without the intervention of public officer.
>
> (Tocqueville 1835, vol. 1: 290)

The fear of the cities is a fear of organized insurrection, the explosive riots of the marginalized, the crime and random violence of the dispossessed.

Fear of the urban masses has fastened on to disease and crime. Much of the fear of the lower class was and, to a lesser extent, still is condensed in the image of the city as a source of disease. The health of the city became a metaphor for society's moral hygiene and moral welfare. Cities have always been a place for disease. People are the main carriers of contagious diseases and cities are congregations of people. The late-eighteenth and nineteenth centuries saw increasing concern with the health of the city.

Figure 3.3 The city as lonely crowd: *Collins Street, 5 p.m.* (1956) by John Brack (National Gallery of Victoria)

Contagion knew no social boundaries. The diseases of the slums could be passed on to people in the very best neighbourhoods.

There has always been the fear of crime. The city has been seen as the den of crime and lawlessness. Just as moral values have always been declining, so have crime levels always been rising. The city is perceived as the epicentre of social breakdown.

Criticisms of the city embody broader considerations. Cities are the vehicle for wider social comment and deeper political statements. In the nineteenth and early twentieth centuries, criticisms of the city were in effect criticisms of the factory system, the money economy and capitalist relations.

By the twentieth century, the link between urbanization, industrialization and capitalism was becoming less clear. It had become a matter of fact, not of evolution. Criticism of cities became a lament for the loss of community. A consistent theme from the nineteenth century to the present is of cities as the place of atomized, fragmented existences (see Figure 3.3). In Book VII of *The Prelude*, William Wordsworth was writing of the big city as a place where

> Even next-door neighbours as we say, yet still Strangers, not knowing each other's name.

One hundred and seventy years later, even a sympathetic urbanist could note:

Nearly everyone feels himself to be marginal in a metropolis. . . . Cities are scary and impersonal, and the best most of us can manage is a fragile hold.

(Raban 1974: 245)

If Jonathan Raban's *soft city* is where individuals can develop the sense of themselves, it is because in the *hard city* no one cares. Behind individualism lies indifference.

The city has become a source of personal disquiet as well as personal liberation, an ambiguity captured by George Simmel at the turn of the century:

On the one hand, life is made infinitely easy for the personality in that stimulations, interests, uses of time and consciousness are offered to it from all sides. They carry the person as if in a stream, and one needs hardly to swim for oneself. On the other hand, however, life is composed more and more of these impersonal contents and offerings which tend to displace the genuine personal colorations and incomparabilities. This results in the individual's summoning the utmost in uniqueness and particularization in order to preserve his most personal core. He has to exaggerate this personal element in order to remain audible even to himself.

(Simmel 1950: 422)

The city has become the modern symbol of personal fragmentation, the place of the disjunction of our public and private lives, the point of separation of functional and emotional relationships.

In the anti-urban tradition, the city has always been a wilderness. In 1699 London was described as a 'place of wild beasts where most of us are equally savage and mutually destructive one of another'. In 1751 Henry Fielding described the slum area of London as 'a fast wood or forest, in which a Thief may harbour with as great ease as wild beasts do in the deserts of Africa or Arabia'. In 1829 Robert Southey could also describe London as 'at once the centre of wealth and the sink of misery, the seat of intellect and empire and yet a wilderness wherein they, who live like beasts upon their fellow creatures, find prey and cover'.

The city as wilderness echoes down the years. In the USA of the near future, portrayed in the film *Escape from New York* (1981), Manhattan is a prison housing the nation's criminals. The movie gives dramatic visual imagery to the belief of the metropolis as something separate from the rest of the country, an urban jungle of anarchy and crime. The fears of our modern society are given shape and substance by such urban disutopias. The city has become the id of the modern imagination, the place where civilized behaviour is vanishing. In the late-twentieth century, the big city fulfils the same role as the howling wilderness of the sixteenth and seventeenth centuries; a place of base instincts, ugly motives, subterranean

Figure 3.4 The integrated, vertical living spaces of the
Old Town of Edinburgh

fears and unspoken desires, a place which reveals the savage basis of the
human condition and frailty of civilized society.

INNER CITY AND SUBURBS

In 1767 an area of land to the north of the old medieval town of Edinburgh
in Scotland was brought under the control of the City Council. For the next
thirty years, buildings were laid out in three parallel streets ending in
elegant squares. This was the New Town of Edinburgh, which remains to
this day one of the finest examples of Georgian domestic architecture and
town planning. It was not the first such scheme. South of the border, in
London and Bath, similar developments had begun almost fifty years
previously. But in Edinburgh we see very clearly the making of the modern

Figure 3.5 The New Town of Edinburgh with its elegance, symmetry and segregated social groups (compare with Figure 3.4)

city. Prior to the building of the New Town, Edinburgh's population was concentrated in the Old Town where six-storey buildings, clustering around the medieval spine of the High Street and Canongate, housed both rich and poor, commoner and gentry. There were distinctions by building, sometimes even only by storey, but the general picture was of the city as a shared space (see Figure 3.4). The New Town distanced the rich and powerful from the rest of society. The building of classical Edinburgh was the embodiment of an emerging social class making itself through and in its urban space. Edinburgh's New Town may not have been the first but it is one of the most striking examples of how the medieval, shared city was transformed into the separated, horizontally differentiated city of the modern era (see Figure 3.5).

The process has been going on for some time. From the seventeenth century onwards, cities began to crystallize into distinct neighbourhoods. This differentiation has increased throughout the centuries and now in big cities there is an urban mosaic of neighbourhoods, varying by population type, building style, age and status. Every city has its fashionable districts, its no-go areas, districts on the way up, districts on the way down. In each city there are certain districts which figure in the local mythology: places to aspire to, places to avoid, markers on how well or how poorly a household is making out. Choosing one piece of the mosaic rather than another is a personal statement, a mark of success or failure. There are districts specific to each city but the major cleavage in most cities is between the inner city and the suburb (see Figures 3.6 and 3.7). These terms are imbued with much wider social connotations. They are the light and the shadow of the urban scene. To use the term *inner city* is to concentrate on the city of the poor, old neighbourhoods, the city of the historical legacy and the social problem. However, there is a confusion if we use the words in their simple geographical sense. The inner city areas of London, for example, contain Chelsea and Mayfair as well as Brixton and Tower Hamlets, the very rich and the very poor. Similarly, the suburbs house a range of social types, wealthy bankers as well as humble clerks. The terms *inner city* and *suburb* are rarely used in such a precise sense. They are general mythological entities not specific geographical categories.

As myth, the inner city is the dark underside of the city, a place of crime and disorder, a tariff-free zone for traditional moral values. In the nineteenth century it was the place of the working classes, the source of disease and crime, the home of the crowd. In the twentieth it has become the locale of the underclass, a black hole of contemporary civilization.

The suburbs, in contrast, are used to refer to a whole set of alternative values: family, stability, security, a place where people settle down, raise children, become part of a community. The dream of suburbia was the possibility of the good life without the restraints of the country or the anonymity of the city. Throughout the twentieth century a place in the suburbs became a popular goal. It endorsed notions of thrift, family values and community ties. It gave a portion of property, a sense of achievement, a material and symbolic stake in the neighbourhood.

There were critics. In 1932, Thomas Sharp was describing the inter-war world of southern England:

> From dreary towns the broad, mechanical noisy main roads run out between ribbons of tawdry houses, disorderly refreshment shacks and vile untidy garages. The old trees and hedgerows that bordered them a few years ago have given place to concrete posts and avenues of telegraph poles, to hoardings and enamel advertisement signs. Over great areas there is no longer any country bordering the main roads; there is only a negative semi-suburbia.
>
> (Sharp 1932: 4)

Notice the adjectives: dreary, tawdry, disorderly, vile and untidy. To the urban purists, the suburbs were an aesthetic mess. They were also criticized for their supposed conformity and homogeneity. The great urban commentator, Lewis Mumford (1961: 563), dismissed the suburbs 'as an asylum for the preservation of illusion'.

The criticisms tell us more about the commentators than the suburbs. Behind these criticisms lies a concern with the disorderly nature of the suburbs. They were neither urban nor rural and this offended the tastes of those who preferred stable and separate spatial and social categories. The

Figures 3.6 and 3.7 In the twentieth century, the city as symbol has two elements: the inner city (Reading, UK) and the suburbs (Vienna)

suburbs were a zone of uncertainty between the two great ideas of town and country. They inhabited a penumbral position in the social world; they were neither very rich nor very poor, neither upper nor working class. Intellectuals could neither criticize nor praise them in the accepted manner. The suburbs posed a problem for the intellectual.

By the 1970s the suburbs had become part of the physical and intellectual landscape and supporters of the suburbs began to emerge. Hugh Streeton (1971), for example, praised the suburbs as a place where families could find the place to exercise their freedom and use their imaginations. In 1972 Robert Venturi and others were taking seriously the aesthetics of suburban America. The previously despised strip-landscape became a legitimate source of architectural style, one of the sources of postmodernism (Venturi *et al.* 1972). New intellectual configurations were able to include the suburbs as an authentic source of inspiration; they were no longer an unwanted bastard of an uncaring city and an unwilling countryside.

But there were also new criticisms. A feminist critique began to emerge which saw the suburbs as a place of female imprisonment (see, for example, Rothblatt *et al.* 1979). The separate homes all required regular inputs of modern female labour. For some, the suburbs were a symbol of women's banishment to the domestic world of home worker, child bearer and baby minder.

The changing attitudes to the suburbs tell us much about the changing nature of society.

Part II
Ideologies

Introduction

The ideas of the ruling class are, in every age, the ruling ideas.
Karl Marx and Friedrich Engels (1846) *The German Ideology*

Myths annihilate time; environmental ideologies reify space. National environmental ideologies use the myths of wilderness, countryside and city in establishing and maintaining a national identity. Let us take an example. In Chapter 3 we have examined anti-urban attitudes. These have been found throughout different societies at various times. In the 1920s the Nazi party was presenting a 'Nordic' rural image of Germany. The party paper *Volkische Beobachter* described big cities as

the melting pot of all evil ... of prostitution, bars, illness, movies, Marxism, Jews, strippers, Negro dancers, and all the disgusting offspring of so-called 'modern art'.

(quoted in Lane 1968: 155)

Notice how typical anti-urban myths are now used against specific targets. Myths are transformed into ideologies by particularizing general criticisms to specific ends, by recruiting broad arguments to particular political purposes, and by shaping the myths to a definite purpose. Ideologies give myths a time, a place and a purpose.

Ideologies reflect not only the distribution of power in society but also the struggle for power in society. Ideologies bear the imprint of contest, struggle, victory and defeat. The definition of cities, the cultural reproduction of the countryside, and the demarcation of the wilderness are rich in messages of social significance, which bear the stamp of cultural and social power. Environmental ideologies reflect the distribution of power in society, indeed power can be defined, partially at least, with reference to differential impact on the production of ideologies.

The term 'ideology' has been used in a pejorative sense to refer to mistaken beliefs. The underlying assumption here is that my ideas are truthful and scientific, yours are ideology. I do not subscribe to this use.

Ideology is also sometimes used in conjunction with the thesis of dominant ideology. Following on from the early writings of Marx and Engels, a number of writers have used the term 'dominant ideology' to refer to ideas which are seen to justify and legitimate the status quo. The thesis assumes that there is a coherent set of ideas emanating from a homogeneous ruling class, but the ruling class is rarely homogeneous and different factions can produce conflicting sets of interests. Implicit in the thesis is the assumption that people believe the ideologies and act accordingly. It puts the population in the role of passive consumers of ideas and assumes a too simple causal relationship between the production and consumption of ideas.

Given these qualifications, why use the term 'ideology' at all? Why not simply use the phrase 'sets of ideas'? Well, ideology is less cumbersome and, more importantly, it implies a partial set of ideas. To use the term 'ideology' is to make explicit this partiality and selectivity. National environmental ideologies are partial in that they do not necessarily represent the concerns of the whole population. They do not represent an unbroken, unchanged tradition but a *selective, recreated tradition*: selective in the sense that some experiences are considered more salient than others while others are completely ignored; recreated in the sense of reworked at different times in line with broader social changes. The histories of many groups are changed, hidden and misrepresented in this constant process of refinement.

4 Town-birds of the English countryside

The industrial system has brought a great change. The Englishman still likes to think of himself as a 'cottager' – 'my home, my garden'. But it is puerile. Even the farm labourer today is psychologically a town-bird. The English are town-birds through and through, today, as the inevitable result of their complete industrialization. Yet they don't know how to build a city, how to think of one, or how to live in one. They are all suburban, pseudo-cottagey, and not one of them knows how to be truly urban.

D.H. Lawrence (1920) *Nottingham and The Mining Country*

Britain is one of the most urbanized and industrialized countries in the world and has been for almost 150 years. This fact is the pivotal point of any analysis of its environmental ideologies. Notions of wilderness, ideas of countryside and urban attitudes are constantly refracted through this unique historical experience and particular social configuration.

WILDERNESS

Since 1746 there has been no wilderness on the British mainland that corresponds to the American West or the Australian outback. In that year, on a day in April of rain and intermittent sleet, Bonnie Prince Charlie and a group of Highland clans were defeated at Culloden, three miles east of Inverness. The battle, lasting hardly an hour, was not between English and Scots. The battle lines were drawn between, on the one side, predominantly Catholic, Gaelic-speaking, anti-government Highland clans, and on the other, the forces of the Protestant Hanover crown led by the Duke of Cumberland, including English, Lowland Scots and even a few Highland Scots; the MacDonalds fought on the government side. The outcome represented a victory for the Hanover state and assured its monopoly of power over the territory of mainland Britain.

What was defeated on that cold, windy moor in the early spring of 1746 was the last organized territorial resistance to a capitalist system and its state. The Duke of Cumberland's success was a victory for the capitalist

British state over a pre-capitalist communal society. The battle's outcome marked the beginning of the end for a social system based more on kinship obligations and communal ties than commercial relations. After 1746 there was no wilderness in Britain in the American or Australian sense.

After 1746 the Highlands were transformed. It became illegal to wear tartan, play the pipes or carry arms. All cultures need their language. The discouragement of Gaelic was an act of cultural genocide superseded only by the clearances of the early nineteenth century, when the people were thrown off the land to make way for the more profitable Cheviot sheep. Between 1800 and 1840, over 10,000 people were forcibly moved. These people became the basis of the stream of Scottish migrants to the New World of North America, Australia and New Zealand. The Highlands of Scotland are one of the few areas of the world which had less population in 1980 than it had in 1780. In 1775 Samuel Johnson described the Highlands thus: 'where formerly there was an insurrection there is now a wilderness'.

The incorporation of the Highlands into the British state meant a commercial and bureaucratic monopoly of the whole land of Britain. There were areas of mountain and fen but these were areas of extensive agriculture not a wilderness. The wilderness concept, as part of the nation's environmental ideologies, was transferred overseas and, less obviously, to its internal urban condition.

Wilderness and empire

From the seventeenth century onwards, the concept of wilderness was employed in the growing overseas expansion of British commercial and political interests. It sustained and legitimated the colonial adventure which incorporated much of the world's territory into the British sphere of commercial influence and political power. The dominant perception was of a wilderness inhabited by people too lazy or too savage to exploit its resources. Commercial incorporation involved, and was reflected in, racist ideologies. With the hunting-gathering societies, notions of 'savages' and wilderness were regularly employed. With more settled communities, the concept of 'civilized but not quite up to our standard' was used. In both cases, superiority on the British side of the frontier was assumed and was reinforced by the success of Britain, from the seventeenth to the early twentieth century, in becoming the major superpower of the world.

These attitudes continued into the twentieth century, as a young British colonial administrator noted of his older colleagues when he went out to Kenya in 1925:

> when they travelled – which they didn't do a very great deal – they would set up a Union Jack in their camp and rather tend to try and impress the natives with what wonderful things the British were doing for them; the whole idea of the White Man's Burden. I remember one of

these soldiers who, when he travelled north into the country of the Nilotic people, where the men are completely naked, always took with him an Indian trader with a large supply of khaki shorts, which he more or less forced the people to buy from the Indian by selling their goats.

(quoted in Allen 1979: 9)

Three hundred years of world dominance has had its effects on the intellectual life of Britain. Debates about places and people throughout the world have taken place from the position of colonial superiority. Indeed, the geography of the world is described from this position. The Middle East, Far East and South East Asia are spatial adjectives from the standpoint of London. The names persist. The USA fought a war in South East Asia, but for them it was, in fact, more South West Asia. Whole areas of knowledge have been constructed from this perspective. In a most interesting study, Edward Said (1978) has shown how the Orient became a European invention. This distinction continues in the more recent use of the term 'Third World' to describe a separate world. The production of knowledge in the last three hundred years has been affected by this uneven distribution of power and intellectual resources.

There have also been effects on the other side of the frontier. The peoples incorporated into British and European power have had to live with the constant demeaning of their status. Some followed the example from the 1919 *Indian Gentleman's Guide to Etiquette:*

The Indian gentleman, with all self-respect to himself, should not enter into a compartment reserved for Europeans, any more than he should enter a carriage set apart for ladies. Although you may have acquired the habits and manners of the European, have the courage to show that you are not ashamed of being an Indian, and in all such cases, identify yourself with the race to which you belong.

(quoted in Allen 1975: 231)

The making of empire involved attitudes of white (British) superiority and 'native' inferiority. In various forms the racial attitudes persist, sometimes hidden but always there. Some questioned the system. Marcus Garvey (1887–1940), for example, who was born in Jamaica, envisaged 'a new world of black men, not peasants, serfs, dogs or slaves, but a nation of sturdy men working their impress upon civilization and carrying a new light to dawn upon the human race' (quoted in Essien-Udom 1966: 48). Every liberation movement against colonial control had to overcome the undermining of self-confidence brought about by foreign control, collaborative elites and disowning intellectuals. Garvey spoke for third world people everywhere when he told the blacks of America: 'Up, up, you mighty race'.

Local elites in the colonial situation were put in a position of having a foot in both camps. Bright youngsters were often educated in English and

English ways. English language and literature have been enriched by creative schizophrenics such as V.S. Naipaul, Wole Soyinka and Salman Rushdie. The ambivalences continue. In Jamaica the most successful politicians are still those whose skin colour is dark but not black. A *café au lait* complexion is suitably ethnic but white enough to invoke images of authority, power and status.

Overt, demeaning racism was not the only discourse to emerge from the colonial experience. While some simply saw savages, others saw noble savages. While some saw inferior societies, others saw exotic social arrangements that developed characteristics which were constrained at home. These others were the romantics whose writings also inform the discourse of the 'Third World'. Just occasionally the romantics had the opportunity to do more than just write. In 1874 the group of islands now known as Fiji became a Crown Colony. The colony's first governor was Sir Arthur Gordon. He was a romantic, but now a romantic with power. He made it illegal to sell native land and opposed the use of native labour in the plantations. Today over four-fifths of the land is still held by Fijians and this land is the bedrock of a flourishing Fijian culture and a rich communal life. Tension does exist between the two ethnic groups, the Fijians and the Indians, who were imported to work on the plantations. This surfaced most clearly in the military coup of 1987. But compare Fiji with Hawaii, where less than 5 per cent of the land is owned by the indigenous people.

Empire involved a professional class whose job it was to maintain the whole edifice. This professional class, whose cultural spokesman was Rudyard Kipling, evolved codes of behaviour based on the ethos of service, hard work and strength of character, all in the pursuit of maintaining a British-defined social order. In the twilight of empire, the champions of this class took on a more strident strain as they could see themselves, despised abroad, rejected at home, becoming an historical anachronism with no place in the new society and uncomfortable in the old country. Their ethos, however, has not completely disappeared and continues in the expedition business. The nineteenth-century belief in the redeeming qualities of hard work and service has been translated, in the post-empire world, into the positive, character-shaping qualities of Third World expeditions. The explorers of the nineteenth century went to map the world, the modern equivalent go to find themselves. An historical link between the two eras is the Royal Geographical Society (see Figure 4.1). Established in 1830, it was concerned with geographical exploration connected to British commercial interests and political designs. Exploration discovered territories and allowed them to be opened up for development.

Today the Society supports expeditions. In 1980 it sponsored an expedition to Karakoram and in 1988 supported a trip to North West Australia. These official sorties now have the status of scientific trips yet they still have a *Boy's Own* feel and attract those people who are happiest

TENTS

FOR THE COLONIES.

Fitted with VERANDAH, BATHROOM, &c.

As used by most eminent Travellers, and supplied to H.M. Government for East, West, Central, and South Africa, &c.

SPECIAL TENTS FOR EXPLORERS & MOUNTAINEERING

COMPLETE EQUIPMENT.

CAMP FURNITURE WITH LATEST IMPROVEMENTS.
AIR AND WATERTIGHT TRUNKS.
UNIFORMS AND CLOTHING OF ALL KINDS.

"Consult with Messrs. Silver & Co., who know exactly what is needed for every part of the Globe."—*Extract from* "*Notes on Outfit,*" *by the Royal Geographical Society.*

Figure 4.1 Advertisement from the *Colonial List Advertiser*, 1931 – note the native on hand to boil up water

living under canvas, working in remote areas under tropical skies, plagued by mosquitoes, within a community of khaki-clad, wide-brim-hatted scientists. The whole venture is legitimized with reference to the modern religion, the pursuit of 'scientific knowledge'. The Society also acts as a clearing house for and supporter of smaller expeditions by undergraduates, school parties and young people making trips to the Third World. The Society holds the reports of these expeditions. They make interesting reading. One wet Tuesday in November 1987, I spent most of a morning and all of an afternoon in the Society's Library in Kensington Gore, London, reading through some of the reports of the last twenty-five years.

There were the scientific ones, such as the London University Ceylon Expedition of 1963 which wanted to look at the effect of hot weather on work but found that, compared to the field trials of the UK army in Aden, the local community lacked 'the regimentation and obedience to instruction'.

There were the *Boy's Own* adventures, such as *Srinagar Through Zanskav To Marrali On Skis*. The Old Harrovians' Himalayan Expedition of 1983 were revived when '"Tea, Sahib" came the cheerful cry as Aany Furer, our smiling sherpa, opened up the tent flap'. There were the disappointed:

> We were both amused and perhaps a little disappointed to find that in the cafés were the now traditional jukeboxes and it was even possible to buy Coca Cola!
>
> (Churchdown Lapland Expedition, 1965)

There were the intrepid fieldworkers:

> The inhabitants of Markha and Zanskav were extremely curious about my presence and so I had to [*sic*] difficulty in getting them to sing for me. In fact they were more than willing to do so. . . . I was taken into someone's house and given bowlful after bowlful of the Chary, the local alcoholic beverage. I emerged hours later having learnt how uncongenial high altitude and early morning drinking are.
>
> (Cambridge Ladakh Expedition, 1985)

There were the committed:

> If I wanted to understand the village, I needed to go to the other side, to the people and even more important – I had to see the village in operation . . . to see if and where I might make some contribution.
>
> (Expedition to India by Sixth Form Group from
> Hampton School, 1984)

There were the positively lyrical:

> On leaving camp after dark I think we all used to look with affection at our little community. The lighted tents standing together encompassed by the wilderness.
>
> (Expedition to Central Lahal, 1955)

These expeditions were partly funded by local and national businesses such as BP, Barclays Bank and Jobs Diary. The funding probably arose from friends of friends on the Board but they still indicate a belief by business in the character-forming experience of expeditions. The expeditions had varying aims, different goals, but they all shared the assumption that the Third World was another world – a place for a rite of passage, a testing ground for the executive class.

The wilderness within

The use of wilderness imagery and language within Britain has always been linked to questions of social control and public order. In the seventeenth century the term 'Indians' was adopted, from the experiences of the colonies in North America, to refer to the forest dwellers in the Forest of Dean. They were called Indians because they were outside formal social control and constituted areas of resistance against the established order. To call them Indians was to highlight their danger and to justify punitive actions. There have been three groups who have consistently received this designation or its equivalent in contemporary Britain.

The nationalist Irish have been a problem for the British state for four hundred years. While they have not been called Indians, they have been the subject of jokes. The typical 'Irish' joke shows the Irish to be stupid.

Question   How do you brainwash an Irishman?
Answer   Piss in his wellies.

Question   What do you call an Irishman with a Ph.D.?
Answer   A liar.

Question   Did you hear about the Irishman who hijacked a submarine?
Answer   He asked for a million pounds and a parachute

There are libraries of Irish jokebooks which repeat the basic theme. The jokes have varied in detail over the years but, from the time of Cromwell to the present day, the intention has been the same. The jokes separate out the Irish from the space of civilized society. The Irish are not only different, runs the subtext of these jokes, they are inferior. The jokes are the popular response to the difficulty that the British have had in incorporating the Irish. The jokes are not innocent of political connotation.

Like any anti-personal jokes, anti-Irish jokes have a sly quality. The perpetrators, when questioned, can go on the offensive with remarks such as, 'Don't you have a sense of humour, then?' But such jokes are a form of attack. Anti-Irish jokes are a potent way of sub-humanizing the population.

The rapid and large-scale industrialization of the nineteenth century created a new group in British society, the urban working classes, who were seen as a potential threat to the established order. The country had become 'two nations', the image used in Disraeli's 1845 novel, *Sybil*:

> between whom there is no intercourse, and no sympathy; who are as ignorant of each other's habits, thoughts and feelings, as if they were dwellers in different zones, or inhabitants of different planets; who are formed by a different breeding, are fed by a different food, are ordered by different manners, and are governed by the same laws.

There have always been the rich and the poor but the urbanization of the working classes meant a separation from the closer control of more rural communities and a separation into distinct urban neighbourhoods. The working-class city became a source of mystery, a source of fear. While David Livingstone went to Africa, Henry Mayhew, Charles Booth and the like were exploring darkest London. A whole category of reporters became established whose job it was to inform the middle classes of the life of the masses. Like early anthropologists, the reporters told their audience about the urban other. The reports ranged from the salacious, through the empirical to the reforming. Sometimes they were combined, as in *The Bitter Cry of Outcast London* written by the Revd Andrew Mearns in 1883. The Revd Mearns was concerned to highlight the appalling housing conditions of the poor in London and his tract dealt with this theme by noting at some length and detail the gross immorality and promiscuity resulting from overcrowding. Social concern and mild titillation helped to achieve a wide and influential circulation. In the next year a Royal commission was established, which informed 1885 and 1890 Acts, both entitled *Housing of the Working Classes*.

The power of dramatized reporting continues to influence. Some eighty years later, in 1966, the BBC showed a powerfully realistic drama, *Cathy Come Home*, about homelessness. The Housing Minister of the time, Arthur Greenwood, ordered a private showing for all his officials and the public response led to a strengthening of the pressure group Shelter, a group which has been an important voice in all subsequent housing debates.

Middle-class fear of the urban other has fastened on to images of crime. The fear of crime, as much as the experience of crime itself, has been a powerful social force. In an excellent corrective to the belief in a crime-free, golden age of the recent past, Geoffrey Pearson (1983) has shown that it has been a constant theme since mid-Victorian times. It is, in effect, associated with the emergence of a residentially separate, urban working class. The working class, separated out from the middle class in their own residential districts and evolving a separate popular culture were seen by many Victorian commentators as the natives within (see Figure 4.2). The term 'thug' was adopted from India to refer to urban crime at home. An article in *Reynold's Newspaper* of 14 August 1898 fumed against those who worried too much about the 'barbarians of the wild Soudan but ignore far wilder barbarians they may find within a few paces from their own street doors'.

The young male working class has been a particular focus for concern, from the 'peaky blinders' of Birmingham in the 1890s to the Teddy Boys of the 1950s. Lacking deference, full of energy and with disposable income, they were the folk devils of the recent past. New candidates emerged in the post-1945 period with the onset of Asian and Afro-Caribbean migration from former British colonies.

In 1948 the SS *Empire Windrush* brought 492 immigrants from Kingston, Jamaica to London. They were brought in as cheap, much-needed labour. In official statistics they were referred to as New Commonwealth immigrants. Forty years later, there were about 1.8 million New Commonwealth immigrants concentrated in the inner areas of the big cities. They constituted less than 4 per cent of the total population and yet, for some, they, and in particular the young male Afro-Caribbean community, posed a great threat. Twenty years after the SS *Empire Windrush* landed, Enoch Powell, a Conservative MP in the Midlands, made a now famous speech on immigration. He spoke of a nation building its own funeral pyre and said

GOING OUT TO TEA IN THE SUBURBS
A Pretty State of Things for 1862.

Figure 4.2 A cartoon from *Punch* (3 January 1863): fear of crime in the cities is not a recent phenomenon. This expedition has an uncanny resemblance to colonial expeditions.

that he could see the 'Tiber foaming with much blood'. In the 1970s and 1980s young blacks, like the peaky blinders of the 1890s or the Teddy Boys of 1950s, became the urban folk devils. The moral entrepreneurs had a new villain:

> The mugger was such a Folk Devil; his form and shape accurately reflected the content of the fears and anxieties of those who first imagined, and then actually discovered him: young, black, bred in or arising from the 'breakdown of social order' in the city; threatening the traditional peace of the streets, the security of movement of the ordinary respectable citizen; motivated by naked greed. ... In short, the very token of 'permissiveness' embodying in his every action and person, feelings and values that were the opposite of those decencies and restraints which make England what she is.
>
> (Hall *et al*. 1978: 161–2)

The black inner city has become the most recent wilderness, inhabited by the 'primitive others', a 'threat' to traditional values, a source of 'social disorder'. The debates about the inner city of the 1980s mirror, in an uncanny way, much earlier debates about the unruly colonies.

So-called civilized societies perhaps need a wilderness. It acts like a Freudian sink of repressed and forbidden feelings, the ultimate source of evil or good, an atavistic reservoir of very strong positive and negative imagery. In the expansive phase of British imperialism, the wilderness was transposed overseas and far away to alien peoples in foreign lands. In its waning phase, the wilderness is the dark continent of the inner city.

A GREEN AND PLEASANT LAND

A landscape of power

I have a map, first published in 1776 probably as part of a book, which consists of three route maps from Edinburgh. I bought it because one of the routes passed through Tullibody, the village of my family where I lived until I went to University. The routes show only the terrain and the location of the local gentry. Tullibody figures on the map only as the location of a Kirk and of one Colonel Abercrombie, whose descendants still own land in the area. One of my uncles worked for a while in their local leather factory. The map says nothing about the other people of the village. They were given the cartographic condescension of silence. They were unmarked and unrecorded. The map is a landscape of power.

The English countryside, like my map, is a landscape of power whose 'mythic' properties are comparatively recent in origin. From the time when my map was printed to the Napoleonic wars, there was a growing population which meant a rising demand for food. In association with technological developments this led to the first agricultural revolution involving technological changes, which allowed farmers to improve soil fertility, reclaim wasteland and develop new breeding techniques to produce fatter sheep and healthier cattle. There was a dramatic increase in the extent and intensity of farming. The landscape was transformed by the enclosure movement. Enclosure meant the enclosing of open fields and the privatization of common pastures. It had been going on for centuries but was becoming more common by the seventeenth and eighteenth centuries. In the latter half of the eighteenth and early part of the nineteenth century, enclosures were increasing: five and a half million acres, approximately 20 per cent of England's total acreage, was enclosed between 1760 and 1820. Enclosure was effected through an Act of Parliament. The usual procedure was for the large landowners and farmers to settle their differences beforehand. They then applied to Parliament for permission to enclose and a bill was brought to Parliament. Objections were heard and three commissioners were nominated to investigate the claim and to allocate land. The system was geared for the benefit of the wealthy.

Take the case of Croydon, as noted in Hammond and Hammond (1948). On 7 November 1796, a petition for the enclosure of 750 acres of open and common fields and 2,200 acres of common marshes, heaths, wastes, woods, lands and grounds was received and a bill was presented on 8 May 1797. Petitions were heard from local farmers and from one Richard Davis and others on 26 May. These stated that 'the said Bill goes to deprive the Inhabitants of the said Parish and the poor thereof in particular, of certain ancient rights and immunities granted to them (as they have been informed) by some, or one, of the Predecessors of his present Majesty, and that the said Bill seems calculated to answer the Ends of certain Individuals.' The petitions were rejected and the bill received royal assent on 19 July 1797. The land was then divided up. The biggest landowners alienated most of the common land. Of the 2,950 acres, only 215 acres was left for the use and benefit of the poor. According to Dr Benjamin Willis, with the benefit of thirty years' experience of enclosure:

> By the destruction of the common rights, and giving no renumeration to the poor man, a gentleman had taken an immense tract of it and converted it into a park, a person in the middling walk of life had bought an acre or two, and though this common in its original state was not so valuable as it had been made, yet the poor man should have been consulted in it.
> (*Third Report of the Select Committee on Emigration 1826–7*: 309)

Even Arthur Young, who had been a powerful advocate of parliamentary enclosure and was made secretary of the Board of Agriculture when it was established in 1793, became disenchanted. In 1800 he wrote, 'I had rather that all the commons were sunk in the sea than that the poor should in future be treated on enclosing as they have generally been hitherto' (quoted in Rude 1972: 40).

The enclosures were the imposition of a new commercial order, an order in which traditional obligations to villagers and the local community were broken. Land was privatized and the landscape was transformed into a commercial space of regular, hedgerowed fields. The so-called 'typical' English scene, of a patchwork of green fields, is in origin the spatial imprint of an eighteenth-century commercial enterprise. Through the enclosures, the landowners obtained more land and strengthened their power while those of the 'middling walk of life' also gained. For those at the bottom, the enclosures meant a loss of traditional rights. The result was the break-up of the peasantry and the creation of a rural proletariat very dependent on cash wages. It is ironic that the typical English countryside, the super-charged image of English environmental ideology, which can still conjure up notions of community, unchanging values and national sentiments, is in reality the imprint of a profit-based exercise which destroyed the English peasantry and replaced a moral economy of traditional rights and obligations with the cash nexus of commercial capitalism.

While transforming the countryside into an ordered mosaic of bounded fields, the same powerful groups were also creating the other major environmental icon, the English landscape garden. One was for profit, the other for delight, but both were an exercise in power.

Aesthetic sensitivities shifted throughout the eighteenth century. In garden design the move was away from tight, enclosed spaces, with geometric lines of vegetation, towards a more expansive sweep of turf and trees, with vistas of lake, lawn and copse. The fashion for parkland scenery set around the big country house can be seen in the meteoric rise of the landscape designers, William Kent, Lancelot Brown and Humphrey Repton. Let us concentrate on Brown. Born in 1716 in Kirkharle in Northumberland, Brown was apprenticed as a gardener on the estate of a local landowner, where he was given a grounding in the essentials of landscape management. In 1740 he became undergardener at Stowe in Buckinghamshire. The main designer was William Kent, one of the first to give gardens a more 'natural' look. He had travelled in Italy and knew the poet Alexander Pope, who had written that 'All gardening is landscape painting' (quoted in Mainwaring 1925: 127). The style that Pope and Kent championed was known as the picturesque, literally 'after the manner of paintings', in particular the arcadian landscapes of Claude Lorraine and Gaspar Poussin who were immensely popular in eighteenth century England.

In 1749 Brown set up his own business and moved to London where he could meet the landowners who visited London. His first contract was gained in 1751 and from then until his death he was continuously in employment and always in demand. No self-respecting eighteenth-century landowner could remodel his country seat without calling for Brown, who gained the nickname 'Capability'. Brown worked on almost 150 estates and undertook some of the largest 'improvements'. The complete remodelling of Blenheim gardens in the 1760s was one of the largest projects, entailing an expenditure of £30,000 (in today's figures the equivalent of £750,000).

Brown opened up gardens so that all was landscape. Lawns came from the edge of the house and merged into the surrounding fields through the use of ha-has, sunken fences which kept in grazing animals but left the traverse of the eye undisturbed. Depth was added by clumps of woodland, set into the parkland or following sinuous curves along the top of ridges. Brown favoured lakes and was forever damming streams and turning brackish ponds into graceful lakes. Brown became rich and successful. He purchased a small country seat, was appointed High Sheriff of Huntingdon in 1770, and sent his son to Eton. He died in 1783, a wealthy man.

This parkland scenery was achieved at some cost. In 1752 a Joseph Damner, later to become Baron Milton and 1st Earl of Dorchester, purchased Milton Abbey and estates in Dorset. In accordance with the fashion of the time he employed Brown to landscape the area around the site of his new house. There was one problem. The medieval village of Milton Abbas lay right beside Damner's property and schoolchildren from the grammar school used to steal his fruit and trespass on his ground. His answer was to obtain Parliamentary legislation to move the school to Blandford, buy up all the village property, demolish all the buildings and

Figure 4.3 Nuneham Park

Figure 4.4 Less than two miles away from Nuneham Park is the 'displaced' village of Nuneham Courtenay

rehouse the inhabitants in a new village up the hill away from the house. The new village can be seen to this day – a sharp geometry of regular one-storey, box-like cottages, an unsettling mix of rustic cottages in straight, regular lines.

It was not just the *nouveaux riches* like Damner, unburdened by ancient obligations, who were razing villages. When Lord Harcourt decided to abandon the ancestral home at Stanton Harcourt, he chose to build a new house on a knoll overlooking the Thames at Nuneham Courtenay (see Figure 4.3). Work began in 1756. The ancient village of Newham was destroyed and the villagers were moved to a new village, discreetly out of sight of the house (see Figure 4.4). The next Lord Harcourt employed Brown in 1777 to landscape the views from the house.

Oliver Goldsmith presented an alternative view of the landscape changes. In his poem *The Deserted Village*, first published in 1770, Goldsmith tells the story of the demolition of a mythical village, Auburn, which was probably based on the destruction of Newham and the rebuilding of Nuneham Courtenay.

> The man of wealth and pride
>
> Takes up a space that many poor supplied;
> Space for his lake, his park's extended bounds,
> Space for his horses, equipage and hounds;
> The robe that wraps his lambs in silken sloth;
> Has robbed the neighbouring fields of half their growth;
> His seat, where solitary sports are seen,
> Indignant spurns the cottage from the green.

The poem is an eighteenth-century version of those investigative TV documentaries where pictures of the dispossessed poor are contrasted with the filthy rich. It is a marvellous piece of committed poetry, completely over the top at times, but no worse for that.

> But times are altered; trade's unfeeling train
> Usurps the land and dispossesses the swain;
> Sweet smiling village, loveliest of the lawn,
> Thy sports are fled, and all thy charms withdrawn;
> Amidst thy bowers the tyrant's hand is seen,
> And desolation saddens all thy green:
> One only master grasps the whole domain.

The desire for 'Brown' landscapes was a matter of aesthetic sensibilities underwritten by social and economic power. Garden design was concerned with seclusion and exclusion. The big houses were isolated from local communities by turf and wood. Seclusion was obtained by exclusion. Commanding positions were exactly that, sites of command, centres of power separated from the peasantry by seas of grass and fences of trees.

The paradox is that the twin elements of the 'typical' English country-side, small regular fields and rolling acres of parkland, were not the result of centuries of unending, conflict-free tradition, as is commonly supposed and regularly presented, but of a radical change in power relations. It was and is a landscape which carries the inprint of power.

The holders of power were the landed aristocracy, masters of rural domains, who formed an elite group in eighteenth century Britain and whose power persisted throughout the nineteenth century. At the apex of the social hierarchy were the 300-strong families who together owned a quarter of England in individual parcels of over 100,000 acres. Their country houses were the intersections of national and local power. Their position is neatly summarized as:

> a most delicate and precarious balancing act between several sets of opposing extremes. In their family arrangements they had had to steer between the pursuit of too many and too few heiresses; between producing too few and too many children; between allowing too little or too much individual discretion in the disposal of property; between too generous expenditures which ran up debt or too miserly expenditure which generated contempt; between overbuilding which created a seat too expensive to live in, or underbuilding which led to status derogation. In their behaviour toward other classes they had had to steer between too generous paternalism towards tenants which would erode revenues and too ruthless profiteering which would undermine deference; between too ready an acceptance of the new rich which would dilute numbers and values and too rigid rejection which would stimulate class antagonisms. In their political capabilities they had to manoeuvre between too gross an exploitation of public offices which would engender popular opprobrium and government inefficiency, and too ready a welcome to reform which would substitute merit for influence and thus might erode one basis of their family fortune, between the cherished ideals of popular sovereignty and the rule of law, and a practical arrangement which preserved power in élite hands.
>
> (Stone and Stone 1984: 421–2)

Below this group were the rural gentry, about 3,000 strong, who owned estates of between 1,000 and 10,000 acres. Their power was much more localized and they helped to run the shire counties. These two groups had an absolute majority in Parliament until 1885 although there had been some accommodation to the new urban and industrial realities before then. The repeal of the corn laws in 1846, for example, marked a recognition of urban interests. Thompson (1963) has argued that reform was made by the aristocracy, who were mindful of their metropolitan and national interests and responsibilities, and accepted by the gentry who were 'constrained to accept from conservative hands changes which they would have resisted to the death if proposed by middle-class radicals' (Thompson 1963: 24).

Table 4.1 Ownership of selected landed estates in England, 1873 and 1967

| Owner | Acreage | |
	1873	1967
Marquess of Abergavenny	28,000	1,000
Earl of Aylesford	19,500	5,000
Marquess of Aylesbury	55,000	6,000
Lord Brocket		4,500
Lord Brassey	4,000	4,000
Marquess of Bath	55,000	10,000
Duke of Beaufort	51,000	52,000
Viscount Bolingbroke	3,300	4,000
Lord Bolton	29,200	18,500
Viscount Blakenham		580
Mr E. Brudenell	15,000	10,000
Lord Brabourne	4,100	3,000
Sir W. Bromley-Davenport	15,600	5,000
Lord Brownlow	58,300	10,000
Marquess of Bristol	32,000	16,000
Earl of Carnarvon	35,500	6,000
Lord Clinton	34,700	26,000
Viscount Cobham	6,900	400
Viscount Cowdray		17,500
Baron Crathorne	5,600	4,000
Sir J. Craster	2,800	750
Earl of Durham	30,000	30,000
Earl of Derby	68,900	5,000
Earl of Devon	53,000	5,000
Duke of Devonshire	138,500	72,000
Lord Egremont	109,900	20,000
Marquess of Exeter	28,200	22,000
Earl Ferrers	8,600	250
Lord Feversham	39,300	47,000
Fulford of Fulford	4,000	3,500
Duke of Grafton	25,000	11,000
Earl of Harewood	29,600	7,000
Earl of Huntingdon	13,500	
Marquess of Hertford	12,200	8,000
Lord Iliffe		10,000

Source: Perrott (1968) and Newby (1979)

The *economic* power of the landed interest began to falter in the last quarter of the nineteenth century. An agricultural depression, from 1873 almost to the turn of the century, meant falling rents and dwindling revenues. A Liberal government elected in 1906 began an assault on the entrenched power of the landed interest. The tide had turned. The great estates began to break up. Before 1914 only 10 per cent of farmland in England and Wales was owner-occupied, but this figure rose to 36 per cent by 1927 and to almost 80 per cent by 1980. It is now the fashion to mourn the passing of the great estates as they disappear into historical irrelevance. This is not quite the case. Table 4.1 provides a comparison between 1873 and 1967. There is a decline in many cases but there are still significant holdings. Although statistics on ownership are hard to come by and difficult to interpret, Massey and Catalano (1978) suggest that almost one-third of land in Britain is still in the private estates of the landed nobility.

In contrast, the *cultural* power of the landed interest is undiminished. The image of the country seat became the zenith of ambition for the rest of society. Those moving up the hierarchy saw a rural setting as the pinnacle of their rise and a mark of their arrival. Throughout the eighteenth, nineteenth and twentieth centuries, most people who have made serious money have tended to obtain a country property. Those who made money in India built nabob mansions in the home counties, industrialists purchased estates, and money made in the city was consumed in the country. The purchase of a rural property was not only a mark of wealth but also a badge of respectability, taste and decorum. The country property was the socially sanctioned method of conspicuous consumption. Industrialists who made their money from iron, engineering, cotton, coal and beer bought rural estates and country seats. Take the case of the Tennants, as chronicled by Simon Blow (1987). In the late-eighteenth century, Charles Tennant was an apprntice weaver at a mill outside Glasgow. He invented a chemical bleach and eventually had the largest chemical manufacturing plant in the country. He made a fortune yet kept his radicalism. His son bought an estate, built a country seat and collected pictures. In turn, his son, who was made Lord Glenconner by Asquith, had that odd assortment of children which bedevils those whose connection with money is in its spending not its making. One son took to drink while another dressed in women's clothing and fell in love with the poet Siegfried Sassoon. The Tennants provide a morality tale of the decline of the industrial spirit.

In 1902 Rudyard Kipling bought a house in the country, a seventeenth-century manor house. The imperialist had returned to the home counties. As he wrote to a friend,

> England is a wonderful land. It is the most marvellous of all foreign countries that I have ever been in. It is made up of trees and green fields and mud and the gentry, and at last I'm one of its gentry.
>
> (quoted in Carrington 1956: 286)

The 'at last' suggests a lifetime goal had been reached: service in the colonies rewarded by the status of gentleman at home.

The image persists into the late-twentieth century. A profile of the millionaire Alan Bond noted:

> Bond left the City . . . and drove to Oxfordshire where he has bought the estate village of Glympton for £11m. He and his colourful wife 'Red'

Eileen bought the 2,000-acre estate to realise Bond's dream, now that he is 50, of becoming a county Squire in the land of his birth.

(*Independent*, 12 November 1988)

I also recommend reading any of the many articles and books on manners produced in the 1980s. Just one example is an article in the *Observer* magazine of 4 September 1988, entitled 'Mind Your Manners'. The writer sought to indicate the correct manners in polite society. 'Polite society' was defined as the owners of country seats. The lead photograph was of a tweed-clad couple, on the steps of their country home, welcoming brash townies. The message was: how do we turn these *nouveaux riches* folk into well-behaved members of the elite? The most obvious way is to buy a home in the country, or at the very least to know how to behave during a weekend in the country; and in order to play the part, to get kitted out in green wellies, jackets, thick-soled shoes and Viyella shirts, all in a fawning copy of the Balmorality of the modern Royals. It was not a spoof article. The author of the article assumed that rural living was and still is the unstated yet universally accepted desired state, the preferred end point, the zenith of good taste and status credibility.

Balmorality

The Royals have been key figures in establishing consumption patterns and preferred ways of life. They have been influential in establishing and reinforcing the 'country' ethic. Let us consider just one example. The most imaginative act of the nineteenth-century environmental ideology was the creation of the Highland myth. Queen Victoria was a keen reader of Sir Walter Scott and was steeped in myths of Scotland. In the 1840s she purchased a laird's house in upper Deeside which was subsequently Germanized by Prince Albert into Scots baronial, a pseudo-gothic pile of crenellated towers and battlements. The Queen ordered all of the staff to wear kilts in a tartan designed by herself and the Prince. Balmoral became a Disneyland for the monarchy, a place of make-believe, a never-never land, a tartanized Scotland emptied by clearances. Beneath the genuine interest was a soft gooey centre, a sentimentalization of the Scots' historical experience. The country had become a playground. In her diary of 8 September 1842, the Queen noted:

> Albert went off at half-past nine to shoot with Lord Breadalbane ... returned at half-past three. He had had excellent sport and the trophies of it were spread out before the house – nineteen roe deer, several hares and pheasants, and three brace of grouse; there was also a capercailzie that had been wounded.

The next day Albert went out again

at twenty minutes to three, having had very hard work on the moors, wading up to his knees in bogs every now and then, and had killed nine brace of grouse. We lunched then we went to the drawing room, and saw from the window the Highlanders dancing a reel.

(quoted in Pocock, undated: 185–6)

By slaughtering the wildlife and watching the natives, the Royals created a fashion for shooting-lodges in the Highlands. More than that, they helped to create the myth of a Highland Scotland which represents, in condensed form, the wider creation of the British countryside.

A landscape without figures

The countryside became, and still is, the most important landscape in the national environmental ideology. It holds pride of place. In England the two meanings of country, as countryside and nation, are collapsed into one another; the essence of England is popularly thought to be the green countryside – the enclosed fields, the secluded/excluded parklands of the country houses, and the small villages. The nineteenth-century landed elite may have lost economic power in the twentieth century but their symbolic power is still evident in this view, which is widely believed at home and increasingly marketed abroad. The countryside has become the 'real' England, the 'unchanging' England. It has become the land of retreat from an increasingly urban and overwhelmingly industrial society, the place to escape modernity.

The country became a haven for the rich because it had been emptied of people. It was a landscape without figures, cleared by enclosures, an agricultural revolution, and steady mechanization which had stripped the fields of labour. There were almost 1.5 million agricultural workers in 1851 but only 240,000 by 1981. The respective percentage of the labour force employed in agriculture declined from 22 per cent to 2 per cent. The urbanization and industrialization of British society decanted the rural population, leaving a vacuum to be filled by imaginative reconstructions of rurality. There was some resistance.

The locals of the countryside had been, by and large, beaten into submission by historical events, though there had been resistance against the commercialization of agriculture. On 28 August 1830, a threshing machine was destroyed. This was the first act of what became known as the Captain Swing riots. The destruction of the new machines and the burning of ricks was an act of defiance, a rage against the tide of events. The response was harsh. The state authorities executed nineteen people, imprisoned over 600 and transported 481 to Australia. Later an attempt to set up an agricultural union by labourers in Dorset in the early 1830s was quashed. The six 'martyrs' of Tolpuddle were arrested in 1834 and transported to Australia. Eventually, however, an agricultural labourers' union was established and achieved tremendous growth in the 1870s. Demands for wage increases helped to boost the membership to 120,000 by 1873. The motto of *Press forward, push onward, rise upward* is strangely reminiscent of the cry of Marcus Garvey. The strike called by the union in 1873 was met by a farmers' lock-out and intimidation of workers. The strike was unsuccessful. The story of class relations in the British countryside since then has been one of occasional acts of resistance met by the more successful power of the landed interest. Agricultural trade unionism became an established fact in the twentieth century but it was never able to provide a high standard of living for agricultural workers, who were always on the wrong end of the supply–demand equation.

The story is not of continual defeat, however. There were some successful examples of rural resistance. Let us return to the place where we started this chapter, the Highlands of Scotland. During the clearances, families were removed from the land. Some emigrated, some moved south, but some obtained land on the narrow coastal strips of the Highlands and Islands. In the mid-nineteenth century there was a huge demand for seaweed. It was needed for chemical production. Many landowners settled people on crofts – smallholdings too small to live off without another source of income – and these crofters provided the labour for seaweed collection. Agitation for security of tenure and reduced rents emerged in the 1870s. It was part of a nationwide, though uncoordinated, land reform movement. In the Highlands it was influenced by an early form of liberation theology. The deeply religious, Gaelic-speaking community drew biblical parallels for land reform and saw divine justification for security of tenure (see Meek 1987). Tension increased in the 1880s. In Skye, in 1881, a rent strike was called. Evictions took place and resistance against the evictions led to a skirmish which resulted in the despatch of a gunboat and the arrest of four crofters. The land war spread to other islands and the mainland. The Parliamentary response was to establish the Napier Commission to look into the causes of the social unrest. The report published in 1884 identified lack of security of tenure, loss of land (taken for sporting purposes, as the wealthy followed the lead set by Prince Albert) and too high rents. Social unrest continued and, in the 1885 general election, four pro-crofting Members of Parliament were elected. Gladstone's government responded with the 1886 Crofters' Holdings Act which gave security of tenure, and the right of bequest to one member of the family. Subsequent Acts of Parliament, in 1911, 1955 and 1976, further codified the unique status of crofters.

Crofters not only have individual plots of land but also share communal spaces of foreshore and grazing ground. Crofting is patterned into a more communal lifestyle and strictly commercial considerations have been tempered by wider social considerations and obligations. There are now 14,000 crofters and 17,000 crofting units throughout the Highlands and Islands of Scotland, a reminder and a demonstration of a communal alternative to purely commercial farming. Crofting is a way of life, an act of defiance, a statement of cultural resistance against Balmorality. For most of the twentieth century it was seen as a pre-capitalist remnant but in the more ecologically aware last quarter it provides a glimpse of what a post-capitalist economy could look like.

The power of landscape

The ideological importance of the countryside has meant that it has become separated from purely agricultural considerations. The country-side is more than just a place for farmers to grow crops, raise animals and make money. It is a place of broader cultural significance and deeper ideological meaning, a place redolent with historical association, percep-tions of nationality and intimations of community. It has become a place of wider political significance. The landscape of power has become the power of landscape to evoke feelings, generate emotions, provide causes. Two important causes have been access to the countryside and the look of the countryside.

As the nineteenth century wore on, there was a concern to widen access, an attempt to democratize the countryside. The National Trust, for example, was established to halt further enclosure of common land and to provide open spaces for urban workers. There were also explicitly socialist movements, such as the Clarion Clubs of the 1890s, which combined socialist rhetoric with environmental awareness. These clubs believed in getting away from the towns and cities into the fresh air of the countryside. The aim was 'to bring the town dweller more frequently into contact with the beauty of nature; to help forward the ideal of the simpler life, plain living and high thinking' (quoted in Prynn 1976: 68). The Rambling movement of the early twentieth century was a popular-based attempt to increase access to the countryside. In April 1932, a mass trespass by 500 ramblers on the Duke of Devonshire's grouse moors in Kinder Scout, Derbyshire led to a battle between estate workers and ramblers. The wild scenes of Kinder Scout have since passed into Rambling folk memory but they were part of a sustained commitment to open up the countryside. The attempt was successful. The Access to the Mountains Act was passed in 1937 and the Countryside Act of 1949 helped to establish national parks. The war has been won but battles persist as farmers close off rights of way and ramblers resist.

Since 1945 there has been a second agricultural revolution in Britain. Farming has become even more mechanized, more capital-intensive and more chemically based. Farms have grown bigger, hedgerows have dis-appeared, trees have been felled and meadows ploughed. Underwritten by public subsidies, modern farming has transformed the old landscape of power.

The impact of these changes is noted by the following two letters from the letters page of the *Guardian*.

Sir, I live in a beautiful and remote spot under the White Horse Hill, surrounded by open countryside. On occasions, I visit my daughter who lives on the Pepys Estate, Deptford – the two locations could not be more dissimilar.

However, I have noticed that, while the dawn chorus here in Uffington is now almost non-existent, it is positively deafening (provided you get up in time before the traffic) in the concrete wilderness of SE8. Ten years ago it was not so. Could it be that Rachel Carson's Silent Spring has overtaken the countryside and that the sensible, streetwise birds have winged it to the crop-spray free city?

(Guardian, 14 April 1988)

Sir, Within hours of our arrival in Cherbourg last week, we had seen hedgerow after hedgerow studded with primroses, cowslips, violets, and great drifts of pink and white wood anemones. The following day we passed fields full of milkmaids and small pale daffodils.

All these pleasurable sights brought back vivid memories of a similar Easter trip through mid-France three years ago.

On each occasion I mentally pictured the contrast between this feast of wild flowers and their conspicuous absence along the verges of rural England. In my own county, cowslips are now almost nonexistent or occasionally one catches glimpses of snowdrops in small bunches or a patch of primroses. Why such a difference between one side of the Channel and the other? I can only assume that the English spray weedkiller farther and wider than do the French.

No doubt this produces more or less wild-flower-free crops, but now that we appear to be producing too much of everything agriculturally speaking, couldn't we at least leave the hedgerows free of chemicals so that flowers start to bloom again in French profusion along English country roads? – Yours wistfully

(Guardian, 29 April 1988)

The new agriculture changed the look and the feel of the countryside, turning it more obviously into a place of wealth generation for farmers rather than a nature spot for observers. The paradox was that the main sites for broom and blackberries, butterflies and bats, birds, flowers and mammals became not the countryside but railway cuttings, road verges, derelict inner city sites and Army ranges. The real sanctuary for nature became those places untouched by farmers' hands.

Perhaps the most trenchant analysis of the environmental inputs of these agricultural changes came from Marion Shoard who wrote:

the English countryside has been turned into a vast, featureless expanse of prairie. Its surface is given over either to cereal growing or to grass monoculture, fuelling intensive stock clearing. This new English landscape can offer little delight to the human eye or ear. It cannot sustain

Whose land is it anyway?

The proprietors' interest in the countryside, which is expressed in the Country Landowners' Association and the National Farmers' Union, adopts a disdainful attitude towards the conservationist movement. So far it has refused to discuss seriously the proposition that an owner's rights in his land are subject to an over-riding public interest.

Countering the assault on the countryside

Axe on agriculture

The Tory Party is rapidly becoming aware of the vote-winning possibilities in conservation issues.

Reaping the profits of greed

agriculture threatens the environment

WHOSE LAND IS IT ANYWAY?

Fields and forests are big business, but the public has a right to enjoy them. Keep the basic principles in view, says *Kay Batchelor*, and we can reach a happy compromise

green lobby

Rare plants lost

Probe reveals scandal of pesticide spraying

GEOFFREY LEAN and ARTHUR OSMAN report on a deadly problem for country dwellers.

Scores of people throughout Britain are being poisoned by clouds of pesticides sprayed from planes and helicopters, an *Observer* inquiry has established.

The scandal threatens to eclipse straw-burning as the most controversial public nuisance for country dwellers, but although agriculture Ministers have promised to strengthen safety rules for other aspects of pesticide use, their proposed legislation contains no provisions for aerial spraying. Friends of the Earth is launching a campaign to persuade them to tackle the problem.

A land farmed into the ground

Countryside siege

Figure 4.5 Newspaper cuttings from the 1980s, reflecting attitudes towards modern agriculture and its damage to the environment (taken from a range of newspapers and journals, including the *Guardian*, the *Independent*, the *Observer*, the *Sunday Times* and *Good Housekeeping*)

our traditional wild flowers, birds and animals ... unless something is done to curb agricultural intensities, virtually the whole of the countryside will be no more than a food factory by the early part of the century.

(Shoard 1980: 10)

All three commentators quoted share a sense of loss for the traditional countryside. Shoard's book is entitled *The Theft of The Countryside*, a title

Figure 4.6 Mompesson House, Salisbury, built by Charles Mompesson in the early eighteenth century, is a typical National Trust property. It is a big, imposing place, housing the accumulated wealth of the bourgeoisie. It represents history from the perspective of the rich and successful.

which captures the sense of resentment that 'our' countryside has been sold off for economic gain. Her next book, published in 1987, was entitled *This Land is Our Land: The struggle for Britain's countryside*. The countryside is more than a food factory, it is a cultural resource (see Figure 4.5).

The desire to preserve and recreate the traditional landscape of rural England is strongly felt by an overwhelmingly urban population. It is given an institutional force in the form of such bodies as the National Trust. The Trust emerged from the concern of Victorian radicals to save the countryside and allow access to town dwellers. Because of taxation, dwindling resources and changing fashion, many big country houses were coming up for sale. Under a special Act of Parliament in 1937, the National Trust was allowed to hold land and investments for the upkeep of property and it began to buy up country houses. By 1988 it owned 87 (see Figure 4.6). In the second half of its life, the National Trust has become concerned with the preservation of the landscape of power.

Kenneth Clark said in an address to National Trust members in 1970:

The world of great houses and peaceful village streets and decent market towns once seemed absolutely inviolable. Now it has largely

vanished and is continuing to vanish at an incredible speed. But a great part of us – our lives, our language, our lyric poetry – belongs to that world. What a misfortune if these parts of our national life were without visible confirmation. *The National Trust not only provides great pleasure it also plays an important part in stabilizing and unifying our society.*
                    (quoted in Fedden and Joekes 1973: 26, emphasis added)

The homes set in the Brown landscapes are now seen as elements of a shared culture, part of a nostalgic creation of an organic community. The National Trust, with over a million members and a staff of 2,000, not only evokes the past but also creates it.

Most societies go into the future with a rearview-mirror on the past. This is particularly pronounced in Britain because in the past it was *the* imperial power. Now it is only one more 'major power' lacking its former global economic and military might. In Britain the past is a happier, more secure time than the present or the future. The countryside is what most people see or want to see in the rearview-mirror. The landscape of power has become the power of landscape to embody 'national' sentiments of former glories, past power and world dominance.

BABYLON AND JERUSALEM

In the early nineteenth century, according to Mark Girouard (1985), two conflicting images of the city began to appear. The first was the city as Babylon, the city as a wild and wicked place. The second was the city as Jerusalem, the city as an earthly paradise. These images condensed the ambivalence felt in England towards cities. Table 4.2 shows the main polarities.

Table 4.2. Urban polarities

City as Babylon		City as Jerusalem	
rural	*urban*	*urban*	*rural*
Community	Mob	Community	'Society'
Order	Disorder	Freedom	Repression
Retreat	Work	Progress	Regress

The city as Babylon

Cities have always been crowded, dirty, noisy places. By the nineteenth century it was becoming more noticeable. Cities were growing by leaps and bounds. In 1801, no city in Britain outside of London had a population greater than 100,000; by 1891 there were twenty-three such cities. The landscape was being transformed into a townscape, as villages grew into towns, towns into cities and cities into urban conglomerations beyond the ken of any individual. The population of London increased from 850,000 in 1801 to 4.2 million in 1891. The urban increase was both absolute and relative. London had only 8 per cent of the nation's population in 1801 but 14.5 per cent in 1891. This urban growth came about through massive rural migration. Cities were sustained by a stream of incomers from the villages and the countryside. It was not simply a redistribution of population but a reordering of social relations and a shift in the locus of power. The movement of people from rural areas to the towns involved a loss of power for the rural landed interest who had effective control of life in the countryside through their ownership of the land, employment opportunities and the church. For the Establishment, the rise of towns meant a decline in social control. Urban populations were less constrained by the obligations and controls of rural society. For the rich and powerful the city became the home of the mob. Robert Southey, in his *Letters from England* (1807), noted:

> A manufacturing poor is more easily instigated to revolt. They have no local attachments; the persons to whom they look up for support they regard more with envy than respect, as men who grow rich by their labour: they know enough of what is pressing in the political world to think themselves politician: they feel the whole burthen [*sic*] of taxation which is not the case with the peasant, because he raises a great part of his own food: they are aware of their own numbers, and the moral feelings which in the peasant are only blunted, are in these men debauched. A manufacturing populace is always ripe for rioting – the direction which this fury may take is accidental. In 1780 it was against the Catholics, in 1790 against the Dissenters. Governments who found their prosperity upon manufacturers sleep upon gunpowder.
>
> (quoted in Coleman 1973: 35)

The city was the scene of the dislocation of new and threatening social forces. The industrial cities massed together people who had little say and no power beyond the collective presence. As the cities grew and people became separated out in distinct residential quarters, the urban other replaced the primitive other in the cosmology of the rich and powerful and the merely frightened. In 1842, in a *Report on the Sanitary Conditions of the Labouring Population of Great Britain*, Edwin Chadwick noted that:

> the statements of the conditions of considerable proportions of the labouring population of the towns into which the present enquiries have been carried have been received with surprise by persons of the wealthier classes living in the immediate vicinity, to whom the facts were as strange as if they related to foreigners or the natives of an unknown country.

The poorer citizens were then, and remain today, natives of an 'unknown country' which is feared or romanticized, the subject of urban fieldtrips and anthropological observations. The people of the inner city are the modern savages, disconnected from the more 'natural' rural community.

In the city as Babylon, the urban centres are places of disorder, to be contrasted with the order of the countryside and rural society. Such disorder is evidenced in the lack of religion, lack of morals and rising crime. The English distaste for the city is part of that general mood of anti-urbanism which we have already discussed in Chapter 3. However, it took a particularly potent form in the nineteenth century because of the large-scale urbanization and industrialization. The cities became the storm centres of the Victorian age and, for their critics, they were the site of social breakdown. By the mid- to late-twentieth century, it was the new suburbs that fitted this role. For the anti-urbanists, the burgeoning suburbs disrupt the landscape while their inhabitants do not fit into familiar categories. Anti-urbanism or anti-suburbanism is one critical response to the new and unfamiliar; it is a dismissal of modernity, a contempt for the contemporary.

To see the city as Babylon is to make the contrast between the city as work and countryside as retreat. Britain's towns and cities were the centre for the enthronement of industrial capitalism. For the many opponents of capitalism and the new industrial order, the cities became an important point of attack. Two contrasting positions can be identified. The first is embodied in Friedrich Engel's classic account, *The Condition of the English Working Class in England*, first published in Germany in 1845 and in English in 1892. This book links the emerging economic order with the developing urban order. Engels was at pains to show the link between space and society, city and economy, capitalism and urbanism. It is still a readable account, unsurpassed in its careful documentation and broader theorizing. Few made the connections that Engels did. The second position is exemplified by Charles Dickens. In *Hard Times*, first published in 1854, Dickens paints a picture of a northern industrial town. Coketown was based on his earlier visit to Preston. Throughout the novel, Coketown is used as the embodiment of an unfeeling materialism, a concern with profit at the expense of human feeling and social community. Dickens raises our sympathy but, unlike Engels, gives no real political shape to our emotion. It is not simply that Dickens was writing a novel and Engels a social analysis, their differences were more of political inclination than literary form. To be an Engels, one needed to have an encompassing theory of society and a commitment to radical social change. Few had the knowledge or the inclination. It was much easier to criticize the obvious places rather than the more opaque processes.

The city was something to escape from. There was lack of concern with the city amongst many of the rich and powerful. In 1988, when a journalist asked an ordinary Londoner about the state of London, he replied:

I think it is dirty because the British are dirty. They drop things. In this country there is the culture of the countryside: as soon as you have made your pile you move out of town. I think one of the reasons London is such a poor place is that not enough nobs live there. They all live outside.

(quoted in Perera 1988)

The retreat from the city by the well-to-do has been protected by the British planning system. The system of land use controls which has grown up in this century, at first hesitantly in the 1920s and 1930s, then forcefully codified in the 1947 Town and Country Planning Act but subsequently weakened, has taken as its main aim the protection of the countryside. The system developed as a means of delaying, stopping or channelling urban growth (see Figures 4.7 and 4.8). Cities were necessary evils to be tolerated but not encouraged. The conversion of rural to urban land use was hedged in by regulations and sanctions. The 'preservation' of the countryside has been bought at the cost of high prices for new homes squeezed into high-density plots and separated from workplace areas. The controls did not apply on the other side of the urban–rural divide. The belief in agricultural fundamentalism was so strong that few controls were placed on the agricultural sector. As one observer noted, farmers were not only exempt from local taxation,

but they can uproot Saxon hedgerows, erect farm buildings and turn meadows into arable prairie, without informing, let alone seeking permission from, the local authority.

(Moseley 1984: 156)

The city as Jerusalem

One of the most interesting poets in the English language is William Blake (1757–1827). He had all the gritty individuality of a self-taught and genuinely creative artist. He was always a rebel. He supported the French Revolution and his radicalism continued throughout his life, unlike that of his poetic contemporary, Wordsworth. He was a deeply religious man who saw God as a figure of tyrannical authority and Jesus as the symbol of spiritual goodness. He was an engraver, painter and poet. His early poetry is beautiful and lyrical, his later work more sombre with images in a darker hue. One of his late poems is *Jerusalem*, written between 1804 and 1820. It is a long, rambling monster of a poem which reads at one point:

And did the countenance divine
Shine forth upon our clouded hills?
And was Jerusalem builded here
Among these dark Satanic mills?

Figure 4.7 The March of Bricks and Mortar, an engraving by George Cruikshank (1829): the image is of the nasty town despoiling the defenceless countryside.

Figure 4.8 The image in Figure 4.7 is repeated in this illustration for an article entitled 'The rape of rural England' in the *Sunday Telegraph*, 8 May 1988

I will not cease from mental fight,
Nor shall my sword sleep in my hand,
Till we have built Jerusalem
In England's green and pleasant land.

Two phrases from this quote are now part of the English language: *dark satanic mills* has long been used as a metaphor for the blackness of industrialization while *green and pleasant land* has been the countervailing image of the rural idyll. Blake's image of building a new and better city, a Jerusalem, has a long history stretching back to the Book of Revelation.

There have always been attempts to build alternative cities. In the late-eighteenth and nineteenth centuries, various planned communities were established (see Bell and Bell 1972). The urban masses themselves also sought to create their own communities within football and cricket teams, friendly societies, and trade unions. Wherever people are ignored by society they tend to make their own communities. Compared to the aggressive competitiveness of society, these communities were based on co-operation and sharing.

The Rochdale Pioneers in 1844 established a model of consumer power in which members of the co-operative society received a dividend from the profits and which was to develop into the Co-operative Wholesale Society. Most northern industrial towns had building societies, self-help schemes in which people pooled their savings in order to buy or rent housing. Throughout the towns and cities of industrial Britain, communities of collective self-help were created and maintained. By the late twentieth century, the communities of these institutions had been incorporated. The Co-op had become just one more High Street chain store, while building societies had become major financial institutions little different from the High Street banks. But the process of community formation continues in British cities, whether it be in the black co-ops of the inner city or the self-help schemes of the unemployed.

Underlying the view of city as Jerusalem is the theme of the city as liberating experience. Individual expression has always been easier in cities. The urban not so much cultivates individuality but, in its in-difference, allows it to grow. In Britain as elsewhere, going to the city to find one's true self is one of those myths that motivates individual behaviour. In Britain, however, collective liberation has been as important, if not more important, a theme as private salvation. Urbanization along with industrialization created the working class and they in turn sought to control the cities. Socialist parties in Britain have had, at least since the mid-nineteenth century, most support in the cities. The creation of a socialist tradition has municipal roots. The cities of Britain, with their public housing schemes, public parks, public transport scheme and full range of municipal services, reflect the imprint of a more socialist culture than the rest of society. It is not too fanciful to speak of an attempt, varying in intensity, direction and commitment but ever present, especially in the non-confirmist movement, to create the city of Jerusalem in urban Britain.

There were more secular attempts at building the good city. For the Victorians, with their ultimately optimistic and progressive view of history, the city for all its faults was something to be celebrated, and celebrated it was in the municipal buildings, bridges, railway stations, galleries, roads and harbours. The nineteenth century saw some of Britain's finest commercial architecture. In that century, the city was a site of progress. In this century, there has been deepening ambiguity towards modernity; a sort of optimistic pessimism which only half believes in the present and distrusts the future, an acceptance that progress may not mean civilization. In this intellectual climate there is growing reverence for nature and renewed distaste for the city. Not everyone has turned their back on the city. Two models of urban utopia have persisted in the last hundred years, associated with two different people.

Ebenezer Howard (1850–1928) wrote his book *Tomorrow: a Peaceful Path to Real Reform* in 1898. It was reissued four years later under a different title, the more famous *Garden Cities of Tomorrow*. In his book Howard fused the American homesteading tradition with a form of municipal socialism. Howard saw the social ills in both of the main places of the late-Victorian period, the city and the country. The former had slums and appalling environmental conditions while the latter had a better environment but few job prospects. The answer was to combine the advantages of both in a Garden City. These should be set up in the countryside where land was cheaply available. A green belt should be set around the city, although new towns would be located nearby, linked by a rapid transit system. Within the Garden City the residents would own the land. Increases in land values, brought about by economic growth, would thus accrue to the local community and could be used for providing community facilities, for example swimming pools. In his theory, Howard wedded a new environmental context to a different social order. Unlike many other visionaries, Howard's ideas were put into practice. The Garden City Association was set up in 1899, followed by the Garden City Pioneer Company in 1901. In 1903 the first experiment was begun in the City of Letchworth, north of London. In 1919 Welwyn Garden City was started and the Garden City idea took root in sections of the town planning movement. In the optimistic days of the post-1945 period, the proponents of Garden Cities were successful in gaining a national commitment to the scheme. In 1946 the New Towns Act became law and in the next thirty years twenty-eight Garden Cities, or new towns as they were now called, were built. These new towns, built by central government, gave flesh to much of Howard's environmental image but they were deprived of their social vision. The new towns became large-scale environmental schemes but muted social experiments. What for Howard were to be local initiatives became examples of central government policy.

In Howard's scheme the social and spatial were resolutely interwoven; ideas of place coincided with and were mirrored in ideas of society. In the implementation, however, design and land use planning considerations became more important as the schemes were shorn of their radical virility. In the work of Le Corbusier (1887–1965), by contrast, the physical design considerations were the key. Like Howard, Le Corbusier's thinking was a reaction to the urban conditions of his time. Looking around Paris in the first third of this century, Corbusier could see the shabby urban prospect. However, he reacted against the Garden City solution. Not for him the trek to the countryside. He was against, as he put it, 'sending us out into their fields [Garden Cities] to scrabble earth around a lot of hypothetical onions'.

If behind the voice of Howard we can hear the North American homesteading tradition with its innate distrust of the city, then behind Le Corbusier is the chatter of the intelligentsia disdainful of the uncouth countryside. Rather than going outwards, Le Corbusier's scheme was to pile the city on top of itself. His scheme for a city of three million was for a central area with huge, sixty-storey blocks for offices and administration, raised on stilts to allow the free flow of traffic movement. Grouped around the city centre were to be residential areas consisting of twelve-storey blocks, surrounded by landscaped parks. Within the blocks, shopping and recreational facilities were to be provided and policemen were to patrol the corridors and foyer; the lifts were to be well-maintained and adequate soundproofing was to be constructed. There were sociological undertones to the architecture. Le Corbusier had a belief that residential areas could become some kind of commune in the old French radical tradition. The self-contained residential blocks were to be the environmental context for the new communes.

Many of Le Corbusier's ideas were implemented. His designs were given life and substance in Britain in much of the mass housing schemes proposed in the post-war period. The ever-innovative London County Council's Architect's Department sent a deputation to Marseilles to visit Le Corbusier's *Unité d'habitation* in 1951 and those lucky enough to get on a trip to the South of France came back impressed. The architectural seed was thus sown. In the late 1950s and early 1960s, the architects' designs for high-rise blocks were in congruence with other interests. The big construction companies were eager to develop the new industrialized building systems and in this they were aided by central government, which gave subsidies to local authorities. The larger the residential building, the greater the subsidy.

High-rise living proved to be a disaster. Many of the dwellings were badly constructed and poorly designed (see Figure 4.9). Tenants began to face problems of damp and condensation, as black fungus grew on the walls and the smell of damp pervaded the rooms. The blocks were built on the cheap, with little or no community facilities, and were set in poorly

Figure 4.9 Shoddy Jerusalems: Park Hill, Sheffield, built in 1960, and other high-rise schemes have given the search for collective urban utopias a bad name

designed environments, often in the middle of urban waste land. They were unpopular and as the better tenants moved out the process of stigmatization continued so that only the most desperate of households would accept a vacancy in the tower blocks. The design utopia ended, in some cases, with the demolisher's dynamite; by the early 1980s many local authorities were blowing up their tower blocks.

By the late 1980s, urban utopia had a bad press. Critiques of architects abounded (see Short 1989). But, more importantly, the climate of opinion has now swung away from top-down utopias. The imposition of blueprints designed for the many by the select few has been rejected as a model of social progress. A move from top-down to bottom-up local initiatives is long overdue. There has also been a more general loss of faith in large-scale social progress which has led to a loss of faith in the city (see Figure 4.10). In the nineteenth century, a Liberal MP, Joseph Cowen (1831–1900), could say:

> The concentration of citizens, like the concentration of soldiers, is a source of strength. . . . When people talk of trade institutions, when they declaim . . . against the noise and dirt of the busy centres of population, they should remember the liberty we enjoy as a consequence of the mental activity and enterprise which have been generated by the contact of mind with mind brought together in great towns. . . . Our towns are the backbone of the nation. They give it strength, cohesion and vitality. Scattered populations are usually ignorant, and oppression is always

Figure 4.10 The popular dream: a house in the countryside close to nature yet within a settled, stable village community. The ultimate goal of many is to leave the towns and cities

most easily established over them. The power of concentration may be abused, has been abused, but when regulated by vigilantly supervised institutions, there is no fear either for the liberty of the individual or the community.

(quoted in Coleman 1973: 165–7)

If the Victorians believed in the city as a place of progress, despite the awfulness of the urban condition, the post-Victorians see it as a place of regress despite the liberating qualities of urban life. We have lost our faith in the city as Jerusalem because we have lost our belief in a collective emancipation.

5 Marching through wilderness

The American people see themselves marching through wilderness, drying up
marshes, diverting rivers, peopling the wilds and subduing nature. It is not just
occasionally that their imagination catches a glimpse of this magnificent vision.
... it is always flitting before their mind.

Alexis de Tocqueville (1835) *Democracy in America*

In the process of nation-building in the USA European notions of culture,
politics, nature and society were employed but there was also a conscious
distancing from the European in an attempt to forge a uniquely American
view. The relationship with wilderness became a powerful symbol of US
identity; the development of agriculture was seen in terms of creating the
American dream while the urban experience was a mark of both progress
and regress in US civil society. (It is interesting to note that the US
dominance is such that the term 'American', which literally refers to the
whole continent is often used when referring only to the USA.) The results
are environmental ideologies which share characteristics with Europe,
because they reflect social similarities and a shared intellectual heritage,
but which also exhibit specifically US preoccupations.

TRANSFORMING THE WILDERNESS

Creating the garden

In 1662, Michael Wigglesworth described the forests of New England as:

A waste and howling wilderness,
Where none inhabited
But hellish fiends, and brutish men.
(quoted in Nash 1982: 36)

This was a very powerful view of the country which has persisted through
the life of the republic. It led to the notion of wilderness as a place to be
transformed into civilization. According to Nash (1982: xi), 'wilderness

Figure 5.1 Across the Continent: Westward the Course of Empire Takes (1868) by Francis Flora Palmer: the title says it all (Thomas Gilcrease Institute of American History and Art, Tulsa, Oklahoma)

was the basic ingredient of American civilization'. It was an image shaped by Christian rhetoric. Many of the early white settlers in North America saw themselves on a religious mission of transforming the wilderness into a garden. The settling of the territory had religious sanctification and spiritual legitimation. The society has changed, but the theocratic zeal and justificatory language has persisted. To this religious framework was added the economic motor of an expanding economy. Throughout the eighteenth and nineteenth centuries, wilderness was seen as a repository of commodities, an opportunity for profitable enterprises. Subduing the wilderness could give monetary gain as well as glory to God; wilderness was an economic resource as well as a test of man's devotion (see Figure 5.1).

After the revolution against British rule, the conquest of the wilderness provided an important symbol of national identity and social cohesion. Much of the discourse condensed around the term 'frontier'. The frontier was the dividing line between civilization and barbarism, a line which marked the balance of power between the forces of the republic on the one hand and untamed nature and savage Indians on the other. The frontier was a reminder of the job still to be done, its extension a record of increasing success.

The most important 'biographer' of the American frontier was Frederick Jackson Turner (1861–1932). In a paper read to a meeting of the American

Historical Association on 12 July 1893, entitled 'The Significance of the Frontier in American History', Jackson suggested that the taming of the wilderness was *the* significant fact in the American identity (Turner 1963). He began by drawing attention to the recent comments of the super-intendent of the Census that, for all intents and purposes, there was no longer any frontier. He developed his theme that 'this expansion west-wards with its new opportunities, its continuous touch with the simplicity of primitive society, furnish the forces dominating American character'. The frontier played a crucial role, according to Turner, because westward movement decreased industrial dependence on Britain; it provided the context for government legislation, especially in the fields of transportation schemes, tariff barriers and land nationalization, and it provided the basis of much organized missionary activity. (The USA still has the most missionary Protestant churches in the western world.) Westward move-ment acted as a safety valve, as 'each frontier did furnish a new field of opportunity, a gate of escape'. By calling forth traits of rugged individualism, the frontier helped to promote democracy. 'American democracy', Turner wrote in a later paper published in 1914, 'came out of the American forest, and it gained new strength each time it touched a new frontier.'

Turner and his frontier hypothesis have been the subject of many books and articles. (For a range see Bennett 1975; Billington 1973; Carpenter 1983; Hofstadter 1970; Jacobs 1968; and Noble 1965). To debate about how right Turner was about the actual effect of frontier is to miss the point. The transformation of the wilderness has exercised a considerable influence on American thought. Turner's frontier thesis encapsulates a powerful motif in American thought. Before 1890 the frontier was part myth and part historical process, after 1890 it was purely myth. Yet the Americans' view of themselves continued to pivot around this myth and it was to be a recurring theme in social criticism and popular culture. Let us consider just a few of the subsequent debates.

Part of the problem of the Depression, according to one historian of the west, W.P. Webb, was the crisis of a frontierless democracy. In his book *Divided We Stand*, published in 1937, he put forward the view that the frontier provided conditions in which individualism, equality and personal liberty could grow and flourish, and the existence of available land was like a safety valve for pressures in the society. The closing of the frontier allowed greater power to fall into the hands of big corporations whose influence was crushing the little man. In a frontierless society, big business was able to gain ascendancy. In a metaphor, whose relevance should be seen in the context of the ending of prohibition only a few years earlier in 1933, Webb summarized the effects:

For nearly three centuries Americans drank deep of the potent wine of the frontier, a wine which produced exhilarating experiences of freedom, adventure and boundless opportunity. It was a long, gay evening, but now America must face the morning after with its headache, moody introspection and pathetic glance at an empty bottle wherein only the tantalising odour of wine remains.

(Webb 1937: 158)

If Webb could use the frontier for discussing the internal order of US society, over thirty years later, W.A. Williams (1969, 1972) could use it with respect to US foreign affairs and particularly involvement in Vietnam. According to Williams, the closing of the frontier meant the end of internal expansion. Since domestic prosperity was deemed to be based on expansion, new 'frontiers' were created overseas, and this expansionist doctrine, endemic to US social thought and political beliefs, delayed internal reform. In essence Williams blames the pull of the frontier ideology for inhibiting the creation of a true democracy. Where Turner celebrates, Williams criticizes.

An important belief in the USA is that Americans are truly American when they (re)create the frontier condition. An incantation of the frontier and the frontier spirit is used to create social cohesion. The romance of frontier is so deep and strong that it can be used to cover a variety of issues. On 15 July 15 1960, John F. Kennedy formally accepted the nomination of the Democratic Party in Los Angeles at the Coliseum with these words:

Today some would say that those struggles are all over, that all the horizons have been explored, that all the battles have been won, that there is no longer an American frontier. But . . . the problems are not all solved and the battles are not all won, and we stand today on the edge of a new frontier – the frontier of the 1960s, a frontier of unknown opportunities and paths, a frontier of unfulfilled hopes and threats.

(quoted in Schlesinger, Jr 1965)

Although Kennedy regarded the term New Frontier with some embarrassment, its success at the time is indicative of the power of frontier imagery. It is a power which remains undiminished and capable of use and constant reuse. Writers in the USA, looking to capture an audience about some social issue, incant the word in various forms: the next frontier, the last frontier, the most important frontier. Captain Kirk of the *Starship Enterprise* used to describe space as the final frontier. The imagery is constantly employed. In Tom Wolfe's *The Right Stuff* (1980) the all-American, all-male, all-white astronauts were the new heroes. The race with the Russians was just like the eternal fight between the good guys and the bad guys. Wolfe's tale and his subscription to the cult of masculinity is just one of the many modern portrayals of the frontiers.

Even radical histories seek to claim the frontier. Marginalized groups look back to their (unrecorded) role in the frontier, almost as if to claim legitimacy for their present demands by noting their role in the great

American experience. Frontier histories of blacks (Katz 1971; Porter 1971) and women (Kolodny 1975, 1984; Myers 1982) are concerned with setting the record straight, but they are also arguing for the rights of blacks and women today by laying the claim of these groups to the great American myth of yesterday.

The frontier has become a vehicle for a wide set of concerns in the USA, a major point of reference, a pivot for public debates which not only describes the past but also evaluates the present and contemplates the future.

Preserving the garden

In the fight against the wilderness there was some ambivalence about the struggle and the outcome. There has always been a slightly sniffy intellectual view of those directly involved with subduing the wilderness. In 1821 the President of Yale, Timothy White, could describe the pioneer as: 'too idle, too talkative, too passionate, too prodigal and too shiftless to acquire either property or character'.

Behind that statement lay an east coast intellectual view of the pioneer as *backwoodsman*, not amenable to the civilizing opportunities of industry, commerce and city living. The struggle against the wilderness was a brutalizing experience, taking the energies of the country into contact with savagery. The view has persisted. Some writers see the root of contemporary problems in the early experience of the pioneers:

> Under the aspect of mythology and historical distance, the acts and motives of the woodchopper, the whale and bear hunter, the Indian fighter and the deerslayer have an air of simplicity and purity that makes them seem heroic expressions of an admirable quality of the human spirit. But their apparent independence of time and consequence is an illusion: a closely woven chain of time and consequence binds their world to ours. .... the warfare between man and nature, between race and race.
>
> (Slotkin 1973: 564; see also Slotkin 1985)

Even amongst those who celebrated the pioneer there were twinges of regret at the destruction of the wilderness. James Fenimore Cooper's tales of the frontier contain the basic ambivalence. His books, which include *The Pioneers* (1823), *The Prairie* (1827), *The Pathfinder* (1840) and *The Deerslayer* (1841), were very popularly received at their time of writing and continue to influence. Cooper's hero, Natty Bumppo, is a pioneer who brings civilization but also inaugurates the destruction of the wilderness. Behind Cooper's ambiguity lies the concern with creating an 'American' society from the wild but also a much broader 'romantic' appreciation of the beauty of the 'American' wild.

In 1849–50 John W. Audubon, son of the wildlife painter J.J. Audubon, travelled from New York to California via New Orleans and overland through Texas, drawing as he went. (His sketchbook is now in the Southwest Museum in Los Angeles.) Underneath his drawing of a landing at the Tuolumne River in California, he wrote: 'Every turn gives some vista of beauty in this Garden of Eden.'

Running alongside the belief in transforming the wilderness into a garden was a body of opinion, sometimes in opposition, at other times part of a general ambiguity, which saw the wilderness already as a garden; a garden which had to be preserved.

Wilderness as Eden has been an important element in US environmental ideologies. It was made up of aesthetic, nationalist, scientific and religious sentiments underwritten by nostalgic regret at the passing of the wilderness. Even as early as 1834 a remark by Daniel Drake captures that feeling:

> the teeming and beautiful landscape of nature fades away like a dream of poetry. . . . Before this transformation is finished, a portrait should be taken, that our children may contemplate the primitive physiognomy of their native land, and feast their eyes on its virgin charms.
>
> (quoted in Mitchell 1981)

Up until the Civil War (1862–5), the moving force of the nation was the expansionist drive and the major public concern was with subduing the wilderness. However, in the last half of the nineteenth century and throughout the twentieth century, the politics of wilderness preservation began to compete with the politics of wilderness exploitation. There was a more receptive audience for an alternative message which touched the sense of regret at the passing of the wilderness. This message was portrayed by painters and photographers.

In the work of George Catlin (1796–1872) we see the career of both a recorder and a defender of the wild. Catlin was a portrait painter from the east. He became fascinated with the Indians and spent much of his life travelling and recording Indian scenes. Catlin linked the destruction of indigenous culture with the vanishing landscape and in 1833 he suggested a national park where the landscape could be

> preserved in their pristine beauty and wildness, in a *magnificent park*, where the world could see for ages to come, the native Indian in his classic attire. . . . a *nation's park* containing man and beast, in all the wild and freshness of their nature's beauty.
>
> (quoted in Mitchell 1981)

Painters such as Albert Bierstadt (1830–1902) and Thomas Moran (1837–1926) gave a grand romantic view of wilderness, a landscape of epic proportions capable of religious and nationalist sentiment. While Europe could boast man-made cathedrals, the USA had older natural rock cathedrals whose architect was the Almighty. The great American landscape became the wilderness scene (see Figure 5.2).

Figure 5.2 Mt Whitney (1875) by Albert Bierstadt (Rockwell-Corning Museum, Corning, New York)

Figure 5.3 This early photograph (1863) of the Yosemite Falls by C.E. Watkins prefigures the later work of Ansel Adams whose photographs also influenced the conservation movement in the USA (C.E. Watkins Collection, Henry E. Huntingdon Library, San Marino, California)

Photographic recorders of the wilder west included W.H. Jackson, Charles Leader Weed and Carlton E. Watkins. Weed took the first photograph of Yosemite in the 1850s, while the photographs of C.E. Watkins in the 1860s helped to get Yosemite established as a protected area (see Figure 5.3). Watkins' photographs were concerned with showing the size and the bulk of nature. The emphasis was on the monumentality of natural forms. There is a direct connection between Watkins in the nineteenth century and Ansel Adams in the twentieth. Both recorded the high sierra and their work was important in influencing public policies for the wilderness.

The images of the artists and photographers were given a scientific basis by the early proponents of the conservation movement who questioned the price of progress in the language of natural science and rationality. George Perkins Marsh (1801–82) not only gave the standard romantic response to wilderness destruction but also elaborated his moral concern with issues of utility and self-preservation. In his very influential *Man and Nature*, first published in 1864, he pointed to the costs of progress on the delicate balance between people and their environment:

The earth is fast becoming an unfit home for its noblest inhabitant, and another era of equal human crime and human improvidence ... would reduce it to such a condition of impoverished productiveness, of shattered surface, of climatic excess, as to threaten the deprivation, barbarism, and perhaps even extinction of the species.

(Marsh 1965: 43)

The words and the message still sound modern to readers of the late-twentieth century. Literary figures also stressed the need for contact with nature. For both Ralph Waldo Emerson (1803–82) and Henry David Thoreau (1817–62), contact with nature was a way of communicating with God, and oneself. 'In the woods is perpetual youth', wrote Emerson in his essay *Nature* in 1836. Emerson, along with Whitman, was important in developing an authentic American voice. Thoreau was less popular in his own era. His famous experiment was to leave the comforts of ordinary people and live in a cabin he made himself beside Walden Pond near Concord, Massachusetts. His record of the experience, *Walden*, first published in 1854, is suffused with both a pantheistic vision which sees all nature as God's handiwork and a social perspective which preaches wariness of human society, customs and mores. 'Observe the hours of the universe, not of the railroad cars', he counselled. It is a message with a large audience in the twentieth century. Thoreau was jailed for refusing to pay taxes. This streak of Yankee independence, combined with a romantic conception of nature and an explicitly political stance, has informed and impressed generations of Americans. He provides an example of self-reliance, self-belief and a love of nature.

Every social movement, to be successful, needs good publicists and in the Scotsman John Muir (1838–1914) the infant conservation movement in the United States had one of the best. He wrote best-selling books and widely read articles, all propounding the need to preserve wilderness. He was an influential figure in having the Yosemite Act of 1890 passed by Congress. The Act created a national forest reserve. In 1892 he was made the first President of the Sierra Club, the main mouthpiece of the early conservation/preservation movement. Muir was successful because he was able to condense the strong romantic and nationalist impulses into a clearly defined goal of preserving grand landscapes and rugged scenery. His environmental monumentalism captured the spirit of the times. Muir had a deep concern with wilderness matched by a fierce desire to influence public policy.

There were strong religious undertones to the notion of wilderness as Eden. This was very important in a country where materialism and spiritualism still fight a vigorous battle, which is largely given over to a truce elsewhere in the capitalist world. Emerson, Thoreau and others gave a religious dimension to the relationship with nature. To love and protect nature was to revel in God's creation. Protecting the wilderness had a religious justification, as Graber (1976) notes:

Much of the political influence of the community of purists stems from the ability of wilderness imagery to flow into the void left by the erosion of spiritual and aesthetic values associated with the countryside and the city. Partially by default, partly by political expertise and partially by strength of conviction, the wilderness ethic and its purist supporters continue to attract adherents and to influence the direction of the environmental movement through the power of a single concept, wilderness as sacred space.

(Graber 1976: 115)

The nationalist and religious undertones help to explain the virility and influence of the wilderness conservation movement in the USA. The defence of the wilderness has been the focal point of American environmentalism.

The dominant nationalist image of the nineteenth century was the defeat of the wilderness. In the twentieth century it had to compete with the image of the wilderness as the very expression of what was uniquely American. Throughout this century, and especially since the 1950s, politicians could rely less on the appeals to 'progress'. The environmental and social costs of progress had been well documented. Environmental groups such as the Sierra Club became successful political forces, achieving purchase from a public sensitized by environment issues. Their main focus in recent years was on the passage of the Wilderness Act, which meandered through Congress from 1955 until 1964. This Act gave legislative form to such concern by declaring 9.1 million acres of wilderness. Since the passing of the Act, more areas have been designated as wilderness and the passage of the Act itself has provided the basis for the creation of more environmental groups. There is now a powerful network of groups and organizations who actively work to preserve the wilderness. This force was felt in the battle of Alaska. Throughout the 1960s and 1970s there was growing development pressure on Alaska from mineral developers and tourist concerns. Alaska became a symbolic battleground between business interests and the increasingly powerful environmental movement. The 1980 signing of the Alaska National Interest Lands Conservation Act, which protected 28 per cent of the state, marked the zenith of the wilderness lobby.

The perception of wilderness as an Eden to be preserved has not held undisputed dominance. In 1981 a change in official attitude was inaugurated along with a new President. The so-called 'sagebrush rebellion' consisted of commercial and government interests seeking to reduce environmental controls and to promote the opening up of the public domain to commercial development.

The rebellion received a setback with the appointment of James Watt as Interior Secretary. By his ability to shoot himself in the foot with his public pronouncements he did more to boost the environmental cause than any one man since John Muir. The experience of the Reagan administration shows that battles will continue to be fought between environmentalists, preservationists, business interests and various government bureaucracies. What is at stake is not just material gain, though that is an important factor, but very different conceptions of the environment of the USA: its uses, its purposes and its position in broader belief systems and ideologies.

Changing perceptions of westward expansion

Hand in hand with the rise of the conservation movement has been a reassessment of the historical experience of the USA. Today the destruction of the wild landscapes, the killing of wild animals and the subjugation of the Indian have become things to be ashamed of, a source of guilt not pride. The pioneers have become less a source of moral virtues to be praised, as in Walt Whitman's *Pioneers! O pioneers!* (1865), and more the source of gnawing guilt about violence and racism, a harbinger of a corrupt society.

> Once upon a time there was an American west. It was part economic and social fact, part myth; while the facts changed the myths survived. . . . The plot, written by historians, repetitiously dwelt on the individual – a modern version of an unrestrained, unfettered Prometheus proclaiming his freedom.
> In the twentieth century, however, the western myth grew increasingly unacceptable. Previously ignored elements crept in, and the tale began to seem full of racial prejudice, violence, frenzied speculation and recklessness towards nature. Individuals shunned responsibility for themselves and for their communities, and began roaming, restless and unfulfilled.
>
> (Hine 1984: vii–viii)

In the rewriting, new heroes have emerged: not the old buffalo-hunting, Indian-killing white men but the Indians themselves.

There have always been supporters of the Indians but through the twentieth century, and especially in the last 25 years, the Indian as popular hero began to develop as a consistent theme in the criticism of white US society. Alternative histories of the West, such as Dee Brown's (1970), took the position of those facing eastward while movies such as *Soldier Blue* (1970) reversed the stereotypes. It was the cavalry who were the savage killers while the Indians were victims of expansionist federal policies and white greed. Such criticism was an integral part of a more general critique of American involvement in Vietnam. Many historians and commentators traced the roots of expansionism in South East Asia to the plains of North America.

The history of the Indian was reinterpreted as a valiant attempt to resist armed aggression by a superior and corrupt force. There has always been a noble savage strand to the American intellectual's response to the Indian. But in the wilderness as Eden paradigm the Indian was seen as part of a more balanced relationship between people and their environment, to be contrasted with the contemporary imbalance. In a book about the Indians of California, published in 1980, the writers could suggest:

> Indians not only lived in nature, but saw themselves as an integral part of it. In native belief, animals had an intelligence equal to man's, as well as human qualities and emotions; and in many mythologies, animals were said to have occupied the earth before man and to have gotten the world ready for humans.
>
> All of nature was thought to be interconnected ... man was seen not as domination of nature but rather as sharing creation and life with the plant and animal forms around him.
>
> In the native peoples of California, who lived here for so very long before the whites appeared, we can see *the true ecological man* – people who were truly a part of the land and the water and the mountains and valleys in which they lived. The environmentalists and conservationists of today feel a kinship with the Indians in their respect for nature, a feeling which at times rises to that of sanctity of the natural world.
>
> (Heizer and Elsasser 1980: 209–220; emphasis added)

Behind those words one can hear the voice of the smog-breathing, freeway-driving, southern Californians looking back to a golden age before the invention of fast-food chains and the internal combustion engine. The Indian has now become the American Adam living in the American paradise.

Calvin Martin, in his book *Keepers of the Game* (1978), forces us to reassess the validity of the image of Indian as ecological hero. He shows, with reference to the Micmac and Ojibwa tribes of eastern and midwest Canada respectively, that the Indian was principally responsible for the over-hunting of fur-bearing animals. The Indians were presented with the opportunity to trade furs with the Europeans for metal implements. This was at a time when there were no longer any moral sanctions against overhunting, because of the collapse of traditional belief systems through disease and the spiritual turmoil associated with contact with the whites. Given incentives and shorn of sanctions, the Indians took part in the unrestrained slaughter of certain game. The Indian went on the offensive and 'Nature, which had once rejected his supplications and frightened him, now lay prostrate at his feet.' (Martin 1978: 109).

The predominant image is of the Indian as ecological hero, a reminder of a golden age, a witness to how far contemporary Americans are out of balance in their relationship to the environment. If Martin is correct, then the Indian becomes more of a classic tragic hero; part victim but also part architect of his own ecological downfall.

CULTIVATING THE GARDEN

In 1811 Thomas Jefferson (1743–1826) wrote to Charles Peale:

> I have often thought that if heaven had given me a choice of my position and calling, it should have been on a rich spot of earth, well watered and near a good market for the production of the garden. No occupation is so delightful to me as the culture of the earth.
>
> (quoted in Peterson 1975)

Jefferson's comments echo a strong theme in American social thought: the cultivation of the garden as an ennobling experience, the natural calling of all good people. The theme resonates through western thought but it was particularly strong in the USA where a powerful belief saw democracy best served by a society of family farms. The defeat of the South in the Civil War meant the eclipse of the plantation as an icon for American democracy. The plantation became instead an image of a vanquished way of life. From the end of the Civil War onwards, the dominant myth of agrarian America has been of the small family farm. Victory and defeat occur in the terrain of ideas just as much as in the field of armed conflict. The defeated in any war lose their myths as well as their battles. The plantation myth persisted but only as an echo of a bygone world not as a model for national identity.

The family farm condensed a number of images. It implied a family group working together on the land, thus involving notions of family togetherness, and co-operation; it implied closeness to the soil and high moral qualities; it conjured up a society based on a free market and free enterprise, where hard work was recognized and rewarded. The cowboy might be the hero of the west but the real bearer of virtue was the small farmer. The image of the family farm implied a whole series of desirable qualities, and the mere employment of the term was to mobilize sentiments of family, freedom, the work ethic and moral goodness (see Figure 5.4).

To encourage agriculture was to ensure desirable moral qualities in the republic. Jefferson, during his term as President (1801–9), completed the Louisiana Purchase in 1803, whereby the USA bought 827,192 square miles from France. Overnight it doubled the land surface of the republic and ensured the agrarian order. For Jefferson it was a safety valve which would avoid the American people becoming piled one upon another in large cities. Later, under the Homestead Act of 1862, men and single women could file claims on 160 acres of unappropriated public land. There were many forces behind the enactment of this Act but, as H.N. Smith: (1950: 170) notes, the strongest was 'the belief that it would enact by statute the fee-simple empire, the agrarian utopia of hardy and virtuous yeomen which had haunted the imaginations'.

False claims and illegal activity undermined the implementation of the Act. By 1890 only 372,659 claims were completed and the land that was

Figure 5.4 Stone City, Iowa by Grant Wood (Joslyn Art Museum)

given was often in inaccessible, infertile areas. The history of the Homestead Act highlights the tensions between the power of the myth and the myth of government power.

In 1810 over 90 per cent of the US population was classified as rural, many were self-sufficient farmers. Even as late as 1880 the farm population was 44 per cent of the total population. One hundred years later this figure had dropped to under 3 per cent. The decline of the importance of agriculture was counterbalanced by the continuing cultural weight given to farming, because to praise the rural was to celebrate the early innocence of the republic.

In 1841 J.B. Lanman could write in *Hunt's Merchants' Magazine*:

> The agriculturalist ... passes a quiet and undisturbed life, possessing ample means and motives thoroughly to reflect upon his rights and duties, and holding a sufficient stake in the soil to induce him to perform these duties both for himself and his country. ... it can scarcely be denied that agricultural enterprise, the basis of almost every form of human pursuit, should be encouraged as a safeguard of a country, the promoter of virtue, and the solid formation of its permanent happiness and most lasting independence.

The ideas have echoed down the years. In 1978, for example, Senator Nelson wrote:

The family farm provides a social environment in which the central virtues of American life are fostered. It is at once a business, a job and a set of family relationships. At best, it does not provide an easy life and in bad times, there are often harsh difficulties. But it provides a good life, and one in which independence, hard work, foresight, cooperation and qualities central to America's needs are fostered. For most of our history, the family farm has been the seedbed of our culture.

(Goldschmidt 1978: vii)

Like Mom and apple pie, the family farm is all that is good, wholesome and decent in American life. It is a partial view. The family farm can also be the scene of backbreakingly hard work, exploitation, repression and cultural backwardness. The massive levels of rural–urban migration, not all being the result of economic forces, partly attest to the desire of many to escape from the rural confines. However, the myth should be seen not as a descriptive tool but as a point of reference in wider cultural discourse which explains and reflects current issues through the prism of an agrarian past.

The machine in the garden

Let us look again at Jefferson's letter (on page 103). On the surface it is eulogizing the agrarian ideal. But note the phrase 'and near a good market for the production of the garden'. It shows an awareness of the commercial nexus which ties the agrarian ideal to market realities. It is an explicit recognition of agriculture as a trade as much as a calling. This is the ambivalence of farming which Hofstadter (1955) refers to as the *soft side* of agrarian ideology and tradition and the *hard side* of business method, profit motive and political pressure group.

This ambivalence has been a consistent feature of painting and literature. Leo Marx describes the fascination for writers of the contrast between the rural ideal and the thrust of agrarian commercialism, especially as signalled in mechanization:

the pastoral ideal remained of service long after the machine's appearance in the landscape. It enabled the nation to continue defining its purpose as the pursuit of rural happiness while devoting itself to productivity, wealth and power. It remained for our serious writers to discover the meaning inherent in this contradiction.

(Marx 1964: 226)

This contradiction continues to exercise a fascination for the artistic impulse in the USA.

The State and the Garden

The farm is the basis of a commercial operation and the farmer is now less of a yeoman farmer and more of a rural capitalist eager to increase profits. To maintain their competitive edge, farmers and the farming lobby have appealed to the family myth in their dealings with the government. Agriculture is a commercial operation involving risks and uncertainty, booms and slumps. Given the political, commercial and symbolic importance of farming, the US government has intervened to protect agriculture. A thumbnail sketch of US agricultural policy would present a picture of continuing government involvement throughout the twentieth century. There has been a whole series of policy measures brought about by the hard side of US agriculture but justified with respect to the soft side.

From the Agricultural Act of 1927 through the Agricultural Adjustment Acts of 1933 and 1937 to the Food and Agricultural Act of 1977, the federal government has been committed to price supports and parity payments, where farmers were assured of payments in line with the best years from 1909–14. By 1985, support measures were costing the taxpayers $15 billion. The family farm myth has been consistently employed to justify rising levels of government support. The preface to the 1977 Act is typical:

> Congress hereby specifically reaffirms the historical policy of the United States to foster and encourage the family farm system of agriculture in this country. Congress firmly believes that the maintenance of the family farm is essential to the well-being of the Nation.

It would be a mistake to see the government's underwriting of agriculture simply as the unfolding effects of a belief of politicians in the myth of the family farm. The political power of farmers has played a part. From 1880 till the turn of the century there was an agrarian revolt, crystallized in the formation of the Populist Party in 1891, which linked agrarian concerns to demands for political reform. In 1892 the party's candidate, James B. Weaver, received just over 1 million votes, (about 8.5 per cent of the popular vote). Although unsuccessful in their own terms, many of the Populists' demands were taken up by the more urban-based Progressives.

In the twentieth century, agrarian movements became less linked to movements of wider reform and social change and more specifically related to sectional demands. Issues of federal farm relief, parity payments, price support measures and help with combating the power of the food monopolies were the central concerns of rural discontent in the inter-war period (see Saloutos and Hicks 1951). In the post-war period, demands revolved around the need for continued support in the face of changing market conditions. The American Agricultural movement was formed in 1977 to organize the concern of the wheat farmers with falling prices. Another round of rural protest was sparked off in the mid-1980s as another price-cost squeeze put the viability of many small farms in jeopardy.

There has also been the organized lobbying of agricultural and food-related industries. To take just one case: the dairy industry, as represented by the Associated Milk Producers, was the tenth-largest campaign contributor to Congressmen in 1984. This paid off. By 1985, government purchase of surplus dairy production amounted to $2 billion. These special interest groups have targeted goals and sophisticated lobbying tactics. The pattern and level of government support for agriculture reflects the operation of these groups as much, if not more, than the consequences of a firmly held agrarian mythology.

The state of the garden

Agricultural policy has been implemented in a society where wealth and power is unevenly distributed. While the small family farm may be the ideological goal of federal farming policy, the reality is somewhat different. The pattern of generous subsidies has benefited the larger farmers. Subsidies and price supports are related to acreage or level of production, not to farm income. Therefore, the larger farmers, who have more acreage and greater production capacity, receive more subsidies. In the 1970s, for example, the 6 per cent of larger farmers received almost 40 per cent of subsidies (Vogeler 1981: 171).

There has been an increasing concentration of agricultural production. The average acreage has increased from 147 in 1900 to 450 in 1979, while the total number of farms has declined from 5,740 in 1900 to 2,333 in 1979. Agricultural production is more and more dominated by the larger farms and, as Table 5.1 shows, these industrialized farms are taking a disproportionate share of farm cash incomes.

Given these trends, it is not surprising to note that the myth of the family farm has been challenged. There have been a number of points of attack which highlight the disparity between the original myth and the contemporary reality. There has been increasing criticism about the rising level of pollution caused by an agriculture dependent upon the fertilizer fix, a trend exacerbated by government price support schemes. Since the publication of Rachel Carson's *Silent Spring* in 1962, there has been a flood of environmental reports about the deleterious consequences of a chemical-based agriculture. Jefferson's original image was of yeomen tilling the soil not agrarian capitalists engineering the environment.

Table 5.1 Farm size and cash receipts, 1977

	% of farms	% of cash receipts
Family farms	90	60
Large and industrialized farms	10	40

Source: Vogeler 1981

Concern has also been expressed, especially by consumers' groups, about the cost of government support. Jeffersonian agrarian democracy was self-sufficient, not the recipient of vast amounts of government subsidy. It is difficult to avoid the conclusion that the farm myth has been employed as a method of coping with critics of spiralling subsidies.

Even critics, however, have partly accepted the myth of the family farm. The object of attack is rarely American agriculture; that would be like attacking the notion of motherhood or patriotism. Instead, the object of opprobrium has been agribusiness. Vogeler (1981), for example, discusses the rise of agribusiness in the USA. His work is similar to many others in that agribusiness is seen as the major source of all evil in the rural world, from depopulation through pollution to the bad working conditions of migrant workers. We should see such arguments in a specific light. The term 'agribusiness' is employed as a counterpoint to the myth of the family farm. If the family farm signifies the soft side of American agriculture, agribusiness is used to describe the hard side and its deleterious consequences, such as pollution and ill-treatment of agricultural labourers. Many use the term 'agribusiness' to point to the hard side of agriculture without disturbing the myth of the family farm.

There has also been some redefinition of what is meant by family farm, in order to retain the moral superiority but ally it to commercial realities. This coping mechanism is demonstrated in a publication of the Food and Agriculture Committee. The committee asked an academic to publish a report on trends in US agriculture. In the resulting publication (Tweeten 1984), committee members could show their disagreement by use of signed footnotes. When, on page 2, the author suggested that farms with annual sales of $200,000 were really large farms and hence, by implication, not family farms, the committee member who owned a farm with four full-time employees could not refrain from noting:

> The typical family farm of 1984 in my estimation is large, does not receive much of the labour from family members and receives a good portion of the total income from non farm sources.

In other words, a real small family farm is neither small nor employs family and it is not a farm. The contortions of logic are necessary in order for commercial operators to lay claim to the myth of the family farm.

The tension between the myth and the market, the hard and the soft side of agrarian ideology, was sharply highlighted in the crisis of small farmers in 1985. In the 1970s, high demand, generous federal support and an eye for profit encouraged farmers to borrow in order to buy land and machinery to increase production. Uncle Sam and world markets, it was thought, could always be relied on to buy the produce. By the 1980s, however, a strong dollar and a worldwide recession caused a slump in demand, which made it difficult to pay debts. Worse still, a Republican administration in 1985 seriously considered reducing federal supports. The dual responses to the crisis are best exemplified in the reaction of the then Budget Director, David Stockman, whose words to a Senate Budget Committee hearing reflected the ideology of the supply side of economics as well as the sentiments of many non-farmers:

> For the life of me, I cannot figure out why the taxpayers of this country have the responsibility to go in and re-finance bad debt that was willingly incurred by consenting adults who went out and bought farmland when the price was going up and thought they could be rich, or went out and bought machinery and assets because they made a business judgement that they could make money.
>
> (quoted in *Time*, 18 February 1985: 24)

In contrast are the sentiments expressed by a writer in the *Los Angeles Times* of 7 April 1985:

> In all the talk today about the farm crisis, everything is said about economics but little about culture – about family farms and the rural way of life as cultural institutions. Small farms support a lifestyle. It's a style that has always been associated with independence, lack of artifice, lack of affectation. In rural areas people take their bearings from the seasons, not the Dow Jones or city magazine editors. They haven't forgotten how to take each other's measure – frauds and fakers are found out quickly enough and consigned to their proper place. Trust in one's fellow man hasn't been completely eroded. Read a small-town police report and weep. They are so hard up for incidents that they print a weekly list of people who left their front doors ajar.
>
> In not helping save the family farm, our government is making a choice for all of us. It is choosing to uproot people whose livelihood bonds them to nature. In the long run, we'll all be less independent, less secure, less grounded.

The second extract lays claim to the myth of the family farm as the environmental symbol of economic purity, social innocence and political democracy. It is a nostalgic response to a corporate, urban, industrial society. We all need a rearview-mirror to give direction in our lives. The family farm is what many Americans like to see when they glance in this mirror, to reassure themselves about where they have come from and to assess their current position.

Because of the structural polarities of belief systems, it should not strike us as a paradox that the most cherished image of an urban/industrial/capitalist society is a rural/agrarian/pre-capitalist world.

THE CITY

The republic was overwhelmingly rural at its birth and this condition was seen by many as the truly American condition. Many agreed with Jefferson when he described cities as 'pestilential to the morals, the health and the liberties of man'. A powerful anti-urban strain in US intellectual thought has seen the city as Babylon (see White and White 1962). But there has been another view expressed by varied immigrant business and reform groups, the city as Jerusalem. Even if it never quite achieved the full flowering of British utopian thought and fabian political practice, at the very least it involved a pragmatic acceptance that if the USA once had an agrarian past it now had an urban present. As Smith (1984: 364) notes: 'All the ambiguities and cruel paradoxes of American life find their symbolic center in the city – all that was most disheartening and all that was most hopeful.'

In few other countries has the city as symbol been so important, because in few other countries has there been such a strong agrarian cultural base in contrast to the many waves of social change washing through the city. The city became, and still is, the terrain for an examination of old values against modern trends and a reaffirmation of established custom against new ways. The city took a particular role in these discourses because what were problems *in the city* were seen as problems *of the city*. Questions of social control, alienation, political power and morality were posed in an environmental language: the prefix 'urban' was partly a shorthand but partly a device for ignoring the social bases of issues. By giving them a spatial designation, the problems *in* the city became the problems *of* the city. The use of the term 'urban' simplified issues of wider social concern, making them easier to discuss but more difficult to address.

The urban experience varied through time and across space. The experience of the city in the west was different, in the late-nineteenth century, to what it was in the north east, and the growth of Los Angeles after the Second World War contrasted with the experience in New York. It is difficult, therefore, to use the term 'urban' in a national context without doing an injustice to marked regional differences. Nevertheless, two general themes can be identified, the city as social threat and the city as opportunity.

The city as threat to social order

The city has always been a place to fear for those in established authority because the city contains marginalized groups, tied neither to the land nor to the existing commercial order. The city houses those who have no power except their presence and their numbers. Jefferson's fear of the city was a fear of class conflict, a continuing and persistant theme in the intellectual response to the city.

Even in colonial America, when the urban population constituted less than 5 per cent of the total population, the seaport cities were the scene of social conflict. Urban street disturbances allowed those excluded from formal politics to participate in public discourse. Women, servants and slaves had a place in the streets if not in the debating chambers. With reference to the late-seventeenth and early eighteenth centuries, Nash (1979) notes:

> Once in motion, the seaport crowd provided nearly every urban dweller a chance to influence the course of events by bringing pressure to bear on the constituted authorities. Crowd actions were frequent enough and effective enough that they achieved a kind of legitimacy of their own. The urban crowd was the watchdog of politics, always ready to chastise or drive from office those who violated the collective sense of propriety or equity. Never wholly legitimized, roundly hated by the upper class, organized and led in mysterious ways that sprang from collective outrage, the seaport crowd served as an effective counterbalance in a political system where men who had secured positions of influence and trust because of their high economic and social position were far from incapable of abusing their power.
>
> (Nash 1979: 36)

The cities contained the groups and the setting for an alternative mode of political discourse. The 'problem' of the city was really the fear of the urban crowd, who posed a serious threat to the established order. Jefferson's distrust of the city was a fear of the European urban experience, where social conflict was sharpened by urbanization. The city was feared as the home of the mobocracy, who could, and did, disrupt 'normal' political discourse and economic transactions. Jefferson's belief was that, without cities, the USA would have a more stable democracy.

The fear of the rabble is also expressed by de Tocqueville who, when visiting New York and Philadelphia, could note in 1835:

> The lower ranks which inhabit these cities constitute a rabble. They consist of freed blacks [and] a multitude of Europeans [who] are ready to turn all the passions which agitate the community to their own advantage.

He gloomily predicted:

> I look upon the size of certain American cities, and especially on the nature of their population, as a real danger which threatens the future security of the democratic republics of the New World.

The fear of the urban crowd, especially for the Yankee Protestants and their spokesmen, increased throughout the nineteenth century and into the twentieth because the cities were overwhelmingly the destination for immigrants, who swelled the ranks of those outside established social customs and political affairs. Between 1820 and 1920, 33 million people migrated to the USA and three-quarters of them ended up in cities (see Figure 5.5). In the largest cities, almost half of the population were either foreign born or of foreign parentage (Ward 1971). And in the last quarter

Figure 5.5 The cities of the USA attracted migrants from all over the world and some, like New York, became vast agglomerations of foreign peoples

of that era, an increasing percentage were arriving from non-Protestant, non-Anglo-Saxon areas. In the 1860s, only 1 per cent of immigrants came from Russia, Austria-Hungary or Italy but, by the first decade of the twentieth century, almost 70 per cent came from these areas. The urban 'rabble' was seen as more of a threat because it was even more different from the religious and ethnic stock of the dominant groups in the society. Religious and ethnic divisions overlaid differences in political power and economic wealth.

One of the most outspoken critics of this new immigration was Josiah Strong (1847–1916). He was a clergyman and General Secretary of the Evangelical Alliance for the United States in New York. He had worked for missionary societies in Ohio, Kentucky, Virginia and Pennsylvania. His diatribe against immigration was his book, *Our Country*, published in 1885. It was very popular; 130,000 copies were sold in five years and individual chapters were reprinted in many newspapers. Strong's book sought to legitimize the continued dominance of the Anglo-Saxon Protestant element in American life which, according to Strong, represented the ideals of civil liberty and pure spiritual Christianity. Although the thesis seems simplistic, and to some abhorrent, Strong employed a formidable talent and no mean writing skill to argue his case.

The USA, according to Strong, was becoming the seat of white Anglo-Saxon power and was destined, because of cultural superiority, to fulfil a world role formerly filled by Britain. However, there were perils to the realization of this greatness; Strong identified immigration, Romanism, Mormonism, socialism and intemperance. The city was singled out because it was here that the perils were focalized and enhanced. Strong referred to the city as the site of social dynamite and noted that there was 'no more serious threat to our civilization than our rabble-ruled cities' (1885: 43). The city was the vehicle for expressing fear about the loyalty to the status quo of those social groups concentrated in the city. As a mayor of New York noted in 1896:

> Foreign immigration, which during the earlier part of the century was encouraged as a necessary means of development ... has become a dangerous element, because much of it is now illiterate and of a character not easily assimilated into the general mass of the people. The magnitude of the problem may be inferred from the fact that we have received 18,000,000 of foreigners in the last twenty-five years, too many of whom are not in sympathy with our institutions, and cannot discharge the ordinary duties of the citizen.
>
> (Columbia University 1896: 82)

Discussions about the city have always been metaphors for expressing fear about the loyalty of marginalized groups in society. At different times, different groups have been seen as the threat; the southern Europeans which so worried Strong have been replaced by the blacks and the Hispanics (see Figure 5.6). Not only have the groups changed but the designation has varied. Nineteenth and early twentieth-century writers could use the term 'city' because cities were small. But as cities grew and the process of suburbanization and residential segregation fine-grained the city, it became more difficult to see issues as city-wide phenomena. Now the key terms were *inner city* and the *ghetto*.

In the wake of black uprisings in the 1960s, the President established a commission to answer three questions: what happened? why? what can be done? The Kerner Commission Report, published in 1968, saw the riots as the outcome of discrimination and segregation. The problems were greatest in the inner-city ghettos:

> The ghettos too often mean men and women without jobs, families without men and schools where children are processed instead of educated, until they return to the street – to crime, to narcotics, to dependency on welfare, and to bitterness and resentment against society in general and white society in particular.
>
> (quoted in Wakstein 1970: 458)

The comments echo the words of C.L. Brace almost a hundred years earlier in his 1872 book, *The Dangerous Classes of New York and Twenty Years' Work Among Them*, when he described New York as:

Figure 5.6 US cities continue to be the destinations for immigrants: this mural in Los Angeles reflects a strong Hispanic presence

> a great multitude of ignorant, untrained passionate, unreligious boys and young men ... who became the dangerous class of our city.

Although the exact words may be different, the theme remains the same: the perceived and actual threat posed by the excluded, marginalized and disconnected minorities concentrated in the cities. When Woody Allen, in *Play It Again Sam* (1973), refers to the city as 'a metaphor for the decay of contemporary culture', he voices an authentic and persistent American concern. If the countryside was the environmental container of the American dream, the city posed its major threat. The wild classes of the city could not be relied on to keep the social peace nor to accept the social order.

Running alongside the establishment fear of the city as a site of social disorder and a place of alternative cultures has been the critique of the city as corrupter of individual and group morality. The two are not independent. Moral judgements have been used to evaluate social minorities, while any threat to social order has been seen in terms of an eccentric position in the moral universe of established opinion.

As a corrupter of individuals, the city as a site of moral impurity was the counterpoint to the lauding of the family farm as a symbol of moral purity. 'The first city', wrote Strong, 'was built by the first murderer and crime and vice and wretchedness have festered in it ever since' (1885: 181).

The mirror image of the agrarian myth, which stated that people closer to nature had more moral lives, was that people concentrated together in cities would do nasty things to each other. In an 1841 edition of *Hunt's Merchants' Magazine*, J.B. Lanman could write:

> The agriculturist, removed from the pernicious influences that are forever accumulated in large cities, and the exciting scenes which always arise from large accumulations of men, passes a quiet and undisturbed life.

He went on to note that agricultural enterprise 'should be encouraged as a safeguard of the country, the promoter of its virtue and solid foundation of its permanent happiness and most lasting independence'. Emerson, in a similar remark, noted that 'cities force growth and may make men talkative and entertaining but they make them artificial'. The notion of the artificiality of urban living persists. On 7 April 1985, a journalist could write in the *Los Angeles Times*:

> I don't like to think about a country farmed by corporations, where all the people live in cities. Who would provide the ballast of things? Every social dislocation would quake through the entire populace, displacing everything, with no cushion anywhere. The raw edge of social change would get sharper. This is largely because cities are deprivation chambers, where people lacking a frame of reference in nature magnify the works of man all out of proportion.

Urban dwellers were, and continue to be, seen as alienated individuals, separated from the social codes which bind people together. The cities were regarded as too big and too variegated, allowing individuals to free-float. There was a strong religious fervour to this criticism and the US cities as Sodom and Gomorrah has been a continuing motif from Josiah Strong to Jerry Falwell.

There is also an academic strand. One of the most influential urban sociologists in the USA was Robert Park (1864–1944), whose writings on the city are still being reprinted in urban sociology and urban geography textbooks. Park noted that the immigrants into the city had lost traditional sources of control:

> The peasant, who comes to the city to work and to live, is ... emancipated from the control of ancestral custom but, at the same time, he is no longer backed by the collective wisdom of the peasant community.

(Park 1952: 24)

This creates the central problem of American political culture: how can these people be assimilated into the American way?

> The social problem is fundamentally a city problem. It is the problem of achieving in the freedom of the city a social order and a social control equivalent to that which grew up naturally in the family, the class and the tribe.
>
> (Park 1952: 74)

This has been the persistent theme in American urban sociology and more widely in American public life. Park reflected a long and continuing line of social observations which concentrates on the city population as lacking traditional sources of moral sanction.

The city was often the locale for a different moral order from the mainly middle-class observer. Immigrant groups had extended families and subtle community networks. Many observers looking for the nuclear family model failed to find it and assumed there were no community bonds. They failed to see the ties which bound individuals with a web of moral constraints. All they could see were anonymous crowds lacking social cohesion. The failure to see beyond the restrictive social models of external observers has been a tragic motif of urban planning in the USA and throughout the world (see Gans 1962).

There is a richness and density to urban living which is not easily caught by crude stereotypes or alien perspectives. And many of the observers and commentators were 'out-of-towners'. The people who write about the city as an independent object of analysis are invariably those who have left the countryside or come from a small town. For convinced urbanists, the city is not something separate from wider social life. Commentators who think *of* the city rather than *in* the city are comparing it with another environment. In such a personal context the city can be contrasted with the more innocent place of youth, a rural arcadia or small town haven of certainty, counterpoised with uncertainties of an adult present.

Consider Frank Lloyd Wright (1869–1959), the Wisconsin farm boy who became a famous architect. He wrote of his arrival in Chicago:

> Chicago, Wells Street Station. Six o'clock in late spring 1887. Drizzling, sputtering white arc-light in the station and in the streets, dazzling and ugly. I had never seen so many lights before. Crowds. Impersonal. Intent on seeing nothing. Somehow I didn't like to ask anyone for anything. Followed the crowds . . . wondered where to go for the night. But again if I thought to ask anyone, there was only the brutal, hurrying crowd trying hard not to see.
>
> (quoted in White and White 1962: 190).

The distrust of the urban crowd, the fear of the mobocracy, never left Wright. America's foremost architect spent his time trying to build a non-city; his most important legacy was isolated houses for a wealthy elite.

The city has been seen as a corrupter of the American dream. The city was the built form of the new capitalist-industrial order; criticisms of the city were and still are criticisms of this order. The urban–rural dichotomy was posed in the form of the city as a place of a hard commercial system, a purely monetary order, to be unfavourably compared to the honest, enduring values of rural communities. It was in the cities, where extremes of wealth and poverty were most visible, where social conflicts were at their sharpest. It was the city that was the setting for the decline of spiritual values and the rise of an uncaring social order.

Evangelists from Strong to Falwell saw the perils in terms of individual sin and the solution in terms of individual moral redemption. There were others who saw it in a broader social perspective. The liberals and socialists saw the 'urban jungle' as the result of unrestrained market forces, the fault of a rampant capitalism with sustainable solutions only possible with wide-scale social and economic reform. In 1904, L. Stephens published *The Shame of the Cities*, based on a collection of articles published in 1902 and 1903 in *McClure's Magazine*. He dismissed the fears of foreign migrants. 'The foreign element excuse', he noted, 'is one of the hypocritical lies that save us from the clear sight of ourselves.' He put the blame on business as the source of corruption of the American dream. This has been a persistent clarion call for the radicals. The problem, however, for the leftists has been the lack of popular support. The majority of the population did not question the urban economic system but simply wanted to redirect its benefits towards themselves.

The cities have had a bad press because large sections of the intelligentsia have expressed anti-urban attitudes. There were exceptions. The cosmopolitans of Manhattan and the sturdy supporters of the big provincial (in the nicest sense of the word) cities such as Chicago and Los Angeles have praised the urban. But the anti-urban strain has been an enduring and important response:

> The American city has been thought by American intellectuals to be: too big, too noisy; too dusty, too dirty, too smelly, too commercial, too crowded, too full of immigrants, too full of Jews, too full of Irishmen, Italian, Poles, too industrial, too pushing, too mobile, too fast, too artificial, destructive of conversation, destructive of communication, too greedy, too capitalistic, too full of automobiles, too full of smog, too full of dust, too heartless, too intellectual, too scientific, insufficiently poetic, too lacking in manners, too mechanical, destructive of family, tribal and patriotic feeling.
>
> (White and White 1962: 222)

The myth of a more innocent past, in the USA as elsewhere, has been associated with the rural and the small town, a pre-urban, pre-industrial past which contrasts enduring community values with the social alienation of the big city. The very strength of this myth has brought forth counter-criticisms.

In the 1920s the novels of Sinclair Lewis (*Main Street*, 1920; *Babbitt*,

1922) poked fun at small-town life, its pretensions and constraints. In Raymond Chandler's world, small towns are places where the law protects the rich, the police are on the make and society is a dog-eat-dog one redeemed only by occasional individual acts of love. The mean streets which Philip Marlowe follows are of a distorted American dream. David Lynch's movie *Blue Velvet* (1987) takes these criticisms further and portrays American small-town life as based on a foundation of warped moral values, corruption, vice and crime.

There are more subtle contemporary criticisms. Garrison Keillor's *Lake Wobegone Days* (1985), which became a bestseller in the USA and was based on a hugely successful radio programme, portrays a very small town in Minnesota, the kind of place where everyone knows everyone else. A careful reading of Keillor, however, reveals a place where creativity and individuality can be stifled in a claustrophobic community. The humour, the wit and the humanity of the writing is underlain by an ambiguity towards the small community – a place where people know everyone else is both a strength and a weakness. The community is a support but, like all supports, it can be inflexible in not allowing things to grow and change. Keillor's next book about Lake Wobegone was entitled *Leaving Home* (1987). The title is indicative of the tension between the attractions of a small town and the need to leave it if real progress is to be made.

Keillor's work is a very sensitive treatment of the big city–small town/ rural dichotomy. More common has been the use by generations of moral entrepreneurs of the urban present as a scene of moral decline counterpoised to the rural innocent past. In this influential discourse, the city is the place where the songs of innocence are no longer heard.

The city as opportunity

In comparison with Europe, the new inhabitants of America had an opportunity to build new cities, free from the constraints of historical legacy. There were diverse experiments at what John Winthrop described as 'building the city on the hill'. In the colonial era, William Penn (1644–1718) had a vision of a small 'green country town' of 10,000 people which was laid out in large lots, a place where religious and political toleration was to be practised. Modern critics focus on the paternalism of Penn and his limited view of political participation (only male Christians could vote or hold office and to the representative assembly was added an appointed council) but in the context of the times, when bigotry and oppression were rampant, the plan was noble and enlightening.

Throughout the eighteenth and nineteenth centuries, various religious and social minorities sought to express their dreams in new settlements. In 1825, the Indiana frontier village of New Harmony was established by Robert Owen and others. Here goods were held in common; private property, religion and marriage were declared evil. New Harmony is the

more radical new world equivalent of New Lanark, established as a model
capitalist enterprise on the banks of the upper Clyde in Scotland in 1784.
New Lanark was the paternalistic capitalist seeking to create a more
uplifting setting for work and moral improvement, New Harmony was a
more communal effort towards total social emancipation.

There have been hundreds of New Harmonys in the USA. From Shaker
and Amish communities in Pennsylvania to Theosophist centres in
California and hippie communes in New Mexico, the American scene
contains diverse experiments in the search for new world utopias (see
Kagan 1975). Their continuing presence is a reminder that the search for
Eden continues.

In 1902 Howard Allen Bridgeman wrote in the *Independent*: 'He is a
dull fellow indeed if his soul is not stirred by the mighty beat of the city
heart.' He repeats an old point – the city as an exciting place – the centre of
civic culture. The same kind of feeling was expressed by Samuel Johnson
when he noted that, 'When a man is tired of London, he is tired of life'.
Bridgeman's point was prefaced by a more specific conception of the good
life:

> As the city man walks busily to his office in the morning or strolls
> leisurely uptown in the afternoon; as he saunters over to his club after
> dinner, or drops into the theatre, he may be pardoned for being proudly
> conscious of the fact that his daily course is not hedged about with
> threatening time-tables; that he has easy access to the best that the rich,
> resourceful city offers in the way of music and theatres, and lectures,
> and preaching, and libraries; that night and day converging streams,
> that take their rise all over the world, are depositing their ample cargoes
> at his very door.
>
> (Bridgeman 1902: 863)

The good city is the one where individuals make and spend money, a vision
of city living enjoyed by the rich, unencumbered male. It is a prospect that
has been an important element in the positive view of the city in American
social thought and political culture. The perception of the city has been
governed by the notion of it as a place where individual wealth can be
accumulated. Urban planning and environmental reform in the USA has
been dominated by the belief in helping business to flourish. The actual
form of this definition has changed through time. We can identify three
broad phases: (i) elite formulation of goals; (ii) pursuit of economic growth
with limited concern for social equity; (iii) desire for growth and social
change.

Elite formulation of goals

Throughout the nineteenth and early twentieth centuries, urban affairs
were dominated by elite formulation of goals and problems. Roy Lubove,

Figure 5.7 Pasadena City Hall, built 1925–7 and designed by
John Bakewell and Arthur Brown Jr, is an exuberant example of
the City Beautiful movement

in his studies of New York and Pittsburg (1962, 1969), documents the way
in which issues of urban planning were defined in response to business
objectives: the 'reluctance to compromise seriously the autonomy of
private business interests determined the character of public interventions'
(1969: 46). As the nineteenth century turned into the twentieth century,
the dominant urban ideology was the City Beautiful, the aesthetic
equivalent of the urban reform movement. The reform movement wanted
to take power away from the city bosses, the City Beautiful movement
wanted to beautify the city. Their vision of beauty drew upon the elements

of classicism in building type and civic ensembles. It was an attempt to give expression to the expanding imperial role of the USA (Klare 1969). The City Beautiful was a vision of a more beautiful urban America which relied on the construction of large civic buildings and broad open spaces (see Figure 5.7). What was good for a municipal elite was considered good for the whole population. The City Beautiful movement is an expression of the political power of the business community with little concern for social equity.

Pursuit of economic growth with limited concern for social equity

Such explicit elitism could not last very long in the more democratic twentieth century. The second phase was the redevelopment of the city centres and the encouragement of suburbanization, as business interests and those of the middle and white working classes coincided. From the New Deal onwards, federal government was involved in funding urban programmes. Although the exact focus of policy changed as administrations changed, the Republicans providing benefits for the rich but cutting back on anything that looked like redistributional socialism to the poor, there was a consensus on renewal in the centre and growth at the periphery. Urban development in the centre was in essence black removal, as low-income, particularly black, groups were displaced in the wake of redevelopment schemes which replaced housing with commercial and industrial properties. The middle class and more affluent working class were helped to make the trek to the suburbs. The massive suburbanization that took place was lubricated by housing subsidies and the highway construction programme. Between 1950 and 1980, the proportion of US population in the suburbs increased from 24 per cent to 42 per cent. Private and corporate interests coincided in the process of suburbanization. Households achieved bigger homes in suburbia while the whole infrastructure of suburbanization, highway construction and purchase of consumer durables, helped to buoy up the US economy. Post-war economic growth was a function and a consequence of large-scale suburbanization. The move to the suburbs became the great American dream, like the earlier vision of the trek westwards. The suburban house became the urban equivalent of the family farm, sharing the same icons of home, family, peace and prosperity. A suburban home signalled one's arrival, one's legitimate place in the social order. It had the right combination of pleasure and sacrifice: enough space to stretch out and relax but enough sacrifice, in terms of mortgage repayments and time spent on the children, to make the pleasure acceptable in a puritan land. The suburbs became the destination and repository of the American dream of individual attainment, family bliss and community harmony. Not everyone accepted the dream. The growing women's movement could see the suburbs as a place of domestic imprisonment for women, a site of domestic labour and exclusion from the larger public world. Not everyone wanted the dream. Single women, childless couples and gays, who refused the suburban option, began to establish their own neighbourhoods in the central city areas.

Desire for growth and social change

The cosy relationship did not include all of the population. The pro-growth coalition did very little for the ethnic minorities trapped in the central cities. The rumblings of this underclass, denied access to the suburbs and badly affected by urban renewal, were heard in the urban riots of the mid-1960s. Between 1964 and 1968, over 300 riots took place in over 250 US cities. Research by Roger Friedland (1982) has shown that rioting was particularly evident in those cities where there had been aggressive urban renewal programmes. The rioting ended but control of the central cities did not always go back to the former elites. From the mid-1960s, urban policy became influenced by questions of social equity as much as by issues of promotion of economic growth. Throughout the USA in this third phase, and especially in the South, ethnic minorities captured control of many central cities. In the city of Birmingham, Alabama, previously the scene of intense white oppression, the first black mayor was elected in 1979.

The new central city bosses of the USA still have a concern with growth. However, they also have a concern with redistributing some of the benefits, in terms of employment practices and community development. In Atlanta, a city where blacks had gained a measure of control, municipal authorities began to redirect spending patterns. In 1960 there were no blacks on Atlanta's payroll. By the mid-1980s, almost 30 per cent of the city's contracts went to black businesses and blacks constituted 65 per cent of the municipal workforce.

The city and individual opportunity

The city as a place of individual opportunity has been a consistent strand in the American experience (see Figure 5.8).

In *Midnight Cowboy* (the 1969 movie based on the novel by James Leo Herlihy), a young man leaves the south to make a living on the streets of New York. His main goal is to become a sexual stud to rich women. The young man stares with wide open eyes when the bus enters New York. Here is where he will make his fortune; here he will find expression, free from the restrictions of a small town. The image of the city as place of opportunity where dreams can be fulfilled is a redolent theme in the popular culture of the USA. In the movies of Woody Allen, Manhattan figures as a place of individual freedom, away from the constraint, pettiness and anti-intellectualism of the archetypal, working class, Jewish family. Manhattan, not Israel, becomes the promised land.

Figure 5.8 The city as privatized, hedonized existence: *A Bigger Splash* (1968) by David Hockney (Tate Gallery). It is the idealization of the city as site of individual achievement and place of pleasurable consumption. Hockney, an English artist, has said that he was attracted to Los Angeles because it had no ghosts; it was unburdened by the weight of history and the work of other artists.

The city as place of individual opportunity was given a particular poignancy in the United States because of the large-scale immigration into the city. Second and third generation migrants were caught between an ethnic past and an American urban present. The representation of this position is a major theme of American culture.

In *The Rise of David Levinsky* (1917), Abraham Cahan describes the experience of a Jewish immigrant from Russia. The novel depicts the material rise of Levinsky but his spiritual impoverishment as he loses his principles. James T. Farrell's *Studs Lonigan* trilogy (1932–5) depicts the experience of a young man of second generation Irish stock in Chicago. The novels trace the corruption of Lonigan and give an example of the American dream gone bad as the young man takes up crime and violence to achieve his purely materialistic ends.

In *The Fortunate Pilgrim* (1964) and *The Godfather* (1969), Mario Puzo presents aspects of the Italian-American experience. Again the concentration is on the family unit and their attempts to achieve material wealth.

In all of these novels there is a theme that the new society creates opportunities but the sense of loss of identity is heightened by a depiction of moral corruption. The American city provided opportunities but at a price; to get on meant to lose either one's ethnic roots or one's moral ballast. The three novelists cited dramatize the ambivalence by concentrating on characters brutalized and desensitized in their pursuit of material wealth. The underlying theme was that the material gains of the city had a high moral price.

If the move to the suburbs was an act of self-sacrifice for the old middle class, then the move back to the city is an act of self-expression for the new middle class. Changes in family size, household composition and consumption patterns, all condensed in the image of the yuppie, are leading to the gentrification of selected neighbourhoods of some central city areas. The imagery of this process is interesting, as notions of homesteading and pioneers are now being translated into an urban context:

> During the 20th century the imagery of wilderness and frontier has been applied less to the plains, mountains and forests of the West, and more to the cities of the whole country, but especially of the East. As part of the experience of suburbanization, the 20th century American city came to be seen by the white middle-class as an urban wilderness, the habitat of disease and crime, danger and disorder.
>
> (Smith 1986: 16)

With the move back to the city the process has come full circle. The ideologies of the early nineteenth century are being mobilized in the late-twentieth century. The belief in transforming the wilderness continues to exercise its power over the American imagination.

6 Two varieties of peoples

In Australia will be seen the savage aboriginals, and ... the civilized white people. These two varieties of peoples differ from each other in all essential particulars. ... The blacks have been for thousands of years roaming over the plains and forest lands of Australia, and have died without leaving any buildings, gardens, farms or erections of a permanent character. The whites have only been here for little more than a century and have everywhere given evidence of their presence by what they produced of houses and other buildings, or farms, orchards, gardens, with all that pertained thereto. While the whites have brought all this about, the blacks during all the centuries of their undisturbed wandering over the wilderness have never even thought of constructing a road, highway, bridge, or street through their camp, or attempted to make a farm, garden, house or manufacturing of any kind.

Unsigned article (1903) *Science of Man*

A threefold division of wilderness, countryside and city fits uneasily with the Australian experience. *Outback* closely corresponds to *wilderness*, but *bush*, used throughout Australia, refers to cultivated and pastoral land as well as to wilderness areas. The usage captures an essential feature of the white Australians' relationship with their environment. Outside of the cities the environment has not been completely conquered.

The Bush has always been viewed by [white] Australians as an alien and hostile land, an enemy to be hacked down, burned away, ploughed under and exploited in any way possible. Perhaps it is simply an act of retribution on an environment in which almost every living thing either bites, claws, scratches, poisons or kills human intruders, and nature itself tries to madden the mind with an endless cycle of droughts and floods.

(Roddewig 1978: 139)

The fuzzy linguistic division between wilderness and countryside that is implicit in *bush* captures the contingency of human control of the environment. The notion of a slender hold over the environment figures as a strong element in white Australian culture. In the novels of Patrick White, the early movies of Peter Weir and the paintings of Sidney Nolan, Fred Williams and Arthur Boyd, the Australian landscape figures as something to be feared as well as admired. In Australia, the bush is a counterpoint to the corrupting properties of urban society while also symbolizing the brutalizing power of untamed nature.

This view of the environment is neither the only one nor the oldest. In Australia, since 1788, there have been two competing environmental ideologies: a recent white one, involving the commodification of resources, and a much older Aboriginal mode of perception and resource evaluation. The history of Australia since permanent white settlement in 1788 is how one achieved dominance at the expense of the other.

THE TAMING OF THE BUSH

> We wrought with a will increasing,
> We moulded, and fashioned and planned,
> And we fought with the black, and we blazed the track
> That ye might inherit the land.
> (F. Hudson, 1908, Pioneers)

In 1788, when the British established a penal colony on the coast of what was later called New South Wales, they came across a society very different from their own. They perceived a wilderness because the indigenous peoples were neither white nor settled and the landscape did not bear the marks of an agrarian society or an industrial order. They saw a wilderness waiting to be transformed by the plough, the introduction of livestock, the mining of minerals and the establishment of towns. For the whites, the land and its resources were a source of wealth and material gain. In the next two hundred years they set about realizing their objectives in pushing the frontier from a toehold on the coast to most of the rest of the vast country. The European attack on the 'wilderness' came from several quarters. Sheep rearing, agriculture, timber extraction and the search for gold all played a role. The push of the farming frontier involved the clearance of vegetation and the break-up of the soil, while the gold diggings badly affected local ecosystems. Writers have referred to a 'a rage against the bush' as farmers and pastoralists cleared the land. The results could be profitable. Here is John Macarthur, writing in 1794 about his farm in Parramatta:

> As to myself, I have a farm containing nearly 250 acres, of which upwards of 100 are under cultivation, and the greater part of the remainder is cleared of the timber which grows upon it. Of this year's produce I have sold £400 worth, and I have now remaining in my Granaries upwards of 1800 bushels of corn. I have at this moment 20

acres of fine wheat growing, and 80 acres prepared for Indian corn and potatoes, with which it will be planted in less than a month.

(quoted in Onslow 1973)

Macarthur was an especially efficient farmer and model employer of convict labour in the new colony. Few could emulate his agricultural achievements but all shared the same goal of transforming the 'bush' into a source of wealth.

The exploitation of resources in Australia became inextricably linked to the British and ultimately world markets. There was, and continues to be, a powerful economic motive in the (white) people–environment relationship over and above subsistence needs. The attack on the bush involved the penetration of market power and the commodification of resources. On the other side of the frontier was a very different conception of the environment.

The Aborigines were not a homogeneous group. The total pre-contact population has been estimated at between 200,000 and 600,000 over the whole land, with groups living in very different environmental conditions and speaking many languages. However, they all shared a deep knowledge of and concern with their environment. Their environmental sensitivity reflected their circumstances. Since they were hunting-gathering groups, they relied upon their local environment to provide them with sustenance and shelter. The importance of the people–land relationship is evidenced in language. The Bicen tribe had four genders: male, female, eatable, non-eatable. This sensitivity was the result of a long, unbroken relationship with the land. Estimates of the length of the Aboriginal presence in Australia ranges from 18,000 to 60,000 years. The people–environment relationship had both a material and a spiritual significance. In the many Aboriginal myths, the people were intimately related to the environment at the time of creation, sometimes referred to as 'the Dreaming' or 'Dreamtime'. In the Dreamtime, spirits – part human, part animal, part vegetable – created the world from a void. All living things and places were the work of these spirits and there was an unending link between people and places, the past and the present, which was codified in myths and re-enacted in rituals. A bark painting of the Dalwonga tribe in East Arnhem Land shows in ochres of red, yellow, black and white the figure of a human form interlocked with pictures of turtles, fish, insects and birds (see Figure 6.1). In this painting, as in all Aboriginal belief systems, people, landscape and animals share the same cosmos.

The arrival of Europeans marked the beginning of the end for the dominance of Aboriginal environmental ideology in the continent of Australia. For the Aborigines, the white invasion involved the loss of the land, the destruction of indigenous cultures and the superimposition of white economic and cultural power. It was not a story of Aboriginal passivity (see Reynolds 1981). There were skirmishes and deaths in the

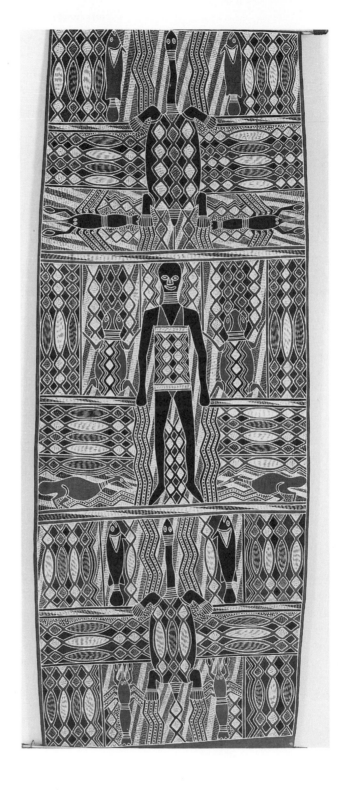

Figure 6.1 Bark painting by member of the Dalwonga tribe showing ancestors of the Yiritja moiety (Australian National Gallery, Canberra)

early struggles of resistance. Later, many of the younger people learned new ways in the schools and cattle stations, away from the age and gender hierarchies of traditional society. In general, however, the extension of European control involved the loss and curtailment of Aboriginal rights and freedoms.

The Aborigines were shot and killed by the early white settlers. When they were less of a threat and more of an administrative problem, they were uprooted from their homelands and herded into missions and government reserves, their lives transformed and regulated by a society in which they had no power and little influence.

It was shamefully late in the twentieth century before there was due recognition of the rights of Aborigines. There was grass roots action in the 1960s, when Aboriginal stockmen went on strike for better pay and working conditions on some of the large cattle stations of the interior. The cause was also taken up by some on the political left in Australia, Aboriginal rights and environmental concern often sharing the same agenda for social reform. There was both black pressure and white responsiveness for change. The image of the Aborigine as noble savage was resuscitated, part of a reassessment of 'wilderness' and national identity. Aborigines were now seen as more ecologically conscious, less demanding of nature, a model of good people–environment relations. A referendum held in 1967 allowed Aborigines to be counted in the census and gave them the vote. Belatedly, the referendum demonstrated a willingness to improve the plight of the Aborigines.

Contemporary issues of Aborigines' rights have focused on the question of land. There had already been some administrative developments in South Australia, where the Land Trust Act of 1966 leased land to Aboriginal communities for up to 99 years through the intermediary of the Land Trust. Under the Act, the Land Trust and the South Australia government shared royalties from mining leases and licences. Almost half a million hectares of land were leased under this scheme between 1966 and 1980.

A major change came with the Milirrpum case. In Arnhem Land in Northern Australia a reserve had been created for Aborigines in 1931. The Chief Protector of Aborigines (note the paternalistic title) had recommended this area because 'the country is very poor, no one requires it, and those who previously have taken some of it have abandoned it'.

By the 1960s this seemingly worthless land was found to contain valuable minerals and the government leased some of the land to a bauxite mining company. The local Aborigines were not consulted. In December 1968 the tribal council and Methodist missionaries of Yirrkala sought court injunctions to prevent mining. One of the elders was called Milirrpum, after whom the case is named. The hearings began in the Supreme Court of the Northern Territory on 25 May 1970. In April 1971 Justice Blackburn reported that he could not issue an injunction against the mining. The case was widely reported and Justice Blackburn's summing up showed an admiration for Aboriginal society but, under European-based law as it stood, he could not order the mining operations to cease.

Although the Milirrpum case was unsuccessful, it influenced the climate of opinion and helped to shape the big change to come. Before the 1972 election the leader of the Labour Party, Gough Whitlam, announced that his party would give land rights to Aborigines 'because all of us as Australians are diminished while the Aborigines are denied their rightful place'. In 1973 the Labour government set up an inquiry, named after its chairman A.E. Woodward who had been the senior counsel for the plaintiffs in the Milirrpum case. The Aboriginal Land Rights (Northern Territory) Act of 1976 contained many of the recommendations suggested by the Woodward inquiry. It allowed Aborigines with primary spiritual responsibility for unalienated crown land to claim ownership, stop mining extraction and negotiate with mining companies over the payment of royalties. It meant that spiritual custodians of the land could become owners in the European sense and that the Australian legal system, basically English in design, was increasingly cognizant of traditional Aboriginal values and land rights. In this sense, the 1976 Act marked a significant departure in almost two hundred years of European–Aboriginal contact.

The legislation has not solved all of the problems. It ignored the plight of landless urban Aborigines, the inhabitants of suburbs such as Redfern in Sydney, or the fringe dwellers of small town, outback Australia. Given Australia's federal system, the 1976 legislation applies only to the Northern Territory. In 1985, Aborigines in Queensland, for example, had yet to achieve meaningful land rights; and even in more enlightened states, a constant battle has been waged between mining and cattle interests on the one hand and Aborigines on the other over the implementation of land rights legislation. In May 1985, as the federal government was seeking to introduce a new land rights bill, the *Canberra Times*, after reporting days of Aboriginal protest on the steps of the federal Parliament, exemplified the white backlash in an editorial on 6 May which called land rights an 'extraordinary privilege' and argued against the costs of 'preserving the benefits of a neolithic culture'. The land rights issue will continue to concern Australian governments for some time to come (see Figure 6.2).

Subtle changes have occurred in environmental attitudes since the white people colonized Australia. In the eighteenth and nineteenth centuries, there was a clear divide between black and white which exemplified very different attitudes to land and nature. Over the course of two hundred years, while this basic cleavage exists, there are now white groups eager to save the wilderness and some Aborigines keen to lease parts of their land to mining companies. Monetary interest and spiritual concerns regarding the environment are no longer a clear black and white issue. Keneally (1983) describes the case of an Aborigine who had given permission for

Figure 6.2 Poster advertising a land rights demonstration in Canberra

mining to take place on a Dreaming site for which he had spiritual responsibility:

> He was the truest knower of the place, he was the respository of all its meaning. He held it, that is, on behalf of all the clan. Immediately upon consenting to the mining agreement his power as an elder was diminished. He was avoided by his people. Two other tribal elders sang up his death. The Jabiluka negotiations had occurred in late 1981. By September 1982 he had gone blind. He did not consult a European doctor about his blindness because he believed that there could be no cure from the justifiable, inevitable singing. At the time of writing he is wasting, his spirit bleeding away. But if its spirit place is broken up for ore, where can the spirit find rest? Perhaps there are other places in the country of his kin to which it may be able to journey. But there is no certainty of that. So that it is not just that he is dying; it is that from within his view of the earth, his soul may be lost forever. . . . The man's grandchildren may have community centres, small industries, four-wheel-drives. The man himself is in hell.
>
> (Keneally 1983: 220)

THE BUSH TAMED

> Take now the fruit of our labour,
> Nourish and guard it with care,
> For our youth is spent, and our backs are bent,
> And the snow is on our hair.
>
> (F. Hudson, 1908, *Pioneers*)

Australia was founded as a penal colony, an antipodean *gulag*. The first settlement was restricted to policeable proportions and all land was initially held by the Crown. In the course of the next 50 years, land was sold off to private estates as pastoralism became more important. The frontier expansion from the coastal toehold reflected the changing relationship between Australia and Britain. Australia became less of a prison and more of a producer of raw materials such as wool, grain and gold.

The move into the interior was based on economic calculations, but it was a commercial enterprise legitimated with reference to a number of ideologies.

From the mid-nineteenth century, there was the development in both Australia and Britain of the view of Australia as a Garden of Eden, a sort of Britain before the fall of the Industrial Revolution. There were several sets of agents in both countries keen to promote such a picture. Farmers in Australia badly needed labour, while shipping companies in Britain badly wanted business. There were also the cultural brokers who, in their praise for Australia, said more about contemporary Britain:

Behind all the admiration for Australia's fresh air, its greenness, its sense of space, its Arcadian innocence and its imagined social harmony, there lurked an unstated comparison with a cold, crowded, polluted, industrialised and socially-divided England.

(White 1981: 34)

Carol Lansbury (1970) shows how the myth of a happy rural life in England was transferred to Australia by writers such as Charles Dickens and Charles Reade in the mid-nineteenth century. Australia became the lost Arcady, a role it still plays for many Britons and Americans. Modern movies, such as *Crocodile Dundee*, continue to propagate the myth. In the nineteenth century the myth had real effects. Between 1830 and 1850, about 150,000 migrants went from Britain to Australia, two-thirds on assisted passage schemes. These people were not only recipients of the myth; many of them in their letters home became effective reproducers. There are very few emigrants who write back to tell their friends and relatives of the disadvantages and constraints of their new life. Few write to say they have made a dreadful mistake in leaving the old country. Most sing the praises of the new land.

There were two different pastoral models employed in the allocation of land. In the first, holding sway until around 1860, the model was of large estates worked by a rural proletariat (see Figure 6.3). One such version of this model was worked out by Edward Gibbon Wakefield (1796–1862). Gibbon developed his scheme while in Newgate prison on a 3-year sentence for abducting a 15-year old girl. It is perhaps fitting that the scheme to transform a penal colony was propounded in one of Britain's more notorious gaols. His plan, published in 1829 as two articles in the influential London newspaper, the *Morning Chronicle*, was to sell off Crown land at a high price. The money raised was to pay for the passage of immigrants, who would be unable to afford the land and thus be forced to work for the landowners. Wakefield had a vision shared by many in Britain, of an Empire held together by ties of trade. The colonies were to be the suppliers of raw materials and food for the mother country. Australia was to function as an agricultural branch plant of the metropolis, with its internal structure a replica of the British rural system of rich estate owners and landless labourers.

The plan was adopted, in part, by the British Government and the 1830s saw the selling of Crown land in New South Wales. The price of five shillings per acre in 1831 was raised to twelve shillings in 1838 and to £1 per acre four years later. Some of the money collected was used to provide assisted passages for immigrants from Britain. In 1834 the British Parliament passed an Act allowing settlement in South Australia; land was to be sold off at a high price, creating large estates and a fund for assisted passages. South Australia was thus a state created for free settlers and not as a penal colony. Even today, many South Australians are proud of the

Figure 6.3 Mr Muirhead's Station (1856) by Eugen von Guérard: a rich landowner surveys his property – his house, garden, wife, children and animals (National Library of Australia, Canberra)

fact that they are not tainted with convict origins and consider themselves to have a higher standard of civic conduct and a better quality of public life.

In the 1860s the model of a rural squirarchy was replaced in public debates by the symbol of the yeoman farmer. The ideal society for rural Australia was now seen as a land populated by small farmers in family units. The small farmer was seen as condensing moral virtue with social stability and efficient farming. From the second half of the nineteenth century until almost the present day, it is this myth which has dominated popular debates and influenced public policies. This shift came about because of social and political changes. The colony achieved a measure of self-government after 1855 and more populist voices were beginning to be heard. 'Land for the people' was a popular mid-nineteenth century cry, a demand bolstered both by successive waves of immigrants seeking a livelihood from the land and by radical urban interests eager to break the political power of the rich landowners, the so-called squattocracy. The immigrants and the radicals were fearful of a countryside closed to further colonization, permanently locked in the hands of the rich and powerful squatters.

The demand to 'unlock the land' was legitimated with reference to the need for more rational farming. Many sought to show how a denser, family farming system would be a more efficient use of the land than the giant sheep runs and huge pastoral leases. These arguments and political pressure successfully influenced public policy and throughout the second half of the nineteenth century various Land Acts sought to create a yeomanry. In 1861, the Lands and Occupations Act of New South Wales allowed any person to purchase between 30 and 320 acres at £1 per acre. A year later the Duffy Act in Victoria allowed any adult male or adult single woman to purchase a block of land of between 30 and 640 acres at a similar price. Comparable Acts in Queensland, Western Australia and South Australia also sought to open up Crown lands to homestead settlement. All these schemes involved deferred payment, in which homesteaders could pay off the purchase price over a number of years. For example, under the South Australia Strangeways Act of 1869, homesteaders could purchase up to 640 acres at £1 per acre on payment of a small deposit, the balance to be paid at the end of four years.

The schemes were only partially successful. There were many abuses by which very large blocks of land were amassed by the wealthy, using phantom settlers. Many genuine settlers could only obtain land with poor soils or in inaccessible locations, and so could not make the farm a paying proposition. In New South Wales, of the 170,000 who had filed an application between 1861 and 1880, only 12 per cent remained by 1880. Michael Cannon (1973) summarizes the story thus:

> Radical writers, an urban middle class wishing to break the squatters' power, and even a few conservatives hoped that strong and independent 'yeomanry' would emerge, replacing the lonely sheep runs with a large population dwelling on self-contained farms. In a few favoured areas this aim was partly achieved. But the general result was the transformation of squatters' leaseholds into freeholds owned by the same men or the banks, the alienation of the choicest parts of the public domain for all foreseeable time, and the rise of a class of wealthy landed gentry whose influence on Australian life has not proved entirely beneficial. Colonial budgets may have been balanced by the irresponsible selling of Crown land, but the social penalties were drastic and long-lasting.
>
> (Cannon 1973: 126)

Despite the failures, the yeoman myth persisted into the twentieth century, aided by a rural reality and an urban yearning (see Figures 6.4 and 6.5). It was evident in the Closer Settlement schemes in which each state introduced legislation to purchase land and resell it in smaller blocks to settlers. A total of 1.3 million hectares was repurchased between 1890 and 1917; the largest amount was in Queensland (318,051 ha), where the scheme was widely publicized in Britain to attract immigrants. Then there were the various Acts which gave servicemen returning from the two World Wars favourable treatment, involving preferential loans in acquiring land for homestead farming. The scheme after the First World War put

Figure 6.4 An artistic codification of the yeoman pioneer: *The Pioneer* (1904) by Frederick McCubbin (National Gallery of Victoria, Melbourne)

Figure 6.5 A similar image is repeated in the 1926 silent film, *The Pioneer*, but here the woman is given a more equal role. (National Film and Sound Archive, Canberra)

over 29,000 returning soldiers on the land. A.B. Facey (1981), in his autobiography *A Fortunate Life*, describes how he obtained a farm under this scheme. By the 1920s, many had failed. In Tasmania, for example, only 800 of the initial 2,000 remained on the land by 1925:

> Under capitalization, the depredations of rabbits, the ruin of the Irish blight in potato-growing areas, and the lack of skill on the part of the ex-soldiers, all put paid to the dream of many a settler.
>
> (Robson 1985: 120)

The yeoman myth is part of the romance of the bush, of the tendency to see it as a place of virtue to be contrasted with the evils of the city. One reason for putting people on the land was to take them away from the city. In the 1880s, various decentralization leagues were established in Victoria and New South Wales to move people and public services away from Sydney and Melbourne. Economic arguments and social values were intermingled. Too-large cities were seen as abnormal, socially dangerous and generators of almost everything from crime and immorality to pollution. Here is a Labour representative in the New South Wales State Parliament of 1905 making a popular country statement:

> get the bulk of our people away from the towns and give them such conditions that young fellows can make homes for themselves and settle down in comfort as soon as they arrive at a marriageable age and there will be no real difficulty then about the declining birth rate. It is the town life and the greater or lesser degree of degeneracy – in the physical as well as moral sense that attends it.
>
> (quoted in Crowley 1973: 84)

These arguments continue to be used. They have been a consistent element in the policy objectives of the Country Party which has invested decentralization 'with a certain mysticism, and in its propaganda decentralization has emerged as the cure for Australia's ills, a panacea for problems in defence, industry, education, health and morals' (Aitkin 1973: 418).

The praise of the bush continues and not only as a politically conservative force. It is one element in the contemporary counter-culture movement. The landscape of Australia is studded with alternative communities, communes and farming co-operatives. Some of these places survive more by means of welfare payments than other economic transactions. There are others where former flower-power groups have become small business people. One example, which I visited in 1985, was the town of Kuranda in the rainforest above the coastal city of Cairns in Northern Queensland. Here the Kosmic Kuranda Kiddies of the acid rock era were running good health food restaurants, growing avocados and aloe vera plants, managing art galleries and selling hand-painted T-shirts. It was an economic lifestyle lacking the formality of centralized socialism or the aggressiveness of corporate capitalism. Kuranda is one of those places which sympathetic visitors cannot recall without generating pleasure and warmth. It evokes memories of a slow lifestyle and a pleasant relaxed atmosphere.

The Australian character and the countryside

The rural experience has figured prominently in the question of Australian national identity. The best known contribution is Russel Ward's *The Australian Legend*, first published in 1958 but reprinted every couple of years since then in popular glossy productions. In essence, his argument is that there is a clearly identifiable Australian character:

> According to the myth the 'typical Australian' is a practical man, rough and ready in his manners and quick to decry any appearance of affectation in others. He is a great improviser, ever willing 'to have a go' at anything, but willing to be content with a task done in a way that is 'near enough'. Though capable of great exertion in an emergency, he normally feels no impulse to work hard without good cause. He swears hard and consistently gambles heavily and often drinks deeply on occasion. . . . sceptical about the value of religion and of intellectual and cultural pursuits generally. He believes that Jack is not only as good as his master but, at least in principle, probably a good deal better, and so he is a great 'knocker' of eminent people. He is a fiercely independent person who hates officiousness and authority. . . . he is very hospitable and above all, will stick to his mates through thick and thin.
>
> (Ward 1958: 1)

Ward argues that these characteristics come from the itinerant pastoral workers of the bush in the early and mid-nineteenth century, when the 'brute facts' of Australian geography, work conditions and convict-based attitudes to authority all created a 'bush ethos' which stressed mateship, self-reliance, communal effort, distrust of authority and contempt for social hierarchies. The attitude of this group was disseminated throughout the wider population through speech and songs and, more formally, through both the writings of the bush school of Paterson, Furphy and Lawson and the rhetoric of the trade union movement which took the ethos of the bushman as part of its hopes, goals and myths. According to Ward, the myth of the bushman continues to exercise a hold over the popular imagination in Australia.

Ward's definition of the typical Australian is of a man and his description of national characteristics is of a particular type of masculinity which stresses male bonding. This is the mateship tradition of Australian society, one consequence of which is a restricted vision not only of the role and importance of Australian women in the national character but also of women's capabilities (Dixon 1983; Summers 1975).

Is there an Australian character and did it really come from the ethos of the bushman? We can never really know; ultimately, these are not arguments susceptible to empirical verification. The more interesting point is the continuing use of a rural 'character' for an urban nation. Despite being one of the most urban countries the dominant self-image is still of a rural Australia.

THE CITY IN THE BUSH

Although the dominant imagery of Australia, as portrayed in films and advertising, is of wilderness, and the popular representation of its history is of Antipodean wild west where men are men and the frontier is beyond the cloudless and unpopulated horizon, the settlement reality is very different. Australia is one of the most urbanized countries in the world. Of the 14.5 million population, 55 per cent live in just five cities: Perth, Adelaide, Brisbane, Melbourne and Sydney. One out of every three Australians lives in either Melbourne or Sydney. The typical Australian family lives in the city; the koala and the kangaroo are only something that they see on the television or at the zoo.

Economic history of the urban hierarchy

The urban hierarchy of Australia is unusual. As Table 6.1 shows, it is dominated by five big cities, followed by only a few medium-sized cities and then a scatter of small settlements. The top-heavy character of the hierarchy is a result of economic history. In the early years of white

Table 6.1 Population distribution in Australia, 1980

States	*Capital city*	*Second largest city*
New South Wales	Sydney	Newcastle
5,126,127	2,876,508	258,972
Victoria	Melbourne	Geelong
3,832,443	2,578,759	125,279
Queensland	Brisbane	Gold Coast
2,295,123	942,836	135,437
South Australia	Adelaide	Whyalla
1,285,033	882,529	29,962
Western Australia	Perth	Bunbury
1,273,624	809,035	21,749
Tasmania	Hobart	Launceston
418,957	128,957	64,555
Territories		
Northern Territory	Darwin	Alice Springs
123,324	56,482	18,395
Australian Capital Territory	Canberra	
221,609	219,331	

settlement it was a penal colony. Prisons are about enclosing people, limiting their space. The early foothold on the coast was confined to a limited area around Sydney. Captain Philip, his marines and convict charges were hemmed in by the nature of their business, by ignorance of the terrain, by fear of the indigenous population and by a need to maintain links with Britain. The colony relied on Britain for food.

Throughout the nineteenth century, more and more of the interior came under white control. The Aborigines used the land for both material and spiritual purposes. The whites used it only for material purposes. White control meant the commodification of the land. Sheep and cattle were grazed, wheat was grown and minerals were mined. These commodities were shipped overseas as Australia became a branch plant of an economic enterprise whose head office was in London.

The regional office was the major city in each state that was the place of transhipment, the centre for local finance and state government. Each state capital grew as a port for the import and export of goods. As more of the interior was commodified and trade increased, so did the big cities. The cities grew larger as the expansion of the trading system increased local earnings, which in turn created the demand for more goods and services. In each of the state capitals there was a process of cumulative causation as the big cities expanded. Tables 6.2 and 6.3 show for Victoria and New South Wales how even today the size of towns declines markedly after Melbourne and Sydney.

In each state, the settlement pattern was of a dominant coastal capital city with a scatter of small towns. Sydney, Melbourne, Brisbane, Adelaide and Perth continue to dominate the commercial and political life of their respective states, a situation criticized by Australia's most famous poet, A.D. Hope, in his 1972 poem *Australia*:

> And her five cities, like teeming sores,
> Each drains her: a vast parasite robber-state
> Where second hand Europeans pullulate
> Timidly on the edge of alien shores.

Table 6.2 Urban hierarchy of Victoria, 1980

City	Population
Melbourne	2,578,759
Geelong	125,279
Ballarat	62,641
Bendigo	52,741
Shepparton	28,373
Warrnambool	21,414
Wodonga	18,142
Mildura	15,763

Table 6.3 Urban hierarchy New South Wales, 1980

City	Population
Sydney	2,876,508
Newcastle	258,972
Wollongong	208,651
Maitland	38,865
Albury	35,072
Orange	27,626
Broken Hill	26,913
Bathurst	19,640

The big cities once established grew as trading centres, points of transhipment, seats of state government, legal and financial centres. A self-perpetuating cycle of growth was maintained, as government policy and public spending was biased towards the state capital. Railway charges, for example, were fixed throughout the state to favour the movement of goods into the capital city, even when other coastal towns were closer. The net result is a series of urban fiefdoms closer in character to Renaissance city states with rivalries just as intense, especially between Melbourne and Sydney (Davidson 1986). The two cities are often used to identify different characteristics of Australia. Melbourne is seen as more cultured and more civilized than brash, hedonistic, corrupt Sydney. Barry Humphries has two stock Australian characters. It is no accident that the drunken cultural attaché, Sir Les Paterson, comes from Sydney while the (previously) more prim Dame Edna Everidge is a resident of Monee Ponds, Melbourne.

The politics of the urban hierarchy

The Australian urban hierarchy is not yet dominated by just one city. The reason for this pattern lies in the politics of the urban hierarchy.

It was only in 1901 that the separate states federated to become one nation. Prior to this, the states were a series of quite separate entities all looking more towards Britain and overseas markets than to each other. Their separateness was a function of distance (Perth is two time zones away from Sydney), economic orientation and inclination. They had different railway gauges, different newspapers and even different rugby codes. Rugby league was played in New South Wales while Aussie Rules, a balletic game of organized violence, had its centre in Victoria.

Each state was like a separate country, with very powerful state capitals responsible for trade, transport, education and the vast bulk of public expenditure. State politicians used this power to maintain urban dominance. In New South Wales, for example, the state government, based in Sydney, fixed the railway charges so that it was always cheaper for wheat farmers to export their produce through Sydney rather than any

Figure 6.6 The centralization of power in the big cities has caused
rural resentment to such an extent that a Country Party has been a
significant feature of the Australian political scene throughout most
of the twentieth century. This cartoon from the *New State Magazine*
(June 1923) captures the images of rural virtue opposed to urban
centralization.

other port in New South Wales. Political power was used to maintain urban
primacy (see Figure 6.6).

When these separate city-states sought to join together for mutual
benefit, in the federation of States now known as Australia, the question of
a federal capital was a tricky one. The reality of population distribution
and political power meant it had to be either in Victoria or in New South
Wales. Three thousand kilometres and two time zones away in Western
Australia there was always less commitment to federation.

On 2 January 1898, a referendum was held to vote on the draft Constitution. The vote was overwhelmingly for Federation but in New South Wales the 62,000 cast for Federation failed to meet the previously agreed minimum of 70,000. This gave some leverage to the State Premier of New South Wales, George Reid. He managed to persuade the other Premiers that the voters of New South Wales needed extra enticement. At the next Premiers' conference, held in January 1899, Clause 125 of the Constitution was made to read:

> The seat of government of the Commonwealth shall be determined by the Parliament, and shall be within territory which shall have been granted to or acquired by the Commonwealth, and shall be vested in and belong to the Commonwealth, and shall be in the State of New South Wales, and be distant not less than one hundred miles from Sydney.
>
> Such territory shall contain an area of not less than one hundred square miles, and such portion thereof as shall consist of crown lands shall be granted to the Commonwealth without any payment therefor.
>
> The Parliament shall sit at Melbourne until it meets at the seat of government.

The Clause was a compromise. New South Wales got the federal capital within its boundary, but Victoria managed to have it far enough away from Sydney so that few advantages could be gained by Melbourne's arch rival. Moreover, Melbourne had the Parliament until a new one could be found.

It was to be 25 years before the Parliament moved from Melbourne. While the broad location of the new capital was fixed, the precise location was hard to find. A Royal Commission report of 1900 examined 23 possible locations. A tour by Senators and Representatives in 1902 looked at sites in New South Wales, including Bombala, Tumut, Lyndhurst, Albury, Armidale, Lake George, Orange, Bathurst and Dalgety. There were all kinds of political arm-twisting as local and federal politicians sought to have the capital located in their area (Pegrum 1983). Local groups entertained the visiting politicians and sought to impress upon them the advantages of their area. Some had fate turn against them. Supporters of the Lake George site had the misfortune of the Senators' tour coinciding with a drought which made the waters of the Lake disappear. This was a bad omen for those empowered to consider adequate water supply a prerequisite for the new capital. After that visit, Lake George was never a serious contender.

The location of politics involved the politics of location, as towns and their representatives sought to win the prize of capital designation. After a number of votes, the site of Yass-Canberra was decided upon by the House of Representatives on 1 December 1908, was confirmed by the Senate and passed into law twelve days later. The new seat for the young federal government was inland on a high limestone plateau. It became known as Canberra.

Planned cities reveal much about a society because they embody responses to past experiences, suggest visions of the good life and generate models for subsequent developments. In Canberra, Australia has one of the most planned capital cities in the world, ranking with Brasilia and New Delhi in its ordered scope and controlled imagery. An examination of Canberra allows us to comment on urban Australia. In the remainder of this chapter the ideologies of urban Australia will be uncovered through a discussion of Canberra.

Canberra developed

Australian cities are not the simple outcome of pure market forces; like all other cities, they have planned elements. Take Adelaide, the principal city and state capital of South Australia. To view it at night from Mt Lofty is to see the neon advertising lights blink out product names from the high-rise central business district. Away from the centre, one can see the patterned street lighting of the lower-density residential areas spreading along the coastal fringe. Between the business and residential areas is a geometric pattern of darkness surrounding the business district. This is Colonel Light's green belt. Established in 1836, it has been nibbled at and breached by roads but 150 years later still provides a green lung for hard-pressed office workers, a place of sport and recreation in a very central position. Such examples of planned, or at least shaped, development abound in Australian cities but they rarely provide metropolitan coherence. Canberra is the exception.

After finally deciding upon the site, the federal government had to build the city. Although there were a few pastoral properties, some large houses and small cottages, for all intents and purposes Canberra was a blank page, with its overgrazed hills, eroded soil and displaced Aborigines; it was perhaps a fitting capital for white Australia. Because it was to be the seat of government, the *Sydney Morning Herald* editorial of the 27 November 1909 expressed the sentiments of many:

> when we begin to build, even though unpretentiously, we should build to a plan nobly conceived and worthy of the setting provided by nature. Even though our capital be small, a unique opportunity offers for making it one of the most beautiful cities in the world.

To this end a design competition was held. It was announced in 1911 and entries had to be received by 31 January 1912. There was a prize of £2,000 for the winner, to be decided by an unnamed board of assessors. This unusual method prompted the Royal Institute of British Architects to call for a ban by architects throughout the Empire and so few British architects submitted. Despite the ban, 126 entries were received and the majority recommendation gave first prize to an American, Walter Burley Griffin.

Griffin's design had two important elements (see Figure 6.7). First, it

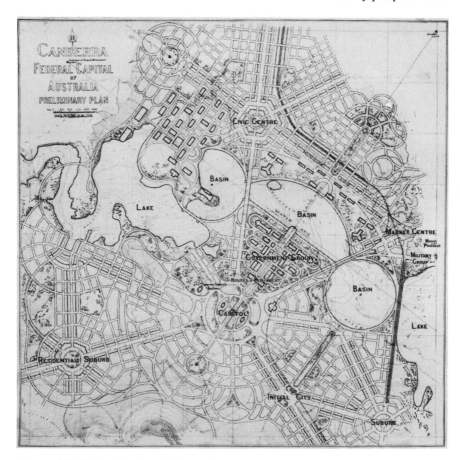

Figure 6.7 Walter Burley Griffin's winning entry in the Canberra design competition, 1912

had elegance. There was a major axis running from a prominent hill site, the Capitol, to Mt Ainslie and bisected by a proposed lake system which Griffin termed the water axis. It was a design of simple geometry, with its lines echoing Haussmann's Paris and the City Beautiful plans of Washington and Chicago where Griffin had worked. It seemed a fitting aesthetic for the architecture of authority. Second, the design had a sensitivity to the site itself, which was lacking in the other entries. Hill sites were utilized, a lake system was proposed and there was an awareness of the harmony between the crisp lines of geometry and the possibilities of the natural setting.

On 12 March 1913, the city was officially named and construction began. The early story was one of disputes. Griffin was appointed Director of Design and Construction in 1913 but there were conflicts with the other officials. By 1920, the year in which Griffin's contract ended, not to be renewed, only £9,000 had been spent. The development of Canberra had been halted by personality clashes and the war effort. Griffin and his wife were outspoken pacifists, a fact which contributed to his waning political favour. Griffin played no further part in the making of the city, but gave his name to a Lake only completed in 1964.

There was some building in the 1920s. The basic layout of Griffin's plan was established, a garden city was produced through extensive plantings and garden suburbs were built. Residential Canberra was low rise, green and open with no front fences, had community shopping centres and lots of trees. Between 1921 and 1924, almost 1,200,000 trees were planted. If the initial design was City Beautiful, then on the ground the place had a softer feel because the Federal Capital Advisory Committee, established in 1921, embraced the designs of the Garden City movement (Freestone 1984).

The terms of Clause 125 of the Constitution were finally completed in 1927, when the Parliament was opened in Canberra on 9 May by the Duke of York. Most of the government departments still remained in Melbourne. Canberra was a small dusty town which just happened to be the Federal capital. Public indifference to the city was evident at Parliament's opening. Officials mad catering arrangements for big crowds which did not appear. The next day, 10 May, 10,000 pies had to be buried in a quiet unrecorded ceremony.

The history of Canberra's development has mirrored the history of the country. The first half of the twentieth century for both Australia and Canberra was a time of depression then war, depression and war again. The city developed only slowly. After the opening of Parliament, some government offices were moved from Melbourne to Canberra but further progress was held back by the reluctance of public servants and the lack of money. Canberra's population on the eve of the Second World War was only 7,000. By 1954, when more of the government offices had made the move, the population was still only 30,000. Streeton (1971) describes the scene in the early 1950s:

> Dismembered parts of it retreated up various hillsides. Tracks led dustily across dry paddocks to lonesome squares of shops. Short bursts of ceremonial boulevard collapsed to cross creeks on narrow wooden bridges, their regiments of elm and fir giving way abruptly to native scrub. A dairy farm on a flat flood plain separated groups of garden suburbs whose mannered geometry and regular government hedges spoke of 'planning' with arcadian monotony and inconvenience. ...
> Visitors agreed with compulsory residents about the 'good sheep station spoiled', the 'seven suburbs in search of a city', the 'city without a soul' or a main street either. Besides golfers and rose growers, only a few rural spirits really enjoyed it, for the mountains and the peace and the trout.

Like the country as a whole, Canberra's fortunes changed in the 1950s. It was the beginning of the long post-war boom, a time of rising incomes and expectations. A Senate inquiry in 1955 suggested a new authority and an increased profile for Canberra and in 1958 the National Capital Development Commission (NCDC) was established to plan, develop and build Canberra as the National Capital. From 1958 to 1986, almost all government offices moved from Melbourne to Canberra. The city took on a more permanent look as the population increased from 40,000 to 150,000 and some second generation and even third generation Canberrans could be found. The old quip that most countries had cities without plans but Australia had a plan without a city was no longer heard. By the 1970s it became legitimate to speak of the city of Canberra.

Canberra and the Australian (sub)urban experience

Canberra is different from other Australian cities in a number of important respects. Most obvious to the visitor is the monumentalism. Within the showpiece Parliamentary triangle of Griffin's design, there is the High Court, the National Gallery, the National Library, the Parliament buildings and various government offices. Many of the embassies are built according to the designs of the respective countries. The embassy of the USA is a Virginian colonial mansion, the Japanese building has all the simple elegance that we expect from that country, including a zen garden, while the Indian embassy looks just the place for a visiting Moghul prince. The net effect is architecture as display, with the work of big-name Australian and overseas architects filling the landscape with a concrete history of post-war architectural fashion: a brutalist block here, a modernist tower there, with a dash of post-modernist whimsy. The result has all the staginess of Disneyland. The buildings are self-consciously on show, distanced from each other and from the life of the city by manicured bush or tarmacadam car-park. In Canberra, as in few other cities, architecture as Architecture is obvious and explicit. The city has become a theme park for modern architecture.

Away from the monuments lie the suburbs, now numbering over thirty, their names a roll-call of Australian public figures – Hughes, Garran, Melba and Florey – with Yarralumla and Tuggeranong a linguistic reminder of another, older, different Australia. The suburbs contain detached, single-dwelling bungalows in a setting of gently rounded streets, gardens which stretch to the road without high fences, and an environment of quietness and vegetation growth overlooked by hills kept as bush. While Canberra shares its general suburban nature with the rest of Australia, its particular form is, to my mind, more pleasant. If civic Canberra has the geometry and the monumentalism of the City Beautiful, of Big-name Architects and Big-scale Planning, residential Canberra has the intimacy and charm of the Garden City, low-rise bungalows and small-scale planning. Much of Canberra gives the feeling that it has enhanced the natural setting and improved upon the pastoral landscape.

Figure 6.8 Melbourne 1985: Australia is a country of big suburban cities

Despite its recency, its planned development and self-conscious look, Canberra is more Australian in its connection with native flora. Formal gardens elsewhere, such as the Domain in Sydney or the Melbourne Botanic Garden, are essentially northern hemisphere gardens under a southern sky. This applies also to much of the greenery of the city in public spaces and private gardens in urban Australia. In Canberra, however, the native flora is much more evident in private gardens and public spaces. Griffin experimented with local plants for landscape potential and the hills surrounding Canberra are covered in gums and eucalyptus. The rage *against* the bush of the last century has been turned into the rage *for* the bush. Canberra now references the Australian bush more than any other city in the world because Canberra's residential growth of the 1960s coincided with a nationalist 'bush' garden movement, when groups such as the Society for Growing Australian Plants proliferated.

Despite the differences, however, Canberra also embodies much of the character of urban Australia. If Canberra is now over thirty suburbs in search of a city, then this reflects the wider society.

Australia is not so much the most urbanized country as the most suburbanized. Almost three-quarters of Australians live in single family dwellings. Away from the central business district, the Australian city is a low-rise spread of dispersed surburbia (see Figure 6.8). The reasons for this pattern are the lack of rented accommodation, the availability of land and the purchasing power of ordinary people. Labour has always been scarce in Australia and so working people have been able to maintain relatively high standards of living. They could afford to be owner-occupiers. Even at the time of federation in 1901, one in every two Australian households were owner-occupiers. In Britain, at the same time, the comparable figure was less than one in ten. The desire for owner-occupation has been a powerful motif in Australian political and social life. Successive governments since the last quarter of the nineteenth century have encouraged and maintained owner-occupation. The desire for a quarter-acre block is the goal of most Australian households. This conjunction of public policy and private desires has transformed the landscape. Residential development has spread out from the edge of the city. Sydney has just less than half the population of Paris but spreads over ten times the surface area.

The overwhelming weight of suburbanization in Australia has stimulated much comment. On the one hand, there have been the critics of the suburbs. Robin Boyd's *The Australian Ugliness*, first published in 1960, refers to the visual mess, the crassness, the overwhelming tackiness and cultural bleakness in

> this halfway area, a cross hatched smudge on the map round each capital city and larger town, in which may be found all the essential drabness and dignity of Australia. The suburb is Australia's greatest achievement (not proudest achievement, there is no collective pride in the suburb, only a huge collection of individual prides).
>
> (Boyd 1980 ed.: 161–2)

The Australian Ugliness is more than just an attack on the suburbs, it is a general critique of visual and especially architectural aesthetics in Australia. It has many interesting insights. It does, however, share a point of association with less sensitive criticisms: a distaste for the lower middle-class British culture which predominates in Australia. For many critics, the Australian suburb with its brick-veneer villas is a solid metaphor for the lower cultural class. Many Australians still believe the myth of a classless society, especially the cultural critics who disguise (from themselves and others) their distaste for the lower orders by taking the general terms *Australia* and *Australian* as their object of attack. A criticism of the suburbs is less dangerous than an out-and-out attack on the 'lower' classes. There are, to be sure, other arguments, for example about the cost of servicing low density sprawl, but the predominance of the suburbs means that discussions about the suburbs are mainly vehicles for discussing unexamined class relations in Australia.

More recently, Kemeny (1983) and others have pointed to the gender consequences of suburbanization. Suburbanization separates residences from employment and particularly limits employment opportunities for women because individual dwellings need large amounts of domestic labour. This reinforces the patriarchal relation in society. Watson and Helliwell (1985) have shown the difficulties faced by single women in a society dominated by the cult of family-orientated, owner-occupied suburbanization.

On the other hand, there are those who applaud the suburbs. If to criticize the suburbs is to put down Australia, then to laud the suburbs is to celebrate Australia. It is not accidental that positive comments about the suburbs are a recent phenomenon, since it is only in the past 30 years that the writing classes in Australia have had enough self-confidence to write positively about their own society rather than disparage the lack of (upper class British) culture. It is no accident that the two writers I now discuss are Australians.

A most vigorous defender of the suburbs is Hugh Streeton. In *Ideas For Australian Cities* (first published in 1970 by the author himself but printed by a commercial publisher in 1971, reprinted in 1973 and revised in 1975), he defends the quarter-acre block because it gives people space and freedom to pursue activities such as gardening, barbeques (the major outdoor experience in Australia), dismembering vehicles, and keeping pets; it allows people to do cheap things by themselves and gives a measure of self-expression to ordinary people. Streeton is aware of the reliance on private vehicles but insists that it provides mobility to many families. Streeton is less comfortable with the feminist critique, perhaps unable to believe the argument about the suburban imprisonment of women. Streeton celebrates the creativity and freedom that the suburbs gives to ordinary people.

Peter Corrigan, an architect and writer, celebrates the suburbs because of their personal expression of individual aesthetics. They may lack visual harmony but they revel in individualism; they may have a simple vocabulary, below professional expectations, but they are, according to Corrigan, a legitimate element of Australian culture.

> Suburbia was ruefully described in the 1960s by Robin Boyd. . . . But the
> values of the bourgeoise Australian dream of a free-standing brick

house with a tiled roof on a quarter acre block of land are being re-examined by a new generation of architects. These values offer no social redemption, but at least they are ours. They owe nothing to the inner city, the outback, or the Dreamtime. The suburbs are not malevolent any more than they are materialistic. They are now being recognised as the Australian communal form that possesses a moral imperative of its own.

(Corrigan 1985: 22)

Corrigan is a post-modernist architect. His views are in contrast with the modernists. Australia's most important modernist architect, Harry Seidler, wrote an afterword to the 1980 second revised edition of Boyd's *The Australian Ugliness*. Seidler's architectural work is all clean lines and formal geometry, which echo the Bauhaus and the international style. The work of Corrigan, in contrast, is more explicit with historical references, has a wider colour range and is softer, more accessible and funnier. Corrigan is also a nationalist. Like Robert Venturi, who seeks to reclaim the commercial strip development of Las Vegas as part of the canon of American built form, Corrigan sees the individuality of Australian suburbs as an important element of Australian national definition.

Both Streeton and Corrigan have brought about a much needed re-evaluation of the social importance and cultural significance of the suburbs. They have shifted the debate away from simple condemnation. But we should be careful of a timid relativism which refuses to criticize suburban tackiness and the harmful social and gender effects of suburbanism. Like Australia itself, the suburbs have much to recommend and much to criticize. Either to dismiss them or only to laud them is to suspend our critical faculties.

Canberra as political symbol

Canberra is more than just a city; it is the physical embodiment of federal power. In Australia, Canberra is synonymous with the federal parliament and the exercise of central government power. Canberra appears in the mass media as the locale for political crises, parliamentary capers and power struggles. Headline writers regularly use phrases such as 'Canberra decides to raise taxes' or 'Canberra says no to new proposal'. All countries have a seat of government but most capital cities are other things as well, a centre of population, a place with a history as well as a present. Canberra's growth has been so recent and the place is still so small and distant that in the popular mind of Australia it is nothing more than the seat of government, a one-industry city where almost 60 per cent of the workforce are public servants. In Australia it is impossible to separate attitudes towards Canberra the city from attitudes towards central government, politicians and public servants. The criticism of Canberra the city is often a

Figure 6.9 Canberra 1986: a view from Mt Ainslie (top right of Figure 6.7), overlooking Lake Burley Griffin, towards Capitol Hill and the new Parliament building

vehicle for a wider discourse on the nature of political power and many of the myths of Canberra are tied up with notions of its being a pampered place, populated with overpaid politicians and underworked public servants. Even its location is in marked contrast to the other state capitals, which are on the coast and so have a maritime climate with a strong beach culture. Canberra, located on a high inland plain, strikes average Australians as lacking in beaches and being too dry in summer, too cold in winter. These images are used as wider metaphors: the inland site is typical of an unnatural city, its winter coldness is a sign of emotional sterility and the dry, hot summer is part of the aridity of a place that is only able to survive by living off the backs of other Australians.

There is also the myth of Canberra as not being the real Australia. It is true that its streetscapes lack historical connectivity with Australia's past. The streets of Canberra are only one meaning thick, they are too recent to have been reused and rebuilt. Canberra references the modern international style of architecture more thoroughly than any other Australian city and thus has few explicitly national points of contact (see Figure 6.9). Through time, different layers of meaning will be attached but, for the moment, Canberra is seen by many as a city separate from the life of the real Australia.

Architecture once used to link Canberra to the rest of the world is now being used to link Canberra to the rest of Australia. In 1988 most, but not all, Australians 'celebrated' 200 years of continuous white settlement. Celebrations were held throughout the land but a major event was the opening of the new Parliament house in Canberra on Capitol Hill, which holds a strategic position in the physical layout of public Canberra. In Burley Griffin's initial report of 1911, the hill was to house a building 'for popular assembly and festivity more than for deliberation and counsel'. However, the site lay empty until the 1970s when it was chosen by a federal government committee to be the site of the permanent federal parliament. A competition was held and the winning design, by Mitchell, Giurgola and Thorp, was announced in 1980. They have created a monumental structure across the hill, linking up Griffin's land and water axes. The building is designed as an embodiment of Australia. The entrance way has a granite block surrounded by water to represent Australia, the island continent, and marble columns have been designed to indicate gum trees, while the red tile roof in the centre and the great verandah reference Australian vernacular architecture. The building is topped by a giant flag of Australia to symbolize allegiance to the nation. There are fears that the new building will lack the informality, the small scale and the accessibility of the temporary parliament. The new building seeks to orchestrate public access, to distance the Prime Minister from the public and to guide people around a consensual image of Australian nationality. It may succeed in this regard. It may not. Structures designed to serve one end may be used for others. What is not in doubt is that one of the most symbolic acts of the Australian bicentennial festivities involved the opening of a government structure in the heart of Canberra, in celebration of Australian nationalism and as an exercise in national symbolism and political mythology.

Part III
Texts

Introduction

We can't interact with the text, we can't affect the development of the text by our own words, since the text's words are already given. That is what perhaps encourages the quest for interpretation.
　　　　　　　Professor Morris Zapp 'quoted' in David Lodge (1984) *Small World*

Texts embody myths and articulate ideologies but they cannot be reduced to them. Texts are produced by particular authors for specific audiences and they are subsequently interpreted by a range of creative readers.

We communicate through texts. They are language made solid, conversations frozen in print and picture. To understand texts is to understand the messages passing between members of society. For our purposes, they provide another insight into the social significance of environmental ideas. Texts may be poems, novels, newspapers, plays, films and television commercials. Here I shall examine three forms: novels, films and landscape painting. I am concerned with 'English' novels, US films and Australian landscape painting and, in particular, with their treatment of wilderness and countryside. Each of them has a sufficiently high degree of self-referencing to make them a coherent unit of study and they provide an extra dimension to the previous, broader chapters on myths and ideologies.

The interpretation of texts can be enlightening but is not easy. They are produced by imaginative individuals. Creative artists condense social concerns, but give them specific, personal shape and substance. The tension is summarized by Sartre (1964: 56): 'Valery is a petit-bourgeois intellectual ... but all petit-bourgeois intellectuals are not Valery'.

There is a need for careful analysis which captures the dialectic of broad social context and individual creative impulse without reading off texts from a socio-economic position or else seeing texts as devoid of wider social meaning and significance.

There is also the problem of causality. Let me illustrate with an example. In 1793, during a tour of northern Scotland, the poet Robert Burns stayed with the Duke of Atholl. During his stay Burns wrote a poem, *The Humble Petition of Bruar Water to the Noble Duke of Athole*. Part of it reads:

Let lofty firs, and ashes cool,
My lowly banks o'erspread,
And view, deep-bending in the pool,
Their shadows' watery bed:
Let fragrant birks, in woodbines drest,
My craggy cliffs adorn;
And, for the little songster's nest,
The close embow'ring thorn.

It was not one of Burns' better poems; one of his biographers refers to it as an 'interesting "occasional" piece' (Daiches 1981: 272). It did, however, have an effect. The Duke did plant trees beside the river. As Margaret Drabble (1979: 69) has noted, 'the trees are now there, one of the most direct testimonies to a writer's influence on landscape'.

The connections embodied in this story are important. We may identify an environmental idea, here expressed in poetic form, and there is the effect, trees were planted. We may identify an idea and an associated effect but we can never be sure that the idea caused the effect. It may have been unimportant or simply one factor amongst many. Can we be sure that the Duke planted the trees because of the poem? He may have been planning the venture for a while, the poet merely giving a nudge to a decision already made on any number of criteria, from rate of return to soil conservation or simply to annoy his wife. Then there is the degree of congruence between the production of environmental images and their consumption. Burns had a romantic conception of nature and countryside. The Duke may or may not have shared this view and his actions could have come from a more technocratic vision of the world. Where Burns saw trees shading the pools of the river and adorning the landscape, the Duke may have seen root systems which improved soil stability, defences against attack or raw timber to be sold for a handsome profit. Producers and consumers may share the same text but can have very different interpretations.

A distinction has been drawn in literary theory between open and closed texts. Closed texts are those which leave no room for the 'reader' to feel other than the stock emotions desired by the 'author'. Open texts, in contrast, are those which allow room for the creative reader. The dominant ideology thesis assumes closed texts whereas, in reality, all texts have both open and closed characteristics.

All of these factors make difficult the interpretation of texts. We can either retreat up into a linguistic fundament – every decoding is another encoding, according to Morris Zapp – or we can be aware of the problems, accept the contingency of our remarks and take a risk.

7 'English' novels

The inescapable fact remains: literature is an aspect of society. It coheres, structures and illuminates many of its most profound meanings. It is, in a particular sense, an institution of society, an inheritance of artistic practices and values, a point of formal interaction where writers and audience meet, a means of social communication and involvement, and a manifest expression of our curiosity and our imagination.

M. Bradbury (1981) *The Social Context of Modern English Literature*

A novel is an impression, not an argument.

Thomas Hardy (1895) Preface to the fifth edition of *Tess of the D'Urbervilles*

As a literary form, the novel is a newcomer. Poetry and drama, dialogues and romances are all much older. The novel is a creation of the modern world and its changing shape, size, form and function tell us much about this world.

In this chapter I will look at selected 'English' novels. I have chosen novels which provide a broad historical sweep and allow me to note some of the connections between changes in literary form and changes in society. The evolution of the novel provides the context for examining the evolution of national environmental ideologies. I have restricted the chapter to two themes, wilderness and countryside.

Like all selections, the choice is partial and biased. I have chosen classic authors, those who have been both influential and widely read. They have all made an important contribution to literary form and to environmental ideologies, but ultimately the choice is a personal one. I have also chosen some of my favourite authors.

TRANSFORMING THE WILDERNESS

'I was born in the year 1632, in the city of York.' So begins one of the first English novels. It was written by Daniel Defoe (1660–1731) who came late to novel writing. Defoe was born in London in 1660, the son of a Presbyterian family. He led a remarkable life. He was a merchant, a government agent and a writer. He attended an academy for dissenters in Newington Green with the idea of becoming a Presbyterian minister. His religious beliefs continued throughout his life and guided his actions. In 1685 he took part in the Duke of Monmouth's rebellion against the Catholic King, James II. Three years later, he supported the landing of William of Orange and continued to write pamphlets in his support. In 1702 he wrote an ironic attack on High Church extremists for not allowing enough freedom to Protestant dissenters. A warrant was issued for his arrest which read:

> Wanted! Fifty Pounds Reward. For the arrest and capture of Daniel Foe or Defoe. He is a middle sized, spare man, about forty years old of a dark complexion and a dark brown coloured hair, but wears a wig, a hooked nose, a sharp chin, grey eyes and a large mole near his mouth.

He was captured, put in the pillory for three days, fined and imprisoned. On his release he was taken up by the influential Robert Harley who was then Speaker of the House of Commons. Defoe was then employed as a government agent, travelling the country and reporting back to Harley. He went to Scotland to influence the negotiations for the 1707 Act of Union. Defoe wrote many political tracts. He was involved in the politics of the day. He supported the Whigs, often by writing supposedly Tory articles! He was treading a dangerous path but a guiding principle was the belief in the Protestant faith and the Protestant succession, plus a sharp eye for survival.

Born into a trading family, Defoe tried his hand at trade. In 1684, when he married at the age of 23, the register noted his occupation as merchant. He became a partner in the stocking trade but also dealt in wine and tobacco. He deserted his business to take part in the Duke of Monmouth's rebellion. He was taken prisoner and only released by the payment of money. This, and the loss of goods captured by the French, led to his first bankruptcy in 1692, with debts of £17,000. He set about paying the debts by starting up a profitable brick and tile business in Tilbury. By 1705 he had reduced his liabilities by £12,000. He had a lifelong interest in trade, first as a practitioner and then after 1705 as a writer. 'Writing upon trade', he wrote in 1713, 'was the whore I really doated upon.' Trade – buying and selling, the noting of commercial opportunities – was never far from his thoughts. His *Tour through the whole Island of Great Britain* (1724) is a commercial survey of the country, an inventory of trading patterns, industry and crafts; it is an early economic geography. A year later came *The Compleat English Tradesman*.

Defoe was a prolific writer. He wrote pamphlets and essays, surveys and arguments, and he contributed to a range of journals. He was a journalist, commentator and propagandist. He was a writer deeply embedded in the arguments of his day, sensitive to shifts in opinion and political power. But late in his life, at the age of 59, he wrote *Robinson Crusoe*, arguably the first English novel. It was enormously popular at the time, both in Britain and abroad, and has remained popular ever since.

This early English novel is not meant to be a novel but to be the recollection, written in the first person, of a real person. It was based on the story of a Scottish soldier, Alexander Selkirk, who lived from 1704 till 1709 on the uninhabited island of Juan Fernández. We do not know if Defoe ever met Selkirk but he would have read the written accounts of his exploits. Although there is a basis in fact, *Robinson Crusoe* is a work of fiction.

In most modern condensed editions, Robinson Crusoe goes aboard a ship and is then shipwrecked on his desert island. In the original longer version, Crusoe is a rebel against his parents, with a love of adventure and an abiding concern to make his fortune. He is a modern hero, the icon of an individualistic, commercial society. He is involved in two voyages and seven trading ventures, especially in South America where he prospers on a plantation. He then persuades his fellow planters to fit out a ship to go to Africa and pick up slaves. The ship is caught in a storm and Crusoe is the only survivor. The novel is firmly set in the contemporary commercial exploitation of the Third World. The narrative then becomes a metaphor for civilizing the wilderness.

After initial distaste at being cast on this 'desert' island, Crusoe sees the benefits:

> I was removed from all the wickedness of the world here; I had neither the lust of the flesh, the lust of the eye, nor the pride of life. I had nothing to covet, for I had all I was now capable of enjoying; I was Lord of the whole manor; or if I pleased, I might call myself King or emperor over the whole country which I had possession of. There were no rivals. I had no competitor, none to dispute sovereignty or command with me!

He surveys the island and begins a calendar. He establishes order in both time and space. He keeps a journal in which he continually invokes the name of God and the hope of spiritual redemption. Spiritual and material progress go hand in hand as Crusoe establishes 'order' on the island.

After twenty-five years alone on the island, 'savages' come to it. He captures one and describes his relationship:

> In a little time I began to speak to him, and teach him to speak to me, and, first, I let him know his name should be FRIDAY which was the day I saved his life. . . . I likewise taught him to say MASTER and let him know that was to be my name. . . .
>
> I gave him a pair of linen drawers . . . a jerkin of goat's skin and I gave him a cap and thus he was clothed, for the present, tolerably well. . . .
>
> I was greatly delighted with him, and made it my business to teach him everything that was proper to make him useful, handy and helpful. . . .

I began to instruct him in the knowledge of the true God. . . .

And now my life began to be so easy that I began to say to myself that could I but have been safe from more savages, I cared not if I was never to remove from the place while I lived.

These quotes culled from the book telescope the colonial venture: Crusoe has given the 'savage' a language, a menial role, a set of clothes and a religion. And, in return, Friday does all of the work! After a 35-year absence, Crusoe returns to England with Friday as his 'faithfull servant'. Further travels ensue, to Lisbon and Madrid, and finally he sells his plantations in Brazil for 32,800 pieces of eight. His fortune is made.

The novel operates at a number of levels. It is an adventure story. For the western imagination it has become one of *the* adventure stories, embodying the theme of retreat, withdrawal and renewal, and then reunion with society. The desert island is a symbol of the wilderness and the recapturing of spiritual wholeness through material progress. The Robinson Crusoe story has become of major significance in western culture. The story has been a template for numerous retellings. It prompted Swift's construction of *Gulliver's Travels* (1726) and has been the setting for many films. Paradoxically, the film which was most faithful to the religious sentiment was *The Adventures of Robinson Crusoe* (1953), directed by the arch anti-cleric Luis Buñuel.

The novel is also the fictionalizing of a specific historical movement. Defoe managed to embody the colonial and mercantile expansion of Britain in his tale of the shipwrecked Crusoe. The story begins with a commercial hero seeking to make his fortune and becoming involved in trading links around the world. Great writers have a habit of being fascinated by the morning spirit of their age. The spirit of mercantile capitalism was developing and strengthening in Defoe's time. At home, the Bank of England was founded in 1694 and the Stock Exchange four years later. Overseas trade was also growing. The East India Company established a factory in Calcutta in 1690 and Defoe was writing when the triangular trade route linked Britain, Africa and the Americas. The expansion of mercantile capitalism is the context for understanding *Robinson Crusoe*. In his conquest of the island, Crusoe condenses the colonial adventure of gaining absolute control over territory, making it commercially useful and subjugating the locals.

Robinson Crusoe also functions as a more general response to the wilderness. In the story, the uninhabited island is a wilderness which is transformed. The island is made habitable, changed from 'desert island' to 'my island' and, in the process, Crusoe is also transformed as he regains his spiritual connections with God. Defoe shares the belief in progress and records the triumph of progress. *Robinson Crusoe* expresses the classical attitude to wilderness.

An opposite view is expressed by the modern writer William Golding. Before looking at his work, however, we must consider the novel which mediates between Defoe and Golding: R.M. Ballantyne's *Coral Island*. Robert Michael Ballantyne (1825–94) was born in Edinburgh to a respectable middle-class family. (His two uncles were printers of Walter Scott; his elder brother a distinguished orientalist.) When he reached the age of 16, his father apprenticed him as a clerk to the Hudson Bay Company in Canada. He returned to Scotland in 1848 and worked for a publishing firm for seven years. In 1856 he wrote an adventure story based on his experiences in northern Canada. This was the beginning of a successful literary career. Ballantyne became a full-time writer and published over eighty books, all of them 'adventure stories for young folks' as he put it.

Ballantyne's books were aimed at the sons of the Victorian middle class. Imbued with a deep religious conviction, he felt he had a moral purpose of educating such boys into codes of honour, decency and religiosity. The high moral tone was redeemed by Ballantyne's ability to tell a cracking good yarn in an accessible and well-fashioned prose style. The attractive writing style is one reason for the enormous popularity of Ballantyne; very much a product of the nineteenth century, his books continued to be read in the twentieth.

Coral Island, first published in 1857, was his third novel. It is written, like *Robinson Crusoe,* in the first person. The hero and 'author' is Ralph Rover who, as his name suggests, is of a roving disposition. In the first chapter he leaves home to go to sea. The chapters are short, none more than ten pages. In the second, he makes two friends, Jack Martin, a strapping 18-year old, and a smaller 14-year old called Peterkin Gay. In the same chapter, there is a storm at sea, by now mandatory for the desert island novel. The three boys are shipwrecked on an uninhabited island in the Pacific ocean. The novel then chronicles their story.

They survey the island by walking round the shore three abreast, with the smaller Peterkin in the middle and Ralph and Jack holding a separate conversation above his head. They find that the island has wild pigs, which they hunt for food. It is a story of unremitting goodness, a sort of muscular Christianity in which the three boys maintain a chivalric code.

> When we did awake it was near sunset and we were all in such a state of lassitude that we merely rose to swallow a mouthful of food. . . . we took breakfast at tea-time, and then we went to bed again, where we lay till the following afternoon. After this we arose greatly refreshed but much alarmed less we had lost count of a day. I say we were much alarmed on this level for we had carefully kept count of the days since we were cast upon our island, in order that we might remember the Sabbath-day, which day we had hitherto with one accord kept as a day of rest and refrained from all work whatsoever.

Like Crusoe, their idyll is destroyed by the presence of the savage other. The savages come in two forms: the native cannibals who come to the island but are repulsed and pirates who kidnap Ralph. After numerous adventures, Ralph manages to escape with the ship and is reunited with his chums. The boys then leave the island and rejoin the outside world.

The book echoes with the Christian evangelistic tradition. At the end, the book praises the wonderful effects of Christianity and becomes little more than a mouthpiece for the London Missionary Society. The effects are noted by a sailor:

> For my part, I don't know and I don't care what the gospel does to them, but I know that when any of the islands chance to get it, trade goes all smooth and easy.

The three boys are bearers of virtue and witnesses to a progressive civilization. The boys spread the Christian message and help to civilize the 'natives' with whom they have come into contact. Like *Robinson Crusoe*, *Coral Island* subscribes to the unity of commercial and religious enterprises. They are both part of a belief in the progressive civilizing force of British expansionism.

Although Ralph, Jack and Peterkin are bearers of a 'civilizing' mission, they are also boys and the book is aimed at a readership of children. The book takes its readership seriously in appealing to the desire in children for occasional defeats of adult authority figures. On the island the three boys escape from the adult world, they make their own world, they defeat the cannibals and Ralph eventually outwits the pirates. All these are metaphors for the defeat of the more oppressive elements of adult authority. At a psychological level the book, like *Peter Pan*, panders to the young person's desire for escape from adult authority, yet for traditional order to be established. *Coral Island* respects a deep psychological desire in a young readership, which perhaps explains its wide and continued popularity.

William Golding was for a time a school teacher. As a school teacher, Golding would have read *Coral Island*. As a school teacher, he also had experience of young boys. The boys of *Lord of the Flies* are not the boys of *Coral Island*.

Born in Cornwall on 19 September 1911, Golding was educated at Marlborough and Brasenose College, Oxford, where he initially read science but changed to English literature. After graduating in 1935, he worked for a theatre company as writer, actor and producer. He joined the Navy in 1940 and saw active service in the D-day landings. After the war he taught English and Philosophy at Bishop Wordsworth's School in Salisbury until 1961. Golding has become a famous and popular novelist. He was awarded the Nobel Prize for literature in 1983. He has become a major literary figure. His first novel was *Lord of the Flies*, published in 1954.

The opening scenes of the novel established the desert island theme. A group of schoolboys are marooned on a desert island. It is not entirely clear how they got there. This uncertainty is the result of a radical change from the first version that Golding sent to publishers. The opening chapter of the initial version describes a war and the flight of the young people aboard an aeroplane. Many publishers turned down the manuscript. In the final accepted version, the opening scene is set on the beach of the island where the boys discuss their plight and choose a leader. The contestants are Jack and Ralph. After Ralph is elected chief, he and Jack and another boy decide to survey the island. They walk three abreast so that the larger boys can speak over the head of the smallest. There are other echoes of *Coral Island* and explicit references abound but, while Ballantyne's Jack, Ralph and Peterkin maintain their chivalry, Christian virtue and decency, the boys in Golding's island display very different characteristics.

The tensions are evident in the three main characters. Jack is strong, tall, physical. Although defeated by Ralph for the leadership, he maintains an independent power base. He has a following amongst some of the boys. He decides to become a hunter, searching for pigs. As the novel progresses, it is clear that he has a destructive blood lust. The pigs in *Coral Island* provided food; the pigs of Golding's unnamed island touch a deeper, hidden need. Piggy, and the name is not incidental to the previous remarks, is the complete opposite to Jack. He is the voice of reason, he echoes adult authority. It is Piggy who hits upon the idea of blowing a shell, initially to round up all the boys and then to use it as a call to a meeting. It is Piggy who criticizes unruly meetings with the scornful remark, 'acting like a crowd of kids'. It is Piggy who says, 'We've got to have rulers and obey them. After all, we're not savages.' It is Piggy who keeps referencing the adult world of responsibility and duties. Where Jack is physical and wild, Piggy is cerebral and weak, the school swot. Torn between these two is the elected leader, Ralph. He is a physical being who swims and climbs with the best of them but, unlike Jack, he has a sense of duty, a connection with the outside world. Unlike Piggy, he has natural authority. He is a modern hero, tormented in his attempt to hold together the fragile society in the face of increasing savagery.

At the beginning, plans are set down but the project begins to falter. The boys begin to neglect their duties, the fire goes out, and there are problems of food and water supply and of adequate shelter. This desert island produces not civilization but bewilderment. Jack and his hunters, now referred to as the savages, become even more dominated by the hunt and the kill. The chant of *Kill the pig, cut his throat* echoes through the island. Jack sets up a rival group whose only goal is killing pigs and enacting hunting rituals. They lose contact with 'civilization' as the scrubbed features of middle-class public schoolboys become caked in grime and smeared with paint. Only Piggy, Simon, two young boys and Ralph are left. Both Piggy and Simon are murdered and the two young boys join the savages.

Where Defoe and Ballantyne see the relationship between people and wilderness as one which produces civilization, Golding portrays a return to barbarism. Where they see progress, he sees regress. Where they see improvement, he sees degradation. Golding's views on wilderness and civilization are complex. In *Lord of The Flies*, civilization is shown to be a thin crust easily exposed by a loosening of sanctions. But civilization itself is shown as a flawed social construct. The external world beyond the desert island is one of war, death and destruction. Golding lived through two World Wars and the explosion of nuclear weapons and was writing at the height of the Cold War. In the novel, an atom bomb has fallen, an air battle takes place unseen above the island and a dead pilot parachutes into the forest to become a source of fear to the boys. Golding's attitude to civilization is made more apparent in his second novel, *The Inheritors* (1955). The novel overturns the conventional view of Neanderthal man as savage figure. The heroes of this novel are Lok, Liku, Fa and Nil, pre-human beings who live close to their environment. Their 'culture' is destroyed by humans who are shown to be aggressive, drunken and rapacious. Golding takes the arcadian view back to prehistory, the golden age was before the time of man.

Towards the end of *Lord of the Flies*, only Ralph is left as a bearer of civilization. He is hunted by the savages who chant as they search for him: *Kill the pig, cut his throat*. Only on the very last page is safety reached, when Ralph comes across a naval officer on the island who has just landed from a cutter anchored offshore. When the officer grasps only the general picture, as the rest of the boys begin to filter down to the beach, he says, 'Jolly good show. Like the Coral Island.'

> Ralph looked at him dumbly. For a moment he had a fleeting picture of the strange glamour that had once invested the beaches. But the island was scorched up like dead wood – Simon was dead – and Jack had. . . . The tears began to flow and sobs shook him. He gave himself up to them now for the first time on the island; great, shuddering spasms of grief that seemed to wrench his whole body. His voice rose under the black smoke before the burning wreckage of the island; and infected by that emotion, the other little boys began to shake and sob too. And in the middle of them, with filthy body, matted hair and unwiped nose, Ralph wept for the end of innocence, the darkness of man's heart and the fall through the air of the true, wise friend called Piggy.

TWO VIEWS OF THE COUNTRYSIDE

The refuge from modernity

Novels construct a world of their own. They draw upon the external world for meaning, but always from a particular viewpoint. In Britain there have been two angles of vision on the countryside. The first is the view from the big house and an important writer in this tradition is Jane Austen (1775–1817). Throughout her work Jane Austen adopts the pro-countryside view:

> The sun's rays falling strongly into the parlour, instead of cheering, made her still more melancholy; for sun-shine appeared to her a totally different thing in a town and in the country. Here [in town], its power was only a glare, a stifling, sticky glare, serving but to bring forward stains and dirt that might otherwise have slept. There was neither health nor gaiety in sun-shine in a town.
>
> (*Mansfield Park*)

The sunshine of her rural world fell only on selected shoulders. The world of her novels is a world of property, power and influence. Like the early cartographer of Tullibody, 'my village', her landscape is of the big house and its inhabitants. The rest are passed over in silence.

Her novels were a product of her age and her background. She was born into a well-to-do family, the fifth of seven children of a clergyman. She lived in the home of her birth, Steventon near Basingstoke, for twenty-five years, then moved to Bath and Southampton. In 1809 she settled into a cottage on the property of her brother at Chawton. Her world was of rural gentry, property owners and their immediate circle. She lived in interesting times. France had been declared a republic in 1792. In Britain there was revolution in the air. The Combination Acts of 1799 banned trade union activity. It was a time of revolution, wars and growing class conflict. The enclosure movement was at its peak and the industrial revolution was beginning to take off. Very little of this appears in Austen's novels. For some, this is a point of criticism, the narrowness of her range a sign of weakness. But this is to criticize her for the size of her canvas rather than the quality of her work. Austen was more of a Vermeer than a Rembrandt. She described her writing as 'that little bit (two inches wide) of ivory, in which I work with so fine a brush as produces little effect after much labour'. Hers is a carefully delineated, finely structured world rather than a sweeping canvas. When giving advice to a niece about writing, she said that 'three or four families in a country village is the very thing to work on'.

She wrote about such families throughout most of her life. Six novels were completed. *Sense and Sensibility* and *Northanger Abbey* were written prior to 1798 but not published until 1811 and 1818 respectively. Between 1811 and 1816 she completed *Pride and Prejudice, Mansfield Park, Emma* and *Persuasion. Northanger Abbey* and *Persuasion* were published posthumously. Together these six books constitute one of the most sustained descriptions of rural gentry, as the eighteenth century turned into the nineteenth.

Jane Austen fictionalizes the dilemmas of the landed elite described by Stone and Stone (see page 71). Let us consider *Mansfield Park*, which first appeared in 1814. Like all her novels it is concerned with positions in society and with social advancement and regression. The opening sentence sets the scene:

> About thirty years ago, Miss Maria Ward of Huntingdon, with only seven thousand pounds, had the good luck to captivate Sir Thomas Bertram, of Mansfield Park, in the county of Northampton, and to be thereby raised to the rank of a baronet's lady, with all the comforts and consequences of an handsome house and large income.

The rest of the novel is concerned with the social pirouettes around the handsome house of Mansfield Park. Marriages are very important in Austen's world. They are acts of love, social alliances and commercial enterprises. 'It is a truth universally acknowledged,' she writes in the first line of *Pride and Prejudice*, 'that a single man in possession of a good fortune must be in want of a wife.' The search for the right partner who fulfils all the requirements is the motor of her narrative. She has a delight in the 'manoeuvring business' of marrying to advantage.

In reading *Mansfield Park*, one is struck by the continual references to property and money. The novelist sets the scene by showing the relative wealth of all the main participants. The Bertrams are rich. Sir Thomas has not only Mansfield Park but also houses in the village and estates in the West Indies. He is also powerful, with interests in Parliament and the right to nominate parsons. This is the economic background to the marriage plans of the young Bertrams – Tom, Edmund, Maria and Julia.

There is also a local landowner, Mr Rushworth, who owns an estate. He has plans for his property: 'It wants improvement . . . beyond any thing. I never saw a place that wanted so much improvement in my life.'

Then there are the Crawfords, Henry and his sister Mary. They are also rich. They visit a relative close to Mansfield Park and their interaction with the Betrams and Mr Rushworth are the backbone of the narrative. Henry Crawford too is very keen on improving and there is a description of his proposals for the future home of Edmund Bertram which tells us much about the social messages signified by landscape improvement:

> From being the mere gentleman's residence, it becomes, by judicious improvement, the residence of a man of education, taste, modern manners, good connections. All this may be stamped on it; and that house receive such an air as to make its owner be set down as the great land-owner of the parish, by every creature travelling the road.

We are left in no doubt of the economic resources and social positions of all the characters. But there is a moral counterpoint to all the manoeuvring for wealth and positions evinced in the ironic descriptions of the characters. With her little remarks, deft descriptions and quiet asides, Austen sums up the moral worth of each of her characters. For example, Miss Mary Crawford's attitude to Tom and Edmund Bertram is described thus:

She had felt an early presentiment that she *should* like the eldest best. She knew it was her way. ... She looked about her with due consideration, and found almost everything in his favour, a park, a real park five miles round, a spacious modern-built house, so well placed and well screened as to deserve to be in any collection of engravings of gentlemen's seats in the Kingdom, ... and of being Sir Thomas hereafter. It might do very well; she believed she should accept him.

Moral goodness is embodied in the figure of Fanny Price, niece to Sir Thomas and Lady Bertram, who was taken in by them when she was 10 years old. For the modern reader, she is one of Jane Austen's least convincing heroines. She is so good, so pure that this reader felt little sympathy. But rather than a character, Fanny is better seen as a moral imperative; she exists as the apex of the moral order, an alternative point of reference to the money order. She refuses a marriage offer from Henry Crawford despite the protestations of everyone and the obvious financial advantages. As punishment she is sent back to her parents' dowdy house in Portsmouth. That is where we found her with the 'sun's rays falling strongly into the parlour, ... to bring forward stain and dirt'. She is vindicated in the end. Henry Crawford runs off with Maria Rushworth (née Bertram). Fanny has been proved right. She is brought back to Mansfield and paradise is regained as she marries Edmund and lives in the parsonage in Mansfield Park. She keeps her morality and achieves the material goodies.

Mansfield Park is a complex novel. The ethical edification is undermined by sympathetic portrayals of the 'immoral' characters and the ironic tone of character description. Only the outsider, Fanny, brought into this social world by an obvious authorial intervention, maintains her dignity while achieving material wealth. All the rest are compromised.

Jane Austen is very aware of the regular compromises involved in social living. Her work provides a detailed description of how individuals move in a social setting. But it is a very circumscribed setting. It is the world of the big house and its inhabitants. For the rest, there is the condescension of utter silence. Like the painting of *Mr and Mrs Andrews* (Figure 7.1), it is a world of prosperity and wealth, yet the making of this wealth goes unrecorded, the social basis of property relations are ignored. Jane Austen associated the big country house with elegance and ease. Of her brother's big home in Kent she noted, 'I shall eat Ice & drink French wine, and be above vulgar Economy.'

Jane Austen achieved some success in her lifetime but her popularity has grown since her death. There are many reasons. She is a marvellous writer, although I think better appreciated the older one becomes. I had to read *Emma* as a first-year undergraduate. Eighteen years of age is not the best time to appreciate her quiet wit and artistry. She is also a female writer and her growing popularity is part of that feminist realignment of our world

Figure 7.1 Mr and Mrs Andrews (c. 1750) by Thomas Gainsborough (National Gallery, London) is a celebration of ownership and power. He stands and she sits, their property displayed behind them – woods, green meadows, livestock, timber stands and rich cornfields. There is no room for the actual workers who stacked the corn. As in the more general idea of the countryside, and in the novels of Jane Austen in particular, the rural workers have been excluded.

view. Her female characters are strongly drawn and her social description of the domestic interiors of country homes provides us with an alternative vision to the male view. But there is also the fact that, for the English reading classes, she presents a life beyond 'vulgar Economy'. She is the novelistic version of those National Trust properties and the accompanying brochures which indicate the aesthetic rather than the social basis to the building and maintenance of Georgian houses and country properties. Jane Austen can give the reader the ease and luxury of a life without work and a society without conflict. A popular reading of her work sees a world populated by dignified social gatherings where individuals are competing for position but everyone knows their place. It is an ordered, safe world. There are temporary discrepancies but the conclusion to all the novels shows the reestablishment of social order.

At one point in *Mansfield Park*, Maria's distaste for Mr Rushworth is summed up in her vision of life after their marriage as:

> doomed to the repeated details of his day's sport, good or bad, his boast of his dogs, his jealousy of his neighbours, his doubts of their qualification, and his zeal after poachers – subjects which will not find their way to female feelings without some talent on one side, or some attachment on the other.

It is a small piece and the mention of poachers can almost pass unnoticed. For Maria, and indeed for Jane Austen, it is something of no real concern. And yet these words constitute a major point of reference in rural social relationships. The Enclosures had given land to the gentry but denied the peasants access to a vital resource. Poaching was a form of class conflict, as peasants tried to gain access to the game of the forests. They had cunning, skill and the prod of hunger. On the other side, the landowners had state power. From the seventeenth through to the nineteenth century, a series of game laws brought judicial terror to the countryside (see Hopkins 1986).

During Austen's lifetime, the conflict sharpened. Five years before she was born, an Act of 1770 stated that any one who killed game of any kind between sunset and sunrise was to be punished with imprisonment of not less than three months; and for a subsequent offence, not less than six months and a public whipping. Thirty years later, another Act stiffened the sentences: those found guilty were to be imprisoned with hard labour and second offenders could be forced to serve in the army or navy. To be caught was to risk prison, the lash and military servitude. Resistance increased as poachers stopped by gamekeepers sought to avoid arrest. When Jane Austen was in Bath, moving in polite society, the Ellenborough Law of 1803 created ten new capital offences, including one for resisting a gamekeeper. When she was finishing her last novel in 1816, another Act passed through Parliament which meant that any armed person found at night in forest, chase or park could, if convicted, be sentenced to seven years' transportation This Act was only repealed in 1828.

Thus, behind the brief mention of poachers lies a brutal system of repression. But Austen's novels have the 'tone of the centre', to use Matthew Arnold's phrase. By refusing to look beyond her social world, Austen presents the vision of a society at peace, in repose, populated by people secure in their positions. In reality, as the game law legislations revealed, it was a world of intense and serious conflict.

The ache of modernity

Jane Austen has always been popular. In her intimate portrayals she has a Vermeer-like quality of translucence, tranquillity and harmony. In her depiction of a world safe from change she provides us with an escape from modernity.

Thomas Hardy (1840–1928) is different. If Jane Austen's vision of rural England is from the drawing room of the big house, then Hardy's is from a three-mile-high location above the county of Dorset.

Hardy was born on 2 June at Higher Bockhampton, a small hamlet in Dorset, the eldest of four children. His father introduced him to music, folklore and nature, and his mother to literature. In his youth he played the fiddle at local dances. He began his working life as an architect but wrote poetry and studied the classics in his spare time. At the age of 22 he went to London, working as an architect, but returned five years later because of ill health. A year later, in 1868, he completed his first novel which he subsequently destroyed. His first published novel came out in 1870. From then until 1896, Hardy made major contributions to the English novel, including *Under the Greenwood Tree* (1872), *Far From the Madding Crowd* (1874), *The Return of the Native* (1878), *The Trumpet-Major* (1880), *The Mayor of Casterbridge* (1886), *The Woodlanders* (1887), *Tess of the d'Urbervilles* (1891) and *Jude The Obscure* (1896). Together they form an impressive recreation of a rural world.

Hardy depicts a fictional region known as Wessex, yet it is a region deeply rooted in a real area of England (see Figure 7.2 and Table 7.1). This area was, and still is, less marked by the industrial revolution than most other parts of Britain. But Hardy does not present the picture of an unchanging rural idyll. Change and conflict are at the heart of his novels.

Hardy takes a wider perspective than Austen, wider in two respects. First, the people of the novels move within and are affected by the physical environment. The novels abound with descriptions of nature. In *The Return of the Native*, Egdon Heath almost becomes a character in its own right, its moods and temper affecting and reflecting the human drama. Hardy's characters move within a physical environment; they are people of the land.

Second, a broader spectrum of people inhabit Wessex: the farmers and the labourers, the landed and the landless, the high and the low. The making of a livelihood is an important element in Hardy's story. His

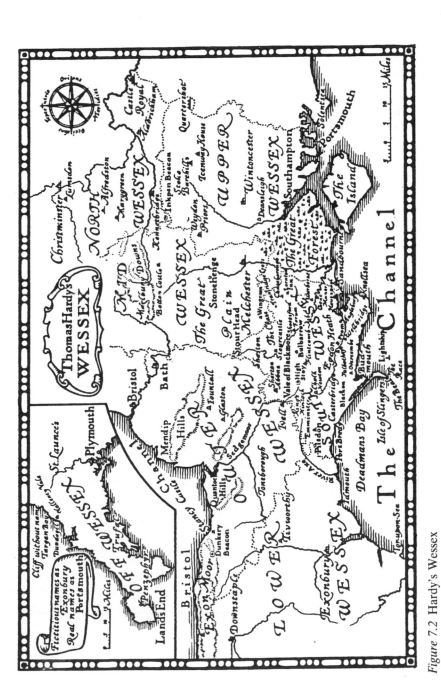

Figure 7.2 Hardy's Wessex

Table 7.1 Hardy's Wessex

Hardy's name	Real name
Abbot's-Cernel	Cerne Abbas
Abbotsea	Abbotsbury
Aldbrickham	Reading
Alfredston	Wantage
Anglebury	Wareham
Badbury Rings	A hill near Wimborne Minster
Budmouth	Weymouth
Bulbarrow	A hill near Sturminster Newton
Casterbridge	Dorchester
Chalk Newton	Maiden Newton
Chaseborough	Cranborne
Christminster	Oxford
Cresscombe	Letcombe Basset
Damer's Wood	Came Wood near Dorchester
Dogbury	A hill near High Stoy
Durnover	Fordington
Egdon Heath	A composite of the heaths between Bournemouth and Dorchester
Emminster	Beaminster
Evershead	Evershot
Exonbury	Exeter
Fensworth	Letcombe Regis
Flintcombe-Ash	Nettlecombe-Tout
Greenhill	Woodbury Hill near Bere Regis
Hope Cove	Church Hope
Kennetbridge	Newbury
Kingsbere and King's-Bere	Bere Regis
Leddenton	Gillingham
Longpuddle	Piddlehinton (also called by Hardy Upper Longpuddle)
Lulwind Cove	Lulworth Cove
Lumsdon	Cumnor
Marlott	Marnhull
Marygreen	Fawley
Melchester	Salisbury
Mellstock	Stinsford and Lower and Higher Bockhampton
Middleton Abbey	Milton Abbas
Nether-Moynton	Owermoigne
Norcombe Hill	A hill near Toller Down
Nuttlebury	Hazelbury Bryan
Oxwell Hall	Poxwell
Port Bredy	Bridport
Pos'ham	Portisham
Quartershot	Aldershot
Rainbarrow	Rainbarrows, a mound north of the Dorchester-Wareham road
Ridgeway	A road between Dorchester and Weymouth
Roy Town	Troy Town

Table 7.1 Continued

Hardy's name	Real name
St Aldhelm's Head	St Alban's Head
Sandbourne	Bournemouth
Shaston	Shaftesbury
Sherton	Sherborne
Shottsford and Shottsford Forum	Blandford
Stoke-Barehills	Basingstoke
Stourcastle	Sturminster Newton
Upper Longpuddle	Piddlehinton
Weatherbury	Puddletown
Wellbridge	Wool
Wintonchester	Winchester
Yalbury Wood	Yellowham Wood

characters are not above 'vulgar Economy'. In contrast with the propertied world of Austen, Hardy gives a voice to those outside the big house. If Austen is the tone of the centre, then Hardy includes the voice of the periphery. Hardy's novels contain two discourses. There is the standard English of the narrative, the voices of the middle and upper classes and the thoughts of all the characters. Then there are the voices of the rural peasantry, whose linguistic presence I find embarrassing to read. It is difficult to understand, yet it lacks the authority of a real rural voice. This is only partly the fault of Hardy. It reflects a wider problem of language. In Britain, as in many other countries, spoken language varies by social and geographic space.

The general picture is presented in Figure 7.3. Authors communicate in novels through standard English – the top of the pyramid. But if a writer wants to incorporate a regional dimension – and Hardy's novels are firmly set in Dorset – then another discourse must be included. However, since all of the narrative is in the standard form, even the thoughts of the rural yokels, these incidents of regional speech stand out as unnatural, untidy and unauthetic. One solution is to ignore the problem and reduce everything to the written form of standard English. This is the modernist solution. The pre-modern solution is to do what Hardy does and include the rural dialogue. It strikes a modern reader as phoney and embarrassing. The post-modern solution is to write the whole novel in the regional accent. This avoids the problem of marginalizing the region but raises problems of comprehensibility. One of the best examples in the twentieth century is Lewis Grassic Gibbon's *A Scots Quair* (1932–4), which is a trilogy of works based in the north-east of Scotland. The narrative contains the words and speech rhythms of the regional language.

Social change and a deeply felt sense of place are the major elements in Hardy's work. Change in individual fortunes is the driving narrative power

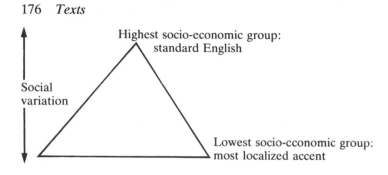

Source: Trudgill (1983)

Figure 7.3 Social and regional accent variation

for his heroes and heroines. In the main, they come from the interstitial area between the rural peasantry and the rural bourgeoisie. Michael Henchard, in *The Mayor of Casterbridge*, is a skilled worker who becomes the mayor of the novel's title. In *Tess*, the heroine is born into rural poverty but is of ancient pedigree. For those who like their novels to end happily, Hardy is a disappointment. He has a deeply pessimistic view of the human condition. Moments of gaiety and laughter are mere interludes, 'happiness was but the occasional episode in a general drama of pain'. The typical Hardy plot shows the rise of a hero or heroine and then their eventual fall as the workings of a sullen fate conspire to grind them into the dust.

Against this pessimistic trajectory, Hardy describes a region and a whole society in the process of change. The transformation of the area and its people is described again and again, depicted in examples of mechanization or changes in work practices or embodied in individuals.

> Between the mother, with her fast perishing lumber of superstitions, folk-lore, dialect and orally transmitted ballads, and the daughter, with her trained National teachings and Standard knowledge under an infinitely revised Code, there was a gap of two hundred years as ordinarily understood. When they were together the Jacobean and the Victorian ages were juxtaposed.
>
> *(Tess of the d'Urbervilles)*

> Reaching the outskirts of the village they pursued the same tracks as formerly and ascended to the fair. Here too, it was evident that the years had told. Certain mechanical improvements might have been noticed in the roundabouts and highfliers. ... But the real business of the fair had considerably dwindled. The new periodical great markets of neighbouring towns was beginning to interfere seriously with the trade carried on here for centuries.
>
> *(The Mayor of Casterbridge)*

In *Tess*, the character of Angel Clare describes the feeling of the age as the 'ache of modernism'. This ache permeates Hardy's novels. The shift from intuition to rationality, from land to capital, rural to urban, religion to science are the polarities that give structure and coherence to Hardy's world view.

Hardy's novels constitute one of the most sustained creations of place in the tradition of the English novel. He gives us a picture of the countryside in transition, a rural region, rich in local ways and customs, being incorporated into a metropolitan society with national codes and standardized life styles. He is, in effect, describing the death-throes of an authentically different rural society. Hardy is the last great English rural writer. He was fortunate to live when the social changes were pronounced and profound, yet there were still memories and traces of an earlier period. Rural novels did not disappear when Hardy left off novel-writing in 1896. Great novelists influence a tradition, they rarely end it. But it has become more difficult to write a rural novel because the rural exists less in reality and more in the imagination. Rural novels have become whimsical or nostalgic, fantastic or realistic but they lack a sense of connection with the real, a connection necessary for genuine art to flourish and develop. In the twentieth century, the rural has became less distinctive, less identifiably different from the urban. The ache of modernity has enveloped them both. The twentieth century signalled many things, one of them being the death of the authentically rural novel.

8 The western

Film has been the most potent vehicle for American imagination ... movies have something to tell us not just about the surfaces but the mysteries of American life.

Arthur Schlesinger, Jr (1979) Preface to
American History/American Film

Although western novels reach a large and faithful audience, it is through the movies that the myth has become part of the cultural language by which America understands itself. ... The central significance of the land is most truly expressed and felt in cinematic imagery.

Will Wright (1979) *Six Guns and Society*

The subject matter of the film genre known as the 'western' is the battle between good and evil in the frontier zone between wilderness and civilization. It embodies general myths of wilderness and countryside and, in particular, US ideologies of nation-building. The western is an important element of Americans' dialogue with their past, their present and their future. Because of the dominance of Hollywood in world cinema, the specific historical experience of the western has also become an important part of popular culture throughout the whole world. Wherever movies have been shown, guys in white hats have been winning the battle with those in black hats. One of the most enduring genres of the most popular art form has been the western.

The genre combines myth and ideology. It is a myth in so far as it condenses themes of good and evil, wilderness and civilization, law and disorder. A range of polarities coalesces around the division between wilderness and civilization in the western. Jim Kitses (1969) identifies individual/community, nature/culture and east/west. Table 8.1 shows the subdivisions. This generality of the western explains its following outside of the USA. There is a continuing dialogue between the western and other film cultures. Western settings are used to portray other people's movies. *The Magnificent Seven* (1960), for example, is a straight rip-off from Akira Kurosawa's (1954) film epic of medieval Japan, *Seven Samurai*. Other film cultures have used the western. *Carry on Cowboy* (1960) is the British low farce outfit employing the fastest *double entendres* in the west. The hero is a sanitary engineer sent to clear up Stodge City. The villain is the Rumpo Kid. Much more (self-consciously) serious are the so-called 'spaghetti' westerns which keep historical referencing to a minimum and violence to a maximum.

Table 8.1 Polarities of the western

The wilderness	Civilization
The individual	**The community**
freedom	restriction
honour	institutions
self-knowledge	illusion
integrity	compromise
self-interest	social responsibility
solipsism	democracy
Nature	**Culture**
purity	corruption
experience	knowledge
empiricism	legalism
pragmatism	idealism
brutalization	refinement
savagery	humanity
The west	**The east**
America	Europe
the frontier	America
equality	class
agrarianism	industrialism
tradition	change
the past	the future

Source: after Kitses (1969)

But the western is also an ideology. It refers to a specific place at a specific time. Westerns inhabit the penumbra between the wild and the settled, the space between nature and civilization and the creation of a territory into a country. The Western movie tradition is a sustained recreation and continual representation of the making of the USA.

Movies in America are, above all else, a commercial enterprise. Companies make them to make money. This is the major constant of the movie industry. However, the companies have to employ various people to make the movies and they need a paying audience. The creative workers and critical audience are the crucial variables of the industry. Fashions come and go, talents emerge, things change. We cannot read off the subject matter of the movies from the profit motive. It is always there like the keel of a ship but it is not the rudder. The dynamic of the industry is the work of creative people to meet the demands of a fickle audience.

All of the major directors and actors in Hollywood have taken part in the western movie tradition. Directors of westerns include Cecil B. DeMille, John Ford, King Vidor, Howard Hawks, Fritz Lang, Sam Peckinpah, Don Siegal, and Mel Brooks, while the range of actors includes Clark Gable, John Wayne, Clint Eastwood, Burt Reynolds, Robert Redford and Paul Newman. Almost all of the major Hollywood talents have had a creative part in the evolution of the genre.

THE EARLY WESTERNS: CELEBRATING THE TAMING OF THE WILDERNESS

One of the first US movies of the twentieth century with a narrative structure was a western, Edwin Porter's *The Great Train Robbery* (1903). It was a sophisticated silent, one of the first films to cross-cut different stories through judicious editing. The film was mainly shot in the railway yards of New Jersey.

Like the pioneers, the western came to portray the movie industry moved west. Southern California had good weather but, above all, it had distance from Chicago and New York. Many film companies used patented cameras and equipment; royalties had to be paid. California was far enough away to avoid the patent detectives. From this beginning grew the Hollywood film industry.

In the second and third decades of the twentieth century, the basic genre of the fledgling Hollywood industry was the western. They were one or two reels long, quickly and cheaply made. They reached huge audiences. In the early teens of the twentieth century, 2 million people were going to watch the movies every day in the USA. It was a cultural form unhindered by the lack of sound. The majority of the audience in many cities could not speak English and the silent movie could transmit plots to non-English speakers. The movies became an important element in the socialization of immigrants.

The majority of silent westerns were made in under a fortnight. The plots were simple, there were identifiable heroes and recognizable villains. The coding of black and white hats stems from this period. The westerns were morality plays in which right and good triumphed over wrong and bad. The values of small-town America were lauded and the virtues of perseverance, decency and good citizenship were given a high profile. The early westerns celebrated the transformation of the wilderness and the coming of civilization. The subduing of the wilderness and the defeat of the Indians and outlaws were portrayed as unalloyed success stories of progress, the coming of civilization as an unqualified virtue.

In the 1920s, a number of silent epic westerns were made. The first was *The Covered Wagon* (1923), directed by James Cruze. The movie was dedicated to Theodore Roosevelt. It was one of the most financially successful silent movies ever made. Set in 1848, it portrays the wagon trail of a group of settlers moving west. They overcome buffalo stampedes, floods and Indians. The film is a celebration of pioneer virtues, given epic sweep by good camera work. The film was unusually long for the time, 103 minutes, and a great deal of effort and money was spent on finding the right location and authentic props. Cruze is supposed to have said: 'There wasn't a false whisker in the film'. *The Covered Wagon* raised the western film into folk history and cinematic art.

The success of *The Covered Wagon* prodded other studios. The head of one, William Fox, wanted a rival movie to be made of railway construction across the USA. He gave the job to John Ford. Ford's real name was John Feeney. Born just outside of Portland, Maine in 1895, he had come to Hollywood in 1914. He worked in the movies as an actor and then as an assistant director in his brother's movies. He became a director with Universal in 1917 on a salary of $75 a week. One of his earliest movies was *Straight Shooting* (1917), in which Cheyenne Harry, played by Harry Carey, portrays an archetypal western hero – the outsider helping family farmers against evil ranchers and saving the day for family, community and civilization.

Ford was successful. In 1920 he signed with Fox at $600 a week and by 1923 was earning $900 a week. Success in Hollywood had quick and tangible results. Of the 50 movies he had made by 1923, 36 had been westerns, so he was well suited for the proposed railway movie, subsequently called *The Iron Horse*. The making of the picture was to be as epic as the story itself. Filming started in 1923 and the budget was half a million dollars, a huge amount then. There were 5,000 extras, 800 Indians and a regiment of cavalry. One hundred cooks were employed to feed the crew as they shot scenes throughout the western states, in the face of freezing temperatures and blizzards. The movie opened in 1924 (see Figure 8.1). It was advertised as 'a romance of east and west, blazing a trail of love and civilization. It proved to be a critical and commercial success, taken seriously by the artistic and academic communities as a stylish rendition of the reality of the west. The audiences loved it. The movie grossed $3 million dollars and made the name of John Ford. He was only 29 when the movie opened. His grandson summarizes the message of the movie thus:

> Although John Ford had taken liberties with the actual events of the building of the transcontinental railroad, *The Iron Horse* was a historical picture that conveyed a strong sense of national pride. It was a celebration of heroic enterprise, of hope, of the country stretching gloriously to its full length.

> (Ford 1979: 34)

With the coming of sound to pictures in 1927, the western went into an eclipse. Throughout the late-1920s and 1930s, the studios were making two

Figure 8.1 A scene from *The Iron Horse* (1923) (National Film Archive, London). Compare this with Figure 5.1.

types of movie: quality movies which had big budgets, big stars, and directors with style, and B-movies which had small budgets, small stars, and directors who were more worried about the length of film produced than its quality. In the 1930s, money was tight. Double features for the price of one gave audiences value for money but gave the studios a problem: they needed a continuous supply of film. This was the *raison d'être* of the B-movie.

Most of the studios made B-movies. They had to, in order to fulfil the viewing hours required by their audiences. Remember that this was all before television. The major genre of the B-movie was the western. There were even some studios, such as Republic, which specialized in B-westerns.

There was one attempt to create a western epic in sound. *The Big Trail* (1930) was the sound equivalent of *The Covered Wagon*. Directed by Raoul Walsh, it was an epic saga of pioneers making their way along the Oregon Trail. The crew travelled 2000 miles through five states and total costs reached $2 million. Unlike *The Iron Horse*, it was a box-office disaster. The *Theatre Magazine* called it 'stagey, melodramatic variety'. In the language of the industry, it died. The leading actor was John Wayne.

The failure of *The Big Trail* and the fashion for musicals and gangsters meant an eclipse of the A-western during the thirties. John Wayne's early career mirrors that of the genre. Wayne, whose real name was Marion Michael Morrison, was born in Iowa in 1907. His parents having come to California, he attended Glendale High School. Prowess at high school football won him a two-year football scholarship to the University of Southern California. In 1927, Wayne's scholarship was not extended and so he went to work for Fox as a prop man. It was while unloading furniture on the Fox lot that Raoul Walsh spotted him, or so the legend goes. He signed a five-year contract with Fox in 1929, on an annually renewable basis. The failure of *The Big Trail* meant that he did not become a big star. Fox did not renew his contract, so he signed with Columbia in 1931 but fell out with the studio boss, Harry Cohn. He scuffed around the smaller studios, working in a number of not very distinguished movies. His career was in the doldrums. In 1938 he returned to Republic and featured in such forgettable movies as *Pals of The Saddle* (1938), *Overland Stage Raiders* (1938) and *Santa Fe Stampede* (1938). He was sometimes working on a movie a week.

The B-movie system had reduced the western to a formula. Outlaws were identifiably evil, the good guys wore the white hats and, after some effort, they killed the bad guys and won the girl. Bad was bad and good was good. The moral universe had no ambiguity. In the small mid-west towns, John Wayne was seen as always on the right and good side. Then came *Stagecoach* (1939), a movie that was to combine the creative talents of John Ford and John Wayne.

THE MATURE WESTERN: THE AMBIGUITIES OF THE TRANSFORMATION

After the success of *The Iron Horse*, Ford continued to turn out good movies, but not another western until *Stagecoach*. He was under a studio contract, which meant that he had to make movies that the studio wanted him to direct. In 1937 he bought the rights to a story, *Stage to Lordsburg*. He worked up a script with Dudley Nichols but could not gain the interest of a studio. Fox, MGM, Warner, Paramount and Columbia all rejected it. Except for cheap B-movie production, westerns were no longer popular, according to the ruling idea. Eventually Ford persuaded a studio. He signed with United Artists in 1937 and began filming in Monument Valley in southern Utah in 1938.

Stagecoach has one of the tightest narratives of almost any western. Geronimo is on the loose in the territory. Through this area travels the stage to Lordsburg. On board is a banker, a whisky salesman, a good woman who is pregnant, a woman called Dallas who has a 'past', a drunken doctor and a gambler. Outside of town, the Ringo Kid/John Wayne hitches a ride. He is on his way to Lordsburg to seek revenge on the Plummers.

The movie follows the journey of the stagecoach and the parallel

Figure 8.2 Stagecoach (1939) (National Film Archive, London)

development of the characters. It is a western odyssey. During the journey, the doctor delivers a baby, the gambler shows that he is a gentleman, Dallas proves to have a heart of gold, and the respectable banker is found to be a thief. Those outside of society are shown to be capable of fulfilling social roles, while the bad people inside society are thrown out. The Apaches are shown as savages who kill settlers and rape white women. They are the bad outsiders who, in a memorable cinematic sequence, attack the stagecoach. The Indians are just about to win when the cavalry arrives. The stagecoach makes it to Lordsburg and Ringo kills the Plummers.

The narrative has a tight structure, with the symmetry of art and the contingency of life. It is a movie but the artfulness is muted, allowing us to 'see' the story not the director. There are a few scenes where we are aware of the camera's presence but the framing of scenes, the mixture of long shots and close-ups, the confidence with details and the bravura action scenes add up to an attractive, economic style (see Figure 8.2).

The characters are general enough to have wider significance – the whore with a heart of gold, the drunken doctor and soiled gambler both still capable of redemption or further decline – but are detailed enough to be autonomous beings. We become interested in their fate. We want to know what happens. The tension is kept high by the knowledge of the feud between Ringo and the Plummers and the encompassing presence of the Apaches. The Indians attack but are repulsed by the army who ride out from over the horizon to save the day. In Lordsburg, Ringo kills the Plummers but we do not see the fight. The build-up to the fight is shown, shots are heard, and Plummer walks out of the saloon. For a second we think that he has won and that Ringo is dead but then Plummer collapses and dies. It is a sequence which has been used again and again. The tensions are resolved in an interesting way. The gambler accused of shooting someone in the back dies bravely but there is still a lingering doubt; the drunken doctor sobers up to deliver a baby but there is the possibility that he will revert to drunkenness; Ringo kills the Plummers but is not jailed. Ringo and Dallas are chased away by Doc and the stagecoach driver. They are Adam and Eve, making a garden from the wilderness; 'saved from the blessing of civilization', as one of the characters says in the final sequence. It is this phrase that is the heart of the mature western. Before elaborating on this theme, let me just note the importance of *Stagecoach*.

Stagecoach is significant in a number of senses. It was the first quality western for almost a decade. Its success revived the genre. Ford had shown that the western was capable of serious treatment. The movie had lifted the western beyond the confines of the studio, the barely credible plots and the cheap scenes. The movie also marked the beginning of the use of Monument Valley as a scene for Ford's westerns. The sharply silhouetted mesas rising above the flat desert plain gave a tremendous cinematic quality to *Stagecoach* and to subsequent westerns (such as *Cheyenne Autumn*, see Figure 8.3). The movie also revived the flagging career of John Wayne. Before *Stagecoach* he was an actor. Now he was a star.

The most important point for our purposes is that *Stagecoach* was the first quality western which dealt with the ambiguity of the transformation of the wilderness into civilization. To be sure, there were the usual elements of celebration. The defeat of the Apache meant the triumph of social order over savagery. But the hero Ringo and his new girl leave Lordsburg. We are made aware that the coming of civilization has its problems. Progress is not an unambiguous process. In subtle ways it is suggested that, in the defeat of the wilderness, we may be losing something important.

Stagecoach stands at a vital point in the development of the western. It marks the development of the genre as cinematic art; *Variety* described the movie quite rightly as 'a display of photographic grandeur'. Above all, it prefigures the mature western, as it records the tension between the celebration and the criticism of the coming of civilization. This tension is at the heart of the mature western.

Throughout the 1940s and 1950s, different aspects of the tension of the transformation were identified. In *The Ox-Bow Incident* (1943), there are

Figure 8.3 Ford's westerns constitute a coherent body of work, part of the unity lying in his use of Monument Valley in Utah. Compare this scene from *Cheyenne Autumn* (1964) with Figure 8.2. (National Film Archive, London)

no heroes. Three cowboys are accused of rustling cattle and are lynched. Later it is revealed that they were innocent. It is a pessimistic movie which portrays the frontier community as a mean-minded, low-spirited mob, fearful of strangers and quick to violent anger. The film, in its attack on the community, predates the more famous *High Noon* (1952), in which the community of Hadleyville deserts a marshal who stands up to four gunmen. Like Arthur Miller's play, *The Crucible* (1953), it can be seen as a morality tale for an America gripped by McCarthyism. *High Noon* was a successful movie. The success was due partly to the subject matter but also to the style of the movie. It had a dramatic tension, with constant cuts to a ticking clock heightening the drama. *High Noon* was a serious western.

Another change in the western was the treatment of the Indians. In *Broken Arrow* (1950), the Apaches are not portrayed as savages. The hero (James Stewart) is a Cavalry scout (note the hero as part insider/part outsider with one foot in civilization, the other in the wilderness) who prevents an Indian war and marries an Indian woman. Now the Indians are seen to have a culture; they are no longer a sullen mass, individual Indians are identified. *Across The Wide Missouri* (1951) extends this theme. Clark

Gable inhabits the wilderness of Colorado in the early 1820s. It is portrayed as a Garden of Eden, with an Indian Eve. The advance of white civilization is seen as the destruction of paradise.

Throughout the 1940s and 1950s, the western became an important film genre. It was a mirror of contemporary society. Not all westerns were serious discussions of American concern. B-westerns continued to be churned out but the introduction of television meant that cheaply made and quickly made series could be portrayed on the small rather than the big screen. Television sounded the death knell of B-movies. In 1958, Republic closed. Less movies were made. Those that were made, however, became increasingly more expensive and attracted some of the best talents. In the 1940s and 1950s major directors such as Anthony Mann, Howard Hawks, Arthur Penn, Fritz Lang, Raoul Walsh, Don Siegel and Henry Hathaway were producing some of their best work with western themes. Big stars such as John Wayne, Glenn Ford, Henry Fonda, James Stewart, Kirk Douglas, Gary Cooper and Clark Gable were hitching on their gunbelts to do what men had to do. It was the western's finest hour. We can see the development of the mature western, with all its ambiguities and in some detail, by considering the career of John Ford. His work spans the early western through the mature western and brings us into contact with the late western.

From *Iron Horse* to *Cheyenne Autumn*

Any discussion of a film director has first to deal with the *auteur* theory. Developed in France in the 1950s, this assigns primary creative power to the director. Thus we have John Ford movies, the movies of Howard Hawks, etc. The theory is an intellectual response to the cinema, an attempt to locate film on the same level as art and literature. To assign a name is to give a film the same status as a painting or a novel. The *auteur* theory is part of the movement to show that movies are an art form, not just the opium of the masses. The *auteur* theorists make an important point in rescuing the cinema from critical neglect. There is still a need for such critical awareness. Many people in British universities continue to think that written texts are culture but cinema is too popular to be art. Novels have been universally appointed a place in the canon of English literature; cinema still has a way to go.

However, the theory as a general model ignores the collaborative group nature of film-making. In one of the best books on contemporary Hollywood, William Goldman (1984) lists seven people who are crucial to the making of a movie: the actor, the cinematographer, the director, the editor, the producer, the production designer, the screenplay writer. To emphasize the point, he shows how a short story is worked up into a movie by interviewing a designer, a cinematographer, an editor, a composer, and a director. The conversations are fascinating and show how putting a screenplay on to the screen is the work of many creative hands and minds.

Having said all that, I still think it legitimate to identify John Ford movies, especially his westerns. The *auteur* theory may be wrong as a generality but it holds true for John Ford and especially his mature westerns. He took a hand in writing the scripts, both formally, in joint script-writing projects, and informally, as he edited the script on location. Ford's western movies have a definite 'feel' to them because of Monument Valley, where most of his later westerns were shot. The stark, wind-eroded monoliths appear again and again in his westerns, providing a constant cinematic imagery. There is also a set of actors who, like Monument Valley, appear as constants – John Wayne, Henry Fonda and Ward Bond are three of the most famous.

Ford's mature westerns came at an interesting time in the history of Hollywood. They were produced just when the studio system, with all its controls, was breaking up and prior to the onset of the star system in which the major actors could not only dictate high salaries but also influence the making of the movie. Ford's westerns constitute a body of work which is recognizable and identifiable. The *auteur* theory is incorrect if it always ascribes primary creativity to the director. John Ford proves the exception not the rule. He became sufficiently successful and powerful not to be overwhelmed by the power of the studio and he was such an expert in filming that final editing by others could not change his intention.

John Ford's heart lay in his western. He made many types of movie but those that were distinctly his were the westerns. We can see the development of his work after the Second World War by considering *My Darling Clementine* (1946). The cavalry trilogy of *Fort Apache* (1948), *She Wore A Yellow Ribbon* (1949) and *Rio Grande* (1950), *Wagonmaster* (1950), *The Searchers* (1956) and *Cheyenne Autumn* (1964). I shall say very little about Ford's craft as a director: his judicious mixture of long shots, pans and close-ups, or his amazing facility with composition not only of big landscapes but also of smaller, more intimate social groups. Nor will I dwell on his faults: his reliance on overlong, often boring, slapstick sequences or his inability to handle women outside of the crude whore/schoolmarm division. My concern here is with Fordian westerns as exemplars of a general trend.

Clementine is a celebration of the taming of wilderness. In this sense it is an early rather than a mature western. The context of the movie is important. It was shown in 1946, just after the ending of the war. The ending of war tends to produce two social movements: a desire to create a new post-war order and a need to recreate the assurances of the pre-war world. *Clementine*, with its return to a celebration of nation-building, reverts to the themes of the early western. It is set in 1882. Henry Fonda plays Wyatt Earp, who is presented as a cowboy. His brother is killed by the Clantons who are definite baddies, black hats, scowling faces,

Figure 8.4 The celebration of nationalism, community and civilization in *My Darling Clementine* (1946) (National Film Archive, London)

obviously people of evil intent. Earp/Fonda goes into the town of Tombstone, which is portrayed as a western version of Sodom. He is appointed marshal and so begins the domestication of Earp, shown by the shaving of his beard and a general cleaning up of his demeanour. He throws away the old cowboy clothes and dons more civilized apparel. The growth of Tombstone's civic culture is shown by his presence at a community dance to celebrate the founding of the church. Ford's heroes have to do two things: ride a horse and dance. The two activities span the requirements of an integrated hero – to be both a cowboy and a member of a community. The basic theme of *Clementine* is the creation of a civilized community (see Figure 8.4). The shoot-out in which the Clantons are defeated is an optimistic climax to the movie.

If *Clementine* celebrates the creation of American community, the cavalry trilogy praises the armed forces. Both the context and the personality of Ford are important in understanding these movies. Again, the war experience allowed a glorification of the armed forces, especially as the Cold War meant that America was on a war footing in ideology as much as military posture. Then there was Ford's continuous fascination with military America. He loved the army and revered the navy. He had a strong streak of military patriotism and his fascination with the world of the military is expressed in the cavalry trilogy of the late-1940s. In 1946 John

Ford, in association with the producer Merian Cooper, set up a production company called Argosy. This was now the way in Hollywood. As the old studio system was breaking down, directors and actors were setting up their own companies to make pictures and then selling them to the studio. The cavalry trilogy were all Argosy pictures, allowing Ford an enormous creative role.

In *Fort Apache* and *Yellow Ribbon*, the Indians are given a more positive portrayal than in earlier Ford movies. The story of *Fort Apache* is the arrogance of an army officer. It shows Lt. Colonel Thursday/Henry Fonda sent to the Arizona frontier. He seeks honour and glory. The Apaches under Cochise break out of the reservation. Their 'slow death' in the reservation, the lack of food and the degradation of their women are shown as causes. The Apaches are now shown as people, not savages, and people with a legitimate grievance. Thursday/Fonda lacks the diplomacy to make peace and his arrogance and lack of tactical skill lead to a massacre of the cavalry.

The theme of Indian resistance is shown again in *She Wore A Yellow Ribbon*. The two parallel stories are of the retirement of Captain Brittles/ John Wayne and the avoidance of an Indian war. The movie begins with Custer's defeat and ends with a reconciliation between the Indians and the cavalry. There is a profound ambiguity here. On the one hand, Ford praises the army yet he is also beginning to see the Indians not so much as baddies but as victims. The real baddies in these two movies are the Indian agents, who do not give the Indians enough food, and the corrupt, non-army whites who sell them guns. The result, especially in *She Wore A Yellow Ribbon*, is praise for the armed forces but an unwillingness to accept their use of force against the Indians.

The ambiguity is resolved in *Rio Grande*, in which the Indians are perpetrators of savage acts. This is the weakest of the trilogy. It is a ponderous, almost embarrassing movie, way below par for Ford. It was only a temporary dip in quality and in the return to the codes of the early western because, with *Wagonmaster* (1950), the Indians are again redeemed as human beings. In this beautiful and simple movie, Ford returns to the old theme of a wagon train of pioneers making their journey to the promised land. This time they are Mormons, who take on two guides, cowboys who are outsiders to the close-knit community. The movie is as taut as *Stagecoach*, with few of the slapstick scenes which mar some of Ford's movies.

The community of the Mormons is expressed in their shared piety and communal dancing. The two guides fill the archetypal figures of old man/ experience/knowledge/maturity and young man/vitality/innocence/learning. The threat to the wagon train is not the Indians but a group of white outlaws – the Cleggs, as blackly evil as they come – who not only take over the train but also attempt to rape an Indian woman. The Mormons and the Indians are both good and in one scene dance together, having previously

Figure 8.5 A farming household looks to the wilderness for the coming of the hero in *The Searchers* (1955) (National Film Archive, London)

struck an agreement that the Mormons could pass over the Navajos' territory in peace. The resolution involves the slaying of the Cleggs, the integration of the two cowboys into the Mormon community and the prospect of entry into the promised land.

In this film Ford does not dwell on the actual conflict between white settlers and the indigenous Indian population. In his middle period, Ford wants to see them both as good. The historical reality was, however, very different, as one side won at the expense of the other. *The Searchers* (1955) takes this conflict as the essential point of reference. It is Texas in 1868. A woman looks out from a verandah. She sees a lone figure riding toward the farm (see Figure 8.5). Ethan Edwards/John Wayne is an archetypal western hero, an outsider with one foot in the community and one foot in the wilderness. Later, all of the men in the community are lured to another area by a group of Indians. While they are on this wild-goose chase, the main band of Indians attacks the farm. They rape and kill the mother and spirit away the young daughter, Debbie, and her older sister, who is subsequently murdered. The narrative force of the film is the five-year search for Debbie by Ethan/Wayne and a young man, Martin. It is a classic western. But there are subtleties to the archetypal plot. Edwards/Wayne is less a hero, more a struggling soul touched as much by savagery as by domesticity. The Indians are shown as people with a culture and in one episode Martin

Figure 8.6 At the end of *The Searchers*, having completed his mission, the hero Ethan Edwards/John Wayne returns to the wilderness (National Film Archive, London)

takes up with an Indian woman. The representation of a vicious cavalry attack on an undefended Indian village represents the other side of the frontier.

Throughout the movie, the two men return in real time and flashback to the homestead. The search in the wilderness is continually contrasted with the domestic setting. The characters of Ethan/Wayne and Martin continue the tension; the old, gnarled half-wild man and the still-innocent, domesticated young man. The tension is resolved when the two men find the Indian party led by Chief Scar, a man allowed the words to say that his son has been killed by the whites. With the help of the cavalry, the two attack the village and recapture Debbie. The final shot is from inside the homestead: the balance now restored, Ethan/Wayne is seen to go off into the wilderness (see Figure 8.6). It is a marvellous film, one of the all-time great westerns, ranking with *Stagecoach*, *Shane*, or *High Noon*. It contains the mythic quality of a quest, the old man/young man theme, the narrative drive of a vengeance motif, all set in a beautiful landscape. The wilderness-civilization theme is central and recurring. Ford celebrates the creation and defence of the white community but begins to mourn the tragedy of the Indians.

The plight of the Indians is the central theme of *Cheyenne Autumn* (1964), a beautiful piece of visual cinema. The dry landscape of Monument Valley figures as a sterile backdrop for the wandering, land-lost Indians. The movie did not do well. The dramatic force was broken by comic sections set in Dodge City, which were used as a vehicle for the star James Stewart, playing Wyatt Earp, in order to attract box office interest. The result was an unsatisfactory mix and a commercial failure. As Ford said,

> I've killed more Indians than Custer and Beecher put together. . . .
> There are two sides to every story, but I wanted to show their point of
> view for a change. Let's face it, we've cheated and robbed, killed,
> murdered, massacred and everything else, but they kill one white man
> and, God, out come the troops.
>
> (quoted in Bogdanovitch 1968: 104)

Cheyenne Autumn was an act of penance, a willingness to see the other side. But it was still within the confines of the mature western. Ford may have been critical of some of the consequences but he was a patriot who celebrated the creation of a white community.

John Ford is an important figure in the western cinema. His vivid composition, his use of landscape as background and metaphor, his pacing of dramatic action and his subject matter raised the western to major significance. He made movies which were both commercial and critical successes. He made both money and art from movies. He created public classics, hailed by critics and film-makers and watched by millions of cinema-goers. He is a notable figure in the cinematic depiction of the settling and defending of America's western frontier. His work embodies the development of the early western into the mature western, while his later films prefigure the late western.

THE LATE WESTERN

In the late western, the wilderness is the Garden of Eden and the coming of civilization is the beginning of the Fall. Elements of this view are found in the mature western but, in the late western, which developed in the 1970s, they become pivotal. In *Cheyenne Autumn*, a cavalry attack on an Indian village is shown but it is a small piece in a mosaic of conflicting images (see Figure 8.7). In *Soldier Blue* (1970), by contrast, the cavalry attack on the Indian village is the dramatic climax of the movie. In the first movie, the attack is part of the continuing conflict between two opposing

Figure 8.7 The change in emphasis of *Cheyenne Autumn* is revealed in this shot: the camera takes the Indians' position, looking out at the army (National Film Archive, London)

forces; in the second, the attack is a massacre of the innocents, an act of genocide.

In the late western, the coming of 'civilization' is the problem, something to criticize not praise. This treatment of the west was part of an explicit self-criticism of America, its way of life and its foreign policy. The western became a vehicle for social criticism.

In the late western, the angle of vision on the Indian is sharply altered. *Soldier Blue* (1970) shows the cavalry as pillaging, raping savages. The subtext here is a criticism of American involvement in Vietnam. The attack on the village is symbolic of America's imperial role in South East Asia and throughout the world.

In *Clementine*, law and order is a force for good, saving the community from anarchy. In the late western, by contrast, law and order is the legitimized power of the establishment. In *Butch Cassidy and The Sundance Kid* (1969) and *Missouri Breaks* (1976), the heroes are up against the forces of corrupt law and order. In *High Plains Drifter* (1973), the whole town is corrupt. Clint Eastwood rides in from the wilderness, exposes the corruption of the place, then rides out. Wilderness is the place of truth and freedom, the town is the place of lies and conformity.

The late western looks to frontier communities for prefigurative elements of contemporary ills. Thus, *Heaven's Gate* (1980) looks at class conflict and *Silverado* (1985) deals with racial issues. Now the frontier land is a place of incubation for the social evils of contemporary America.

The most sustained theme of the late western is the closing of the frontier. In the 1960s and 1970s, a number of 'western' stars were coming to the end of their careers. Their ageing was intimately connected with the theme of the passing of the old west. In *Ride The High Country* (1962), *The Wild Bunch* (1969) and *The Shootist* (1976), ageing stars such as William Holden, Randolph Scott and John Wayne portray old cowboys at the closing of the frontier. In different ways the movies mark the ending of an era. In *The Shootist* (1976), Wayne plays J.B. Books, an ageing gunman (see Figure 8.8). The film is set in Carson City in January 1901. The town has horse-drawn cars, milk deliveries and telephones. Books/Wayne has come there to die, an historical anachronism in a new age, who has outlived his time. In the climax, Books/Wayne goes to the saloon in a horse-drawn car. The public transport system, a sign of civil progress, carries the gunman to his final fight. It is not a great movie but it is an evocative portrayal of a dying man and a dying genre. Wayne died soon after the movie was completed.

In *Lonely Are The Brave* (1962), the 'hero', played by Kirk Douglas, is a cowboy riding a horse, yet he is being chased by police in a helicopter. The man's horse is knocked down by a truck on the motorway. It is a symbol of the end of innocence. In the late western, the closing of the frontier is not a source of rejoicing but a time for sad reflections. Butch Cassidy and Sundance have to leave America, chased out by corporate power. Their breezy personalities have no place in the new economic order. The closing of the frontier marks the ending of freedom and innocence, the defeat of the wild by the tame, the spontaneous by the ordered, and the relaxed by the disciplined. The late western eulogizes the wilderness and damns the coming of social order.

The most successful western of the last thirty years has been *Blazing Saddles* (1974). The conventions of the genre are overturned, with yiddish-speaking Indians, farting cowboys and a black, pot-smoking sheriff. It debunks the myths very successfully in a sustained narrative. The success of *Blazing Saddles* suggests that the western can now only be very successful if it is a parody.

There is always a need for heroes but the western has become a problematic genre for modern heroes. No one wins fame by destroying buffalo, killing Indians or slaughtering Mexicans. Heroes have been displaced to outer space, where guys in white helmets can happily zap guys in black outfits without raising historical sensitivities. The male bonding theme has passed on to the buddy motif of detective stories and road

Figure 8.8 An ageing, dying John Wayne plays an ageing, dying gunman in *The Shootist* (1976) (National Film Archive, London)

movies. Audiences sensitive to gender issues can no longer swallow the male emphasis of traditional westerns where men are men and women are either dance hall girls or schoolmarms, whores or angels.

Few westerns are being made today. Fewer films, in general, are being made. In 1977 it cost an average of $4.6 million to make a movie in Hollywood. Ten years later it cost $17.7 million. Making movies has become an expensive, high-risk activity and westerns are out of fashion. However, like the medieval three-field rotation systems, a period of neglect may do some good. The traditional western, in its early, mature and even late stages, seems to have run its course. Screenwriters may some day look again at that mythic territory between the wild and the tamed. If they are any good and they come up with a new angle of vision, the post-late (post modern?) westerns may be worth watching.

9 Australian landscape painting

Great nations write their autobiographies in three manuscripts – the book of
their deeds, the book of their words and the book of their art. Not one of these
books can be understood unless we read the two others; but of the three the only
quite trustworthy one is the last.

John Ruskin (1884) *St Mark's Rest: The History of Venice*

The artistic response to the Australian landscape is more than just an
aesthetic impulse, guided only by notions of style and decoration. It is as
sensitive to social power as to the fashion of artistic tastes. Painting is
embedded in social relations. If paintings cannot be read off in a simple
manner from the arrangement and exercise of social power, neither can
they be separated. Oil paintings are expensive items bought either by the
wealthy, the corporate or the public art galleries. Their purchase records
the tastes of the rich and the powerful.

Landscape painting is a selective process. Some elements of landscape
are ignored while others are emphasized. Different slants are given to
people–environment relations. An analysis of landscape painting thus
provides us with an entry point into how a society sees its relationship to
that landscape.

I have chosen a range of painters, from the beginning of white settlement
to the present day, which includes individual painters who, by common
consent in the art establishment, are seen as key figures in Australian art.
No large public gallery would feel itself complete unless it had paintings by
each of these artists. Each of them appeared at least once in the lists of
great Australian paintings nominated by five art experts (*Canberra Times*
1985). Their pictures are prominently displayed in all major Australian art
galleries. They represent the dominant art images of the Australian
landscape.

I have taken a chronological approach. There is a coherence to such a
perspective, since each artist draws upon elements of the tradition of
landscape painting and also adds to it. The artists reference one another,
their paintings resonant with paintings of the past and paintings to
come.

COLONIAL VISIONS

There were two artistic responses from the early white visitors to Australia: the romantic and the neo-classical. The romantics saw a land peopled by noble savages in a Garden of Eden. This was the predominant response in the first thirty years, especially from visiting artists who used the Aborigines as a counterpoint to what they saw as a corrupt, effete western society (see Figure 1.6). The longer-term settlers saw it differently; they saw the white presence as a mark of progress, with the development of a white, civil society as being a civilizing mission. Their vision was best expressed by John Glover.

John Glover (1767–1849) was an established artist in England before he emigrated to Tasmania. Born near Leicester, his schoolboy sketches reveal an interest in nature and a talent for drawing. In 1794 he took up the trade of drawing master in Lichfield and undertook sketching tours of Wales, the Lake District and Scotland. Glover was a successful artist. His paintings sold, and sold well. He was made President of the Society of Painters in Watercolour in 1807 and was a founding member of the Royal Society of British Artists in 1823. He exhibited paintings at the Royal Academy.

Like the young Constable, he drew his inspiration from Claude Lorraine (1600–82), a Frenchman who lived in Italy. Lorraine painted the landscape around Rome, in carefully balanced compositions which recalled a golden age of harmonious balance between people and nature. Glover owned several Claudes and sought to become the English Claude. In that direction lay fame and fortune because Claude was enormously popular amongst the English. No Grand Tour was complete without the purchase of a Claude. His paintings became the main reference point for landscape design in eighteenth century England. Many rich landowners sought to turn their estates into three-dimensional Claudes, a case of life imitating art idealizing nature.

Hughes (1970: 41) describes Glover as 'an insignificant eclectic, who had never produced an original brushstroke' during his life in England. The description is a typical Hughes throwaway which is amusing but dangerous, since it is only half right. Glover lacked the originality of Claude but his early paintings were not too bad. They had a less formal organization than Claude and at their best breathed a blue light through the dark under-growth of Claude's Roman landscapes.

Glover fell out of favour by the 1820s. Watercolourists such as John Sell Cotman were more innovative, while the works of Constable and Turner were beginning to prefigure the Impressionists. In 1831 Glover, now aged 64, emigrated to Tasmania, or Van Dieman's land as it was then called. He bought two farms and was given a land grant of 2,560 acres on the slopes of Ben Lomond. The property eventually comprised almost 7,000 acres, centring on the family home of Patterdale, named after a village in Westmorland where Glover had once lived. Glover was part of the first period of land settlement which was dominated by the estates of large landowners.

From 1831 until a few years before his death in 1849, Glover developed his estate and continued to paint. These were not separate activities because Glover the pioneer in a new land influenced Glover the landscape painter.

Glover was one of the first artists to treat seriously the vegetation of Australia. The leaves of the gum tree, the dominant vegetation type, are narrow and turn sideways to the light of the sun. This minimizes evapotranspiration. Glover's trees reflect this quality; they are separate and allow light through. His treatment of Aborigines, in contrast, was poor. They are no more than hunched, black dwarves, poorly painted and little understood. They are not the noble savages of Captain Cook. They are at best a touch of romantic interest, at worst wild savages lacking human individuality. These 'native' scenes were for English tastes. They were invented to meet the demands of English buyers of exotica and the romantic. Glover exhibited 38 paintings in London in 1835.

Aborigines may have figured in the paintings but they had no place in the new white order. Before Glover's arrival, there had been numerous skirmishes between the Aborigines and the new settlers. In essence, the whites wanted the land. The natives were a problem and, one year before Glover arrived, the Lieutenant Governor of Van Dieman's Land conducted a major military operation against them. The plan was to form a line sweeping southwards through the land, forcing them into the Tasman peninsula. The human round-up was not successful. Only two were captured, the rest found a way through the badly coordinated line and some then attacked the soldiers from the rear. But Aboriginal resistance ultimately failed. In 1831, the year of Glover's arrival, the remaining Aborigines were removed to Flinders Island. A depleted group of 36 people were later transferred to a camp north of Hobart. On 8 May 1876, the last full-blooded Tasmanian Aborigine, Trugannini, died there of bronchitis and asthma. (In a bizarre incident, not long after her death, her head was hacked from her body. As an item of ethnographic interest it was sent to Britain. It is still held in the University of Edinburgh.) A whole race had been wiped from the face of the earth in an act of genocide with few parallels. Glover's Aborigines are the ghosts of a vanished race.

Glover also painted pastoral scenes (see Figures 9.1 and 9.2). In *Patterdale, Van Dieman's Land* (1845), we have the landscape sweep of trees, dead and alive, with the sheep and the shepherd indicating signs of pastoral progress, images of economic activity. English buyers in London wanted both the picturesque of the native scenes and good reports of the fledgling colony on the other side of the world. There was also a touch of 'boosterism', as Glover showed that he and the other big landowners were doing well Downunder. *A View of the Artist's House and Garden* (1835) shows the order of the garden, the precision of the settled, in contrast with

Figure 9.1 Patterdale, Van Dieman's Land (*c.* 1845) by John Glover (Queen Victoria Museum and Art Gallery, Launceston)

Figure 9.2 A View of the Artist's House and Garden (*c.* 1835) by John Glover (Art Gallery of South Australia, Adelaide)

the tangle of the gum trees on the hill. This painting is infused with the moral worth of the pioneer in transforming the bush into an ordered landscape. The pioneer was unseen because Glover was not good at painting figures. His skill lay in landscape composition, colouring and the rendering of light as background. His people are dismal failures, wooden, uncomfortable figures. But there was another reason for their absence. Tasmania was a penal colony, the main penal colony of Australia. When Glover arrived, there were 10,000 convicts, almost a half of the total population. When he died, the convict population had risen to 17,700; more than one in every three adults in Tasmania had been transported for a criminal offence. The convicts dug the trenches, made the roads and built the bridges. They were set to work by the government and were assigned to colonists like Glover. They were a central presence in the island. Escaped convicts posed a threat. Glover's son wrote to his brother-in-law in London in 1836 that a party of constables had been sent out to protect them against reported bushrangers (McPhee 1980: 63). When the Glovers went to church, their prayers were disturbed by the clanking of convicts' chains.

The development of Tasmania and of Glover's estate was based on convict labour, people working for their freedom. On his estate, Glover had seventeen male convicts working in the fields and three convict women in the house. This does not appear in Glover's scenes; we see the end result but not the process. In *My Harvest Home* (1835), the plain is rich and fertile, figures are stacking up nature's bounty, a light in the horizon suffuses the whole picture in a pantheistic light, giving a religious tone to the pastoral scene, the blending of God, nature and man (see Figure 2.4). But these figures were convicts, their ankles and wrists marked by penal discipline. Behind the image of an antipodean arcadia lies the reality of an antipodean *gulag*. Glover's paintings show the end result of labour but they are distanced from the reality of forced labour. Glover provides a record of early colonial life but it is a conflict-free, sanitized version of the early years in the colony. It is the view from the big house, watching the natives disappear into a whimper and the 'docile' workers transform the Australian bush into the Australian landscape.

In the work of Eugen von Guérard, the Australian landscape appeared as a mixture of old German romanticism and new commercial realities. Von Guérard (1812–1901) arrived in Australia three years after Glover died. Like Glover, he had trained as an artist in Europe. Born in Vienna into a painting family – his father was a court painter to Francis I of Austria – he studied in Italy and Germany. The news of gold in Australia spurred his spirit of adventure. In 1852 he arrived in the goldfields of Victoria, where he lasted only two years, running out of partners and luck. He returned to Melbourne, wiser but not much richer, and took up his painting career in earnest. For the next 28 years he dominated landscape

Figure 9.3 Tower Hill (1855) by Eugen von Guérard (Ministry of Conservation, Melbourne)

painting in Australia. His output was varied but two important themes were his romantic landscapes and homestead scenes.

Von Guérard had been trained in the early nineteenth-century German romantic school which saw landscape as God's imprint. The most important figure in this school was Caspar David Friedrich (1774–1840), whose paintings have a coherent form and a stillness which bespeaks God's encompassing presence. The role of the artist, according to Friedrich, was to uncover the divine organization behind natural forms. Von Guérard extended this European tradition in the New World. He travelled widely throughout Australia and New Zealand, searching out wild landscapes barely touched by human presence. *Tower Hill*, painted in 1855, was a commissioned work (see Figure 9.3). The enclosed lake gives a symmetrical completeness while the small figures in the foreground emphasize the majesty of nature. The sun's rays coming through the clouds on the top right mirror the tree on the extreme left and both make a connection between sky and earth which completes the wholeness of the scene. Von Guérard received 100 guineas for this picture and also excellent reviews, which made his name in the Australian art scene.

His romantic landscapes intimated underlying patterns and the presence of a divine architect. In *Waterfall, Strath Creek* (1862), the bottom and the top of the picture is connected by the zig-zag geometry of the waterfall (see Figure 9.4). The figure at the top, looking down, is echoed by the two

Figure 9.4 Waterfall, Strath Creek (1862) by Eugen von Guérard (Art Gallery of New South Wales, Sydney)

figures at the bottom, looking up. On either side there is a meticulous painting of the foliage; each leaf is delineated.

Von Guérard received his training when the distance between art and science was much less than it is now. ´Painters regularly travelled with scientific expeditions and in 1862 he accompanied the German hydrographer and meteorologist, Professor Georg von Neumayer, on a trip through northern Victoria. They climbed the highest mountain in

Figure 9.5 Glenara (1867) by Eugen von Guérard (Private collection)

Australia, celebrated in *Mt Kosciusko* (*c.* 1864) In the picture (see Figure 1.4), a figure stands on a flat-topped rock and looks, like the viewer, over a mountain scene of snow and rock outcrop. The highest peaks in the background touch the clouds. The landscape forms a natural cathedral, with the quietness, darkness and intimations of divine presence that are found in great churches.

There was also a more secular side to von Guérard's paintings. His painting career coincided with a long boom in Australian agricultural exports. For the large landowners, the squatters, it was a time of unparalleled wealth. Wool, beef and wheat were in increasing demand in the UK because of sustained economic growth and an agricultural free trade policy.

It was the golden age of squatting and the new wealth was reflected in new buildings, as country houses replaced old slab huts, and 'sheep farms' were turned into 'estates'. Few people wish their misfortunes to be noted but all of us like good fortune to be recorded. Today we take photographs of our weddings, new houses, children and pets. In similar vein, some of the wool kings of late-Victorian Australia commissioned paintings. Von Guérard became the most important pictorial recorder of the squatters' wealth and confidence. *Mr. Muirhead's Station* (1856) is an early work (see Figure 6.3). The house and garden stand in a clearing, an established fact, a statement of pride as the owner surveys his property, wife and children from his horse.

In *Glenara* (1867), the sense of the bush tamed is highlighted by the extensive gardens around the home (see Figure 9.5). These run down the hill, pushing back the gums and grass. The large, imposing house sits in the middle ground, with figures playing in the grass, walking near the verandah, confident and serene. In *Woodlands Homestead on the Wimmera* (1869), now in the Australian National Gallery, Canberra, the house/castle sits in the middle of the picture, at the centre of a commercialized landscape, and squatters proudly ride through their domain, for all intents and purposes English gentlemen surveying their estates. This picture is reminiscent of the eighteenth century English picture of country estates and their owners. The parallels are explicit. The squatters self-consciously sought to copy English traditions. Even their building plans came from England. England provided them with cultural codes and social mores as well as a market for their produce.

AUSTRALIAN LANDSCAPES

For the first three-quarters of the nineteenth century, the development of a pioneer myth was restricted by Victorian attitudes towards the convict basis of early white Australia. There were very few respectable folk in the nineteenth century who wanted to find a convict in their family background. Tasmania is one of the few places in the world where it is an offence to slander the dead, a legacy of the fear of being labelled a convict even when dead. Times change. Heroes and villains have not disappeared, the labels have just been moved around. Now Australians are disappointed if there is not a convict in their family. Everyone wants to find a convict, no one is keen to discover a guard.

By the last quarter of the nineteenth century, there was a new audience of urban dwellers and small settlers and cultural nationalism was competing with the cultural cringe. The connection between nationalist sentiment and environmental imagery was particularly strong in novels, short stories, journal articles and painting. The very influential weekly news and literary magazine, the *Bulletin*, founded in 1880, was an important vehicle for written work. Its early editorial policy was radical and republican, its motto 'Australia for the Australians'. A major contributor was Henry Lawson (1867–1922), who in his stories dignified the earliest (non-convict) pioneers and pointed to the authenticity of a unique (white) Australian experience in the transformation of the wilderness. The experience most commonly portrayed was of a harsh environment tamed by hard work and communal activity. Friendship, or to be more precise in the Australian context, male mateship and the bush figure large in Lawson and other writers of the period, such as A.B. (Banjo) Paterson and Joseph Furphy. In a letter to an editor at the turn of the century, Furphy described his work thus: 'I have just finished writing a full-sized novel; title *Such is Life*; scene Riverina and Northern Victoria; temper, democratic; bias, offensively Australian.'

There was a parallel development in the evolution of an 'Australian' school of painting, the landscape painters of what became known as the Heidelberg School (see Astbury 1985). Two painters are of particular importance: Tom Roberts (1856–1931) and Arthur Streeton (1867–1943).

Born in England, 13-year old Tom Roberts emigrated to Melbourne in 1869 with his mother, brother and sister. He developed an interest in art, winning a prize for landscape in 1873; one of the judges was Eugen von Guérard. He drew for illustrated journals before travelling in Europe between 1881 and 1885, where he was influenced by Whistler and Monet. On his return, he invigorated the Melbourne art scene with an interest in open-air painting, and a concern to paint colour and light. He set up painting camps in Box Hill and Mentone outside Melbourne.

One attender was a local boy, Arthur Streeton, who helped to establish the Heidelberg camp at Eaglemont in 1887. From this outdoor experience of the 1880s came a flood of landscape paintings. Two classics are *The Sunny South* (*c.* 1887) by Tom Roberts (see Figure 9.6) and *Golden Summer, Eaglemont* (1889) by Arthur Streeton (see Figure 2.1) Compared to von Guérard's work, we see in them a change of scale, subject and technique. The landscape has been humanized. Humans are not dwarfed by the landscape, they are part of it. The landscape is not grand but intimate, almost cosy. *The Sunny South* is a celebration of sensual pleasures, one of the earliest Australian paintings of the white nude. The bare bottom which today scarcely touches our sensibilities mightily offended the Victorian prudes of Melbourne. Streeton's painting is a pastoral depiction of a hot Australian summer. A boy tends some sheep but this is not work, merely an Australian idyll. Both paintings reflect the light and warmth of an Australian summer, both are concerned to reflect the light of Australia. Compare this to the minute descriptive brushwork and studio gloominess of von Guérard. *The Sunny South* and *Golden Summer, Eaglemont* are looser renditions, impressionist celebrations of Australia. There is a self-conscious depiction of space and light, an attempt to show Australia as a hedonistic landscape.

In their paintings, Roberts and Streeton concentrated on Australian themes. This was an attempt to define a white Australian identity which was separate from Britain; not only a response to social conflict but also part of a much broader attempt by Australian intellectuals to claim a separate and distinct area for cultural expression. Intellectuals and painters, such as Roberts and Streeton, were defining Australia as a specific area of inquiry because it gave them precedence over foreign imports. The production of an 'Australian' culture and the emphasis on pastoral myths gave protection to local artists in the face of international competition.

The artists' camps in Victoria ended in 1890. The Depression had affected confidence, especially in Victoria where even 'Marvellous Melbourne' saw the long boom turn into a slump. Streeton moved to Sydney in 1890 and shared a studio with Roberts. In 1899 he went to

Figure 9.6 The Sunny South (c. 1887) by Tom Roberts (Art Gallery of Victoria, Melbourne)

Europe, returning in 1924. He continued to paint landscapes. The title of one of his paintings, *Purple Noon's Transparent Light* (1896), came from a line in a poem by Shelley. Streeton later wrote that he worked on the canvas in 'a state of artistic intoxication with thoughts of Shelley on my mind'. The result is a softly composed piece of brilliant colour and a warm tonality which conjures up images of long, languid summer days. The painting was bought by the National Gallery of Victoria and helped to establish Streeton's national reputation. For artists to be successful, they had to sell not only to private owners but also to the public galleries which were becoming very important spenders of art money and arbiters of aesthetic tastes.

Streeton became, and continues to be, one of Australia's most popular painters. He turned out landscape paintings of pastoral Australia well into the 1920s and 1930s. His paintings were seen as the 'real' Australia by many Australians. He dominated popular aesthetic tastes. It was widely reported as a national scandal when the Australian National Gallery refused to buy a Streeton in 1985. It was later bought by a Perth millionaire as an act of patriotic duty. The same Gallery had come in for huge criticism when it bought a Jackson Pollock painting, *Blue Poles*, in 1973 for $1.4 million. There were many reasons for the criticism. It was a useful peg for discussing federal government spending, but a major reason was that an Australian public was so used to the naturalist paintings of Streeton and Roberts that it had little real experience of abstract art. The 1986 exhibition of the Heidelberg School, entitled *Golden Summers*, attracted record-breaking crowds wherever it was shown in Australia.

For Australians, Streeton's landscapes give a solidity to rural nostalgia, an acceptable pictorial representation of the myth of the bush. Streeton is to Australia what Walt Disney is to the USA or John Betjeman is to the older, English middle class.

Roberts' work after 1890 went beyond landscape. He was a fine portrait painter but he is best known for his resuscitation of an older, popular tradition of illustrating outback Australia. Roberts depicted rural Australia in three major works: *Shearing the Rams* (1890), *The Breakaway* (1890–1) and *The Golden Fleece* (1894). All three celebrate outback Australia and, in particular, male labour in the pastoral industries. *Shearing the Rams* (see Figure 9.7) shows the inside of a shearing shed, where men are clipping the sheep. The painting captures the movement in a stylized pose, emphasizing the strength of the men's arms and the communion of labour. It can be seen as a Millet-style depiction of labour with more than a touch of Soviet-style, social-realist celebration of labour. Compare this to photographs of shearing sheds, taken at the same time as Roberts' painting (see Figures 9.8 and 9.9). In contrast to the photographs, Roberts has shortened the length of most shearing sheds, giving a more intimate view with less feeling of the assembly line. His shearers use hand-shears, when most shearing sheds were turning to electric clippers, and he has not included any

Figure 9.7 Shearing the Rams (1890) by Tom Roberts (National Gallery of Victoria, Melbourne)

foremen. Roberts has downplayed the social relations of work, at a time when there was intense conflict between squatters and shearers. The ending of the long boom meant a redirection in profit; squatters responded by cutting wages. The Amalgamated Shearers' Union was formed in 1886 and had some early success. But the squatters formed their own associations and by 1891 had smashed the union. None of this appears in the painting. The men are busy, strong, well fed, neither overworked nor underpaid. There is even a smiling boy in the background to give further reinforcement to the notion of the joy as well as the dignity of labour. *Shearing the Rams* is one of the most reproduced paintings in Australia. It is found in offices and suburban lounges; it is the subject of coffee-table mats and jigsaws. It is an idealized picture of a conflict-free, pastoral Australia, not so much a record of the past but a nostalgia for a past. The picture is so shallow in its relationship with shearing realities that it has allowed a diversity of subsequent meanings to be read off. The workers' movement could see the dignity of labour, the wealthy could see a contented workforce, and nationalists could see an Australia strong and rich, a whole community celebrated in oils.

Figure 9.8 Photograph of sheep shearing shed, taken in the late 1890s (Australian Consolidated Press)

Figure 9.9 Photograph of sheep shearing shed, taken in the 1890s (Australian Consolidated Press)

THE LANDSCAPE OF MODERNIST AUSTRALIA

Each year since 1897, the trustees of the Art Gallery of New South Wales in Sydney have awarded the Wynne Prize for landscape painting. For over forty years, the winner invariably depicted the gum trees, sunlight and rural scene as developed by Streeton and Roberts. Painters of this tradition, such as Hans Heysen and Elioth Gruner, were regular winners. Thus, the pastoral vision of the early Heidelberg School dominated Australian landscape painting.

The first sign of change came in 1942 when Douglas Watson won the Wynne with *Backyards*. It was not well received because of its 'dreary' backyard subject. Criticism reached a peak two years later when Sali Herman's *McElhone Stairs* won the prize, with a picture of a 'rundown' area of inner Sydney. For many commentators of the time, Herman's picture was unpatriotic, a direct attack on Australia as the land of the Golden Fleece and the Golden Summer. Herman's attempt to create a townscape school ultimately failed. The urban has been marginalized in the artistic rendering of Australia. The most successful artist continued to look beyond the cities, further and further into the interior.

In 1947 Russell Drysdale won the Wynne prize with *Sofala*, a study of a small country town in Australia (see Figure 9.11). Where Herman pointed to the urban nature of Australia, Drysdale revised the image of rural Australia. Russell Drysdale (1912–81) was born into an affluent, land-owning, Anglo-Australian family, a type well described in the novels of Martin Boyd (see Klepac 1983). He was born in Bognor Regis, on the south coast of England, and travelled with his family between England and Australia until 1923, when they settled permanently in Australia. He was sent to the Geelong Grammar School, a favourite with the squatters of Victoria, and worked on his uncle's estate in Queensland and as a jackeroo in Victoria. 'Jackeroo' is the term given to a wealthy young man doing a form of rural slumming. Anyone who does not have money and is stuck there permanently is simply a labourer.

Drysdale had eye trouble. In 1932 he went into a hospital in Melbourne and to pass the time did some drawing. He followed up his interest by meeting the art teacher George Bell. In 1933, family business in England allowed him to travel to Paris and this was the first of many visits from which he gained critical stimulus from European modernists. With the help of family money, he became a full-time art student in 1935. He lived for a time in a house in Eaglemont, the same one in which Tom Roberts had worked 50 years before.

It was not until the late 1930s that the personal vision of Drysdale began to take shape. *A Man Reading a Newspaper* (1941) contains the elements of his style: the elongated figure, like a Giacometti sculpture, set against the elements of a dry Australia – all corrugated iron, dead trees, flat landscape and wind-driven water pump – given archetypal form and mythic proportions with touches of surrealism and expressionism (see Figure 2.5).

Figure 9.10 The Drover's Wife (1945) by Russell Drysdale (Private collection)

Drysdale presented a new vision of Australia: a land drier and dustier than the continent of the Heidelberg School, a place where there was a continual struggle against the elements. The man reading his newspaper suggests resignation in the face of adversity, the supreme example of the Australian 'no worries' attitude.

In 1944 Drysdale was commissioned by a newspaper to cover the drought then affecting much of New South Wales. The paintings continue the theme of a harsh, dry Australia. *The Drover's Wife* (1945) shows a woman against the flat horizon and the dead, twisted trees (see Figure 9.10). Although the background is harsh, there is a touch of romanticism, a celebration of the rural values of the small farmer and the soldier-settler family. She is suffering, to be sure, but it is suffering carried with a quiet, stubborn dignity.

Drysdale's work has been a respected part of the Australian landscape painting tradition but it has never been as popular as that of Roberts or Streeton. Drysdale is perceived as unflattering to the landscape and its inhabitants. His work has been criticized as not being the real Australia. So it was with *Sofala* (see Figure 9.11). In 1947, in a trip through New South Wales, Drysdale came across the town. His painting captures the ennui, the transient nature of the built form. The verandahs of iron lace are given

Figure 9.11 Sofala (1947) by Russell Drysdale (Art Gallery of New South Wales, Sydney)

a serenity but there is an indication of the contingency of urban settlement in Australia. The *Bulletin* saw it differently: 'Drysdale's painting, however charitably viewed, is not an understanding – not even an interpretation – but an attack. A clumsy attack' (12 December 1947: 2).

Drysdale continued to travel into outback Australia, extending his range of subjects to the Aborigines and the cattlemen of the interior. With Sydney Nolan and Arthur Boyd, he extended the subject of Australian landscape further into the heart of Australia. It was as if the landscape painters felt driven to go further inland to discover the 'real' Australia. Urban Australia looked like everywhere else but the red heart at the centre held out greater symbolic and aesthetic promise.

Despite his Australian subjects, popular recognition in Australia has eluded Drysdale. His early paintings are unflattering, they show a countryside only just emerging from a deep economic depression and a landscape ravaged by erosion and drought. Drysdale may celebrate the resilience of whites but he highlights their slight hold on a continent older than their dreams and harder than their endeavours.

The Governor-General of Australia lives in a large house in Yarralumla, Canberra, on the shores of Lake Burley Griffin. He is the Queen's representative in Australia, with an important ceremonial role, speaking to ambassadors, politicians, and all manner of community leaders. To be invited to dinner at Government House is an honour eagerly sought by many. In the dining room, on the long walls on either side of the dining table, are landscapes by Fred Williams. He is one of the most abstract of Australian landscape painters yet one of the most popular. He has become the most admired modern Australian painter. Anyone who makes serious money in Australia and has an interest in art will want to have a Williams. No major public institution feels complete unless it has one of his paintings. Fred Williams' landscapes are the acceptable face of modernism in contemporary Australia.

Fred Williams (1927–82) was born in Melbourne. He always wanted to be a painter. At sixteen, he attended the National Gallery School and later the George Bell Art School. In 1956, like many Australians of his generation and inclination, he went to London. He attended art schools, worked as a farmer, visited Paris and painted music hall scenes and some landscapes. The early paintings have the dreary, brown tones of the Euston Road school.

On his return to Australia, Fred Williams began to paint landscapes. 'When I arrived back in Freemantle,' he later told a journalist, 'I was struck by how odd the Australian landscape was, no focal point, so I simply thought, "well, I'll paint it and I'll leave out the focal point".'

His paintings developed from his trips into the Victorian countryside. The progression from *Nattai River* (1957–8) to *Trees on Hillside* II (1964) shows the growing abstraction of Williams' landscape depiction (see Figures 9.12 and 9.13). The basic elements of his more abstract works consist of a background of big, strong blocks of colour, highlighted with small, dense spots of paint. The initial feeling of surface randomness gives way to a definite rhythm and form, which arise from the interposing of generalized form and dense detail, expanses of soft washes and small hard patches of paint.

In *Trees on Hillside* II (1964), for example, there is a brown landscape with a well-defined horizon. A white sky is background to the thickly painted spots of trees. Elements of a particular place have been abstracted into icons of a more general space. The painting is an abstraction of classical proportions, accessible and understandable.

Williams' treatment of the landscape is shared by a character in *Illywhacker* (1985), a novel written by fellow Victorian Peter Carey:

> It was a hot day and the wind was dry. Phoebe sat in the back and reduced the landscape to its most pleasing essentials. She half shut her eyes and allowed her eyelashes to strain out that which was not to her taste. She removed those piles of volcanic rocks, those monuments to the endless work of young soldier-settlers. She eliminated those lovely treeless farmhouses with the sun beating on their shiny gal-iron roofs.

Figure 9.12 Nattai River (1957–8) by Fred Williams (Art Gallery of Victoria, Melbourne)

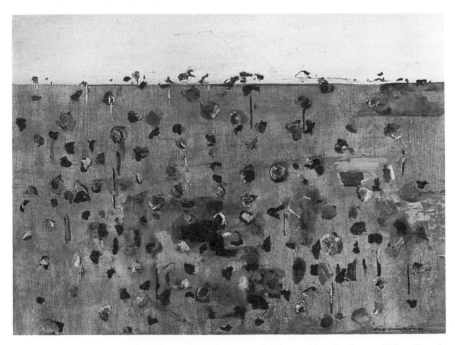

Figure 9.13 Trees on Hillside 2 (1964) by Fred Williams (Art Gallery of New South Wales, Sydney)

Figure 9.14 View from an aeroplane landing at Canberra Airport

She abracadabra'ed the sheep with their daggy backsides. She turned those endless miles of sheep and wheat into something the men who farmed it would never recognise. All she retained was the cobalt blue sky above a plain of shimmering gold. You couldn't make a quid in one of Phoebe's landscapes.

(Carey 1985: 20–1)

Williams, like Phoebe, generalized the countryside, took out the figures and turned it into a landscape unconnected to human endeavours or social relations, a place where 'you couldn't make a quid'.

By the 1970s, his paintings were pared down to even more basic elements. It is important to see the paintings in their technological context. Williams is of the jet era. He is a landscape painter who has looked down on the earth from 10,000 feet in the air. Figure 9.14 indicates one source of William's imagery.

His last major works were the Pilbara landscapes, commissioned by the giant mining company CRA. The Pilbara is a remote area of the north west, in the state of Western Australia, which contains valuable mineral deposits, particularly iron ore. It is perhaps fitting that Australia's greatest landscape painter should paint this landscape. By the 1980s, 40 per cent of Australia's exports were in the form of minerals. Mountains in Western Australia were dug up, taken by rail to the sea and shipped to Japan, to be processed and then sold on the world markets as cars, radios, and videos.

Figure 9.15 Karratha Landscape (1981) by Fred Williams (Private collection of the CRA company, Australia)

The Pilbara commission was a public relations exercise by CRA to help to counter environmental criticisms of their actions.

In 1979 Williams visited the Pilbara and made sketches and gouaches. He did not do the oil paintings until 1981. The following year he died. In *Karratha Landscape* (1981), the view looks across the plain to the hill, reduced to its simplest form, trees bristling along its ridge (see Figure 9.15). It has a more figurative than abstract quality. It is a fresh view of the interior, neither glorifying its remoteness nor expressing melancholy for its aridity. Although funded by mineral barons as a public relations exercise, the Pilbara series manages to transcend its grubby origins.

In his paintings Williams has universalized the Australian landscape. He has taken it out of a specific context and raised it to an ordered beauty. He makes the Australian landscape beautiful, accessible and yet of wider significance.

Maybe that is why his pictures can be found in the dining room of the Governor-General.

ANCIENT MODERNITY

The mineral boom of the 1960s and 1970s, which led to the Pilbara series, also reawakened commercial and political awareness of the other Australians, the Aborigines. Throughout most of the white occupation of Australia, Aboriginal culture was seen, when it was seen at all, as of ethnographic interest only, suitable for glass-case presentation in museums with an underlying model of the steady, linear progress of civilization. Aborigines were a couple of rungs down the ladder and thus only useful as a guide to savage ways, a reminder of how far white society had progressed.

The onset of modernity involved a change in attitude. Traditional societies began to provide models of form and creative impulse to a generation of twentieth-century artists, such as Epstein and Picasso. The work of these and other artists involved not merely a reappraisal of 'primitive' art but a fundamental recognition that it *was* art. The abstraction of modern art reflected many of the forms of 'primitive art' which had been ignored during the dominance of 'realist' painting.

This change was slow to come to Australia. The attitude towards Aborigines of most white Australians was built on a bedrock of institutional and individual racism. At best, it was patronising; at worst, and this was the norm, it involved a denial of their social rights and human dignity. When Margaret Preston (1875–1963), one of Australia's best and most innovative artists, used Aboriginal motifs in her paintings, the response of the *Bulletin* was typical:

> She is allowing the aborigines – a people, she admits herself, too limited in sensibility and technical capacity – to debilitate her talent ... what is really required is the opposite process – the enrichment of primitive art by the infinitely greater technical and spiritual resources of the civilized artist.

> (17 August 1942: 2)

At least the *Bulletin* did admit the existence of such art. More common was its complete exclusion from debates about art. The two standard works on Australian painting, Bernard Smith's *Australian Painting* (first published 1962) and *The Art of Australia* by Robert Hughes (1966, revised 1970 and reprinted in 1984), contain no mention of Aboriginal art. Art, it seems, is only what the white folks do.

Even as late as 1987, a visitor to the Art Gallery of New South Wales in Sydney had a hard job finding any art from Aboriginal Australia. Tucked away below a small sign reading *Tribal Art*, an almost-hidden entrance led to a basement where a few bark paintings and wooden sculptures could be found. The names of the artists were not given and the pieces were behind glass cases. The whole place had a fly-blown, grubby quality which indicated a lack of care and ultimately a lack of respect. Upstairs, in lighter, cheerier surroundings, what immediately hit the visitor coming in off the street was white Australian art, most of it third-rate imitations of second-rate North American and European art. Below stairs in a small, ill-lit room was Australia's most original contribution to modern art and human creativity.

Attitudes are changing. A visitor to the newer Australian National

Figure 9.16 Untitled bark painting by
Dhurritjin Yumbulul (1986) (Author's
collection)

Gallery in Canberra would have less trouble finding Aboriginal art. The art
of Aboriginal Australians is not ghettoized into a tribal section. Canberra
reflects the reassessment not only of the validity of traditional art but also
of its importance as Australian art. The 1960s and 1970s saw the remaking
of white Australian identity and an attempt by Aborigines to gain rights
and respect. Art played an important part. Aboriginal artefacts began to
be sold as 'art', exhibitions were held and purchases were made.
Aboriginal communities could produce artefacts for an expanding market.

There is no one Aboriginal art, there are many Aboriginal communities
with different artistic traditions. In Arnhem Land in the Northern
Territory there is a vigorous school of paintings on bark. In west Arnhem,
the emphasis is on figurative painting, sometimes in an X-ray style which

Figure 9.17 Honey Ant Dreaming (1982) by Mick Tjakamarra (Private collection)

draws on the tradition of rock painting (see Figure 6.1). In north-east Arnhem, the style is more geometric and abstract (see Figure 9.16). In the central desert, in contrast, there is a tradition of sand painting which has been translated on to canvas to produce abstract painting with a geometry of order. So we have to be careful in lumping varied traditions into one general term of 'Aboriginal art'. Ultimately, the pieces are the work of individuals, drawing on traditional forms to make individual contributions.

Despite the differences, there is a general similarity. Art is part of a much broader cultural web linking individuals to specific sites and particular symbols. Each individual in an Aboriginal tribal community has a responsibility, a role to play in the cultural life of the community. In particular, they are given knowledge of specific songs and specific sites. The singing of the songs and the painting of the sites ensures the unbroken connection between the people and their ancestors, between the community and the land.

Figure 9.17, the painting by Mick Tjakamarra, *Honey Ant Dreaming* (1982), can be read in three ways: (i) as a pattern in its own right with colour and form; (ii) as a map of a particular site; (iii) as a work of wider spiritual significance whose meaning is only fully known to other clan members and the artist. In terms of (ii), we can 'read' the painting when we know some of the symbols (see Peterson 1981). The concentric circles are camp sites, the connecting U-shapes are participants in a ceremony, while background colour variation indicates landscape. The painting is a map.

The recent growth and interest in Aboriginal art has a number of implications. It is becoming big business. In 1986, the Papunya Tula Artists Pty Ltd had a turnover of $A400,000, a 33 per cent increase on the previous year. Individual bark paintings, bought for $50 in 1976 were being sold for $1000 in 1986. The middle-men are making money but some of the increased prices are filtering back to the artists' communities, providing much-needed income.

Aboriginal art is now an important part of the definition of Australian national identity. Some white Australians are beginning to realize the artistic and national importance of Aboriginal art as a uniquely Australian art form. Aboriginal art is now being displayed in international cultural events where each country presents its best artistic achievements. Concern is now being expressed at the overseas export of such work and attempts are being made to recover artefacts from overseas collections. The Vatican has the biggest single collection of Aboriginal art, the result of all those mission stations. The Australian government is trying to recover some of the pieces. The attempt to regain these artefacts is an important indicator of cultural nationalism.

The interest in their art is a source of pride and income for Aboriginal communities. Marginalized by a dominant white culture for two centuries, their art now provides them with a measure of dignity, as their works are being given a more prominent place in public galleries and public debates, their motifs are being used by white artists, and their visions of landscape are being taken up by the ecologically conscious. Art is giving Aborigines much-needed respect.

The money from the sale of their art is also giving them self-respect. Art sales allow income support for the outstations movement, which involves people returning to their traditional tribal lands. The money from art sales pays for vehicles and water-boring, equipment so that a more traditional life may be sustained, away from the former mission settlements. There are now over 400 outstations in central Australia.

Art is of political significance. The 'landscape' paintings express the relationship between individuals of a clan and particular sites. In the debates about landownership and mining rights, the paintings become of supreme importance, since they represent an artistic title deed to particular plots of land. The paintings signify spiritual responsibility and traditional ownership and thus provide substance to Aboriginal claims either to stop mining or to obtain royalties. The paintings are of tremendous legal significance.

I entitled this section *ancient modernity* because contemporary Aboriginal art condenses the ambivalence of the old and the new, the traditional and the modern. The basic motifs and 'stories' are centuries old, they refer to a long-standing relationship between people and their land. However, the modern artist is expressing these motifs in new, original and exciting ways. It is a living tradition. Some would say that the commercialization of Aboriginal art is leading to a lessening of artistic integrity. They have a point. There are mass-produced artefacts, tawdry boomerangs and shoddy bark paintings, which are turned out quickly for the expanding tourist market. But work of real value is also being produced and Aborigines are receiving respect and money for their artefacts. The money from sales is supporting the outstations movement, so this is a case of modern tastes supporting a return to traditional homelands. A blanket dismissal of commercialism fails to capture such paradoxes.

The 'old' culture of the Aborigines has something to give to the modern world. I think we can learn something from their spiritual connection with the land. In the Aboriginal traditions, landscape art is not a subject of distanced contemplation. There is not the same distance between artist and landscape as there is in the 'white' landscape tradition. Rather, the painting of the landscape is a work of spiritual communion. Aboriginal art questions the traditional view that we have of landscape. It also forces us to reappraise the notion of artists as specific individuals separated from the rest of the community by training and technical expertise. At a fundamental level, the participative culture of the Aborigines, in which everyone has a creative role, a social importance and community significance, has much to teach us. The notion that everyone is an artist, that everyone has a personal story to tell that is capable of artistic expression, is a profoundly liberating one for our society in which 'artistic creation' is limited to the few. The ancients can help to liberate the moderns.

Guide to further reading

A reader of an earlier draft of this book complained that there was no conclusion. The book just ended, he wrote in a letter to the publishers. This book, however, is not like a sexual encounter leading up to a climax nor like a joke whose structure is geared up to a final punchline. The substance of the book is the exposition itself; the chapters are self-contained, they are not a set of steps leading to a lofty conclusion. There is no neat conclusion, no pithy final statement. The major points have been made in the course of the exposition, indeed they are the exposition.

I can, however, understand the reviewer's concern. We want things to be rounded off, the bow to be neatly tied, the final note to be sung. By way of a compromise, then, the final chapter is a guide to further reading. It is at the end of the book but could just as easily have been at the beginning. It is both an introduction and a conclusion. It is an introduction in that it indicates the sources which have informed the work. It is a conclusion in that it provides readers with a 'map' to help them to explore further some of the themes in the book.

Bibliographies are more often weighed than read. Amongst many scholars there is a feeling that the sheer weight of references is an indication of good scholarship: the more the better. I do not subscribe to this view. My guide, therefore, is a selective one. It concentrates on the sources which I found particularly useful, interesting, or stimulating.

MYTHS

I have yet to find many good books or articles on myths. Part of the problem lies in the elastic nature of the concept. It has been used in a variety of contexts and pulled and twisted to fit a number of debates. With regard to anthropological literature, see G.S. Kirk's *Myth, its Meaning and Function in Ancient and Other Cultures* (1970), the book of readings edited by Edmund Leach, *The Structural Study of Myth and Totemism* (1967), and the grand-daddy of them all, Claude Lévi-Strauss's *Structural Anthropology* (1963). Observers of contemporary society have also used the concept of myth; see, for example, the influential and readable Roland Barthes, *Mythologies* (1972). Much subsequent work is structuralist gibberish, about as digestible and intelligible as overcooked suet pudding. A rare exception is the theoretically informed yet understandable *The Public Culture: The Triumph of Industrialism* (1986) by Donald Horne. Although he is concerned with more general myths of enchantment in modern society, he uses myth in much the same way as it is employed in this book.

The environment

General histories of environmental thought include Clarence Glacken's *Traces on the Rhodian Shore* (1967) and Yi-Fu Tuan's *Topophilia: A Study of Environmental Perception, Attitudes and Values* (1974). Although now dated, Lewis Mumford's *Technic and a Civilization* (1934) is still worth careful consideration. Environmentalism has emerged in recent years as a powerful social force; Timothy O'Riordan's *Environmentalism* (1976) provides a general account, while Necdet Teymur's *Environmental Discourse* (1982) provides a critical analysis of the term and its use in a variety of fields including architecture, social sciences and the media. Have a look at two journals, *The Ecologist* and *Environmental Ethics*.

Wilderness

The first three chapters of Roderick Nash's *Wilderness and the American Mind* (1982) provide an excellent introduction to the general notion of wilderness. The book provides a very useful bibliography. Other general surveys include Dennis Jeans' 'Wilderness, Nature and Society: contributions to the history of an environmental attitude' (*Australian Geographical Studies*, 1983, 21: 170–82) and the book edited by V. Martin and M. Inglis, *Wilderness: The Way Ahead* (1984). On the relationship between religious thought and wilderness, see Part One of George H. Williams' *Wilderness and Paradise in Christian Thought* (1962), the brief but powerful paper by Lynn White, jun., 'The historical roots of our ecological crisis' (*Science*, 1967, 155: 1203–7) and the excellent *Wilderness as Sacred Space* by Lynn Graber (Monograph Series 8, Association of American Geographers, 1976). The role of wilderness in the rise of romanticism is well covered in Christopher Thacker's *The Wildness Pleases: The Origins of Romanticism* (1983) and Hugh Honour's *Romanticism* (1979). A detailed study of the intellectual background to the rise of romantic poetry is given by Marjorie Hope Nicholson in *Mountain Gloom and Mountain Glory: The Development of the Aesthetics of the Infinite* (1959).

Contrasting treatments of the changing perception of nature involved in the development of the scientific enterprise are E.J. Dijksterhuis' *The Mechanization of the World Picture* (1969) and Carolyn Merchant's *The Death of Nature: Women, Ecology and the Scientific Revolution* (1980).

The relationship between wilderness transformation and nationalism are covered by some of the papers in Wolfskill, G. and Palmer, S. (eds) *Essays on Frontiers in World History* (1983). Attitudes to the people of the wilderness are covered in the general study of racist ieology by Michael Banton's *Racial Theories* (1987). Detailed historical studies include Anthony Pagden's *The Fall of Natural Man* (1982) and John Hemming's *Amazon Frontier: The Defeat of the Brazilian Indians* (1987). The noble savage theme is pursued by a number of popular writers. For example, anything by Laurens van der Post on the bushmen of the Kalahari sees their world as a Garden of Eden to be contrasted with the awfulness of the modern world. This theme provides the basis for Marshall Sahlins' brilliant anthropological analysis, *Stone Age Economics* (1972), which seeks to demonstrate that hunting-gathering communities are the original affluent societies, where free time was plentiful and life was rosy.

The countryside

There is no substitute for reading Theocritus and Virgil. Although the form may appear strange to modern readers, they contain the seeds of the pastoral vision. I used the translation of Theocritus by Robert Wells (1987) and the Cecil Day Lewis translation of Virgil's *Eclogues* and *Georgics*. Interesting studies of subsequent developments include *The Penguin Book of English Pastoral Verse* (1974), edited by John Barrell and John Bull, *Pastoral and Ideology: Virgil to Valery* (1988) by Annabel Patterson, and *The Country and The City* (1973) by Raymond Williams. Assessments of the 'truth' of the pastoral vision include *The Rural Idyll* (1989) edited by G.E. Mingay, Fraser Harrison's *Strange Land, The Countryside: Myth and Reality* (1982) and John Berger's *Pig Earth* (1979).

The city

A number of books were mentioned in the text. Let me cite again Jonathan Raban's *Soft City* (1974): it is a well-written assessment of the city as personal experience. Useful historical studies of the city include Mark Girouard's *Cities and People* (1985) and the magisterial *The City in History* (1961) by Lewis Mumford. Peter Hall gives a history of urban dreams in *Cities of Tomorrow* (1989), while David Harvey gives us a Marxist view of the city in *Consciousness and the Urban Experience* (1985). The politic-philosophic basis to different views of the city are considered by Peter J. Steinberger in *Ideology and the Urban Crisis* (1985). You might also want to look at my *The Humane City* (1989).

IDEOLOGIES

Although written more than a hundred years ago, *The German Ideology* (1846) by Karl Marx and Friedrich Engels is worth reading. It still has the energy of two young men angry at the stupidity of their intellectual enemies. The work remains fresh. The same could not be said for most of the subsequent work which has defined, redefined and almost killed the notion of ideology as a working intellectual concept. Exceptions include Raymond Williams' *Culture* (1981) and *The Ideology of Power and the Power of Ideology* (1980) by Goran Therborn.

The relationship between nationalism and ideology is covered in a number of works. Ernest Gellner's *Nations and Nationalism* (1983) provides a useful introduction. In *Imagined Countries* (1983), Benedict Anderson looks at the risk of nationalism in the era of print capitalism; Tom Nairn's *The Break-up of Britain* (1977) looks at the ambivalence of nationalism, while Eric Hobsbawn and Terrence Ranger have edited a book, *The Invention of Tradition* (1983), which shows how the past is invented for specific purposes.

The role of intellectuals in the creation of ideology is given an interesting treatment by Zygmunt Bauman in *Legislators and Interpreters: On Modernity, Post-modernity and Intellectuals* (1987).

Britain

There is, of course, no such place as Britain. As a form of state there is the United Kingdom, which does not (yet) have a king and is not all that united. Then there are the nationalist ideologies of the English, Scots, Welsh and competing Irish. To use the term 'British', therefore, is to coalesce state forms and ideological representations. That is why Chapter 4 opens with a consideration of the experience of Highland Scotland. I have drawn on the work of the popular historian John Prebble and, in particular, on his *Culloden* (1961) and *The Highland Clearances* (1963). Overseas, the experience of Empire had a tremendous effect on attitudes and culture. Eric Hobsbawn's *Age of Empire* (1987) is a splendid survey; *The Lords of Human Kind: European Attitudes Towards the Outside World in the Age of Empire* (1969) is a committed piece of historical writing by V.G. Kiernan, while the books by Charles Allen, *Plain Tales from the Raj* (1975) and *Tales of the Dark Continent* (1979), give us an insight into the British experience of colonial service. The city as a place of native unrest is well covered by Geoffrey Pearson's *Hooligan: A History of Respectable Fears* (1983). In *Man and the Natural World* (1983), Keith Thomas considers environmental attitudes in England in 1500–1800. Howard Newby is one of the most informed writers on rural England; in *Country Life* (1987) he provides a broad social history, while in *Green and Pleasant Land?* (1979) he concentrates on the contemporary period. An effective lament for the loss of rural England underlines the work of Marion Shoard in *The Theft of the Countryside* (1980) and *This Land is Our Land* (1987).

The countryside as spiritual retreat is considered by Martin Wiener in his *English Culture and the Decline of the Industrial Spirit, 1850–1980* (1981). Wiener is very good at showing how the countryside has been used as a counterpoint to industrialism and modernity. Attitudes to cities were profoundly influenced by the experience of the nineteenth century. Let me again mention the *The Country and the City* (1973) by Raymond Williams. The collection edited by H.J. Dyos and Michael Wolff, *The Victorian City* (1973), gives us the historian's viewpoint while almost any novel by Charles Dickens gives us an imaginative reconstruction.

USA

The classic work on the wilderness in US thought is Roderick Nash's *Wilderness and The American Mind* (1982). On European perceptions, see Ray Billington's *Land of Savagery, Land of Promise: The European Image of the American Frontier* (1981) and Hugh Honour's *The New Golden Land* (1965). On the passing of the frontier, have a look at L.C. Mitchell's *Witnesses to a Vanishing America* (1981) J.M. Petulla's *American Environmentalism* (1980) and an interesting biography by S. Fox, *John Muir and his Legacy* (1981).

The line between the settled and the wild has an important resonance in the USA. The importance of Frederick Jackson Turner has been mentioned in the text. Here let me mention the excellent summary by Robert Hine, *The American West* (1984); the feminist perspective supplied by Annette Kolodny in *The Lay of the Land* (1975) and *The Land Before Her* (1984); the literary surveys of R. Slotkin, *Regeneration through Violence* (1973) and *The Fatal Environment* (1985), and P. Fussell, *Frontier: American Literature and the American West* (1965). Barbara Novak provides an interpretation of painting in *American Painting of the Nineteenth Century* (1969) and *Nature and Culture: American Landscape Painting 1825–1875* (1980). The Indian dimension is presented in W.R. Jacobs' *Dispossessing The American Indian* (1985).

The most influential study of agrarian mythology in the USA is by Henry Nash Smith in *Virgin Land: The American West as Symbol and Myth* (1950). Also very important is Richard Hofstadter's *The Age of Reform* (1955). Good general introductions include G.C. Fite's *American Agriculture and Farm Policy Since 1900* (1967), B.L. Gardner's *The Governing of Agriculture* (1981), and H.F. Gregor's *Industrialization of US Agriculture: An Interpretive Atlas* (1982). In *The Machine in the Garden* (1964), Leo Marx considers the effect of industrialization on the agrarian myth and pastoral imagery.

M. and L. White consider the anti-urban strain in US intellectual thought in *The Intellectual versus the City* (1962). Their story is a selective one, as they ignore the radical impulse found in such works as F.C. Howe's *The City: Hope of Democracy* (1905). In *The Urban Wilderness* (1972), Sam Bass Warner, jun. presents a lively general history of the American city; see also Page Smith's *As a City upon a Hill: The Town in American History* (1966). In *Back to Nature* (1969), P.J. Schmitt looks at the arcadian myth in urban America. In *Cities of Tomorrow* (1989), Peter Hall looks at the impulses for urban reform.

Australia

The best single source is the ten-volume, including atlas, *Australians: A Historical Library* (1987). The volumes contain a range of contributions and are very well illustrated. The volumes dealing with the pre-1788 and early colonial periods are easily the best. J.M. Powell has been a persistent analyst of the Australian landscape; have a look at his *An Historical Geography of Modern Australia: The Restive Fringe* (1988).

Australia has been fortunate in having two historians who write marvellously well. There are some who disagree with the political opinions of Geoffrey Blainey but as an academic writing for a popular audience he has few equals. For our purposes, read the impressive trilogy *The Tyranny of Distance* (1966), *The Triumph of the Nomads* (1975) and *A Land Half Won* (1980). Manning Clark is Australia's foremost historian. His *A History of Australia* has appeared in various volumes since 1962. Amongst the younger generations, Richard White, with *Inventing Australia* (1981), is one of the most impressive.

On the early colonial period, Robert Hughes reached a wide audience with *The Fatal Shore* (1986). In *The Road to Botany Bay* (1987), Paul Carter provides a spatial history of the early years of European discovery and colonization. The novelist Thomas Keneally has written a useful account of the interior in *Outback* (1983). Concern with preserving the wilderness can be found in Judith Wright's *Wilderness, Waste and History* (Australian Habitat, vol. 8), and in *Fighting for Wilderness* (1984) edited by J.G. Mosely and J. Messer.

The push into the bush is the subject of Eric Rolls' *A Million Wild Acres* (1981). In *Life in the Country* (1973), Michael Cannon documents the life in rural Australia. In *The Other Side of the Frontier* (1981), Henry Reynolds examines Aboriginal resistance, while in *The Real Matilda* (1983) Miriam Dixon considers the role of women. The ideology of the rural is well covered by B.D. Graham's *The Formation of Australian Country Parties* (1966) and Don Aitkin's 'Countrymindedness: the spread of an idea' (Australian Cultural History, no. 4, 1985).

Histories of urban Australia include Michael Cannon's *Life in the Cities* (1983) and Max Neutze's 'City, country, town: Australian peculiarities' (Australian Cultural History, no. 4, 1985). Perhaps the single most influential book on urban Australia is Hugh Streeton's *Ideas for Australian Cities* (rev. edn 1975). On the early history of Canberra, see Roger Pegrum's *The Bush Capital* (1984). The Garden City movement in Australia is extensively covered in Robert Freestone's *Model Communities* (1989).

TEXTS

One of the most influential, and certainly one of the more readable, cultural analysts is Roland Barthes. In a series of books he has increased our knowledge of texts, their interpretation, status and significance. I have already quoted his book *Mythologies*; also have a look at *S-Z* (1974), *The Pleasure of the Text* (1975) and *Image–Music–Text* (1977). Of the more specifically literary analysts, Umberto Eco is always worth a read; see his *The Role of the Reader* (1979) and *Semiotics and the Philosophy of Language* (1984). An enjoyable way to discover the arguments in the world of literary theory is to read some of the novels of David Lodge. He is a novelist but used to be a professor of English. For our purposes, his most relevant works are *Changing Places* (1975), *Small World* (1984) and *Nice Work* (1988). These books embody the recent history of literary theory, the changing academic fashions and alternative readings of texts. They are also a very good read.

The novel

To put the novels of Chapter 7 in a wide context, have a look at *An Illustrated Companion to World Literature* (1986), edited by Peter Quennel from the original by Tore Zetterholm, and *The Oxford Illustrated History of English Literature* (1987) edited by Pat Rogers.

Information on (dead) authors is available in the *National Dictionary of Biography*. There are whole libraries of books devoted to the selected authors. There is, however, no substitute for reading the original novels.

The western

General introductions to the cinema include G. Must's *A Short History of the Movies* (1981) and the excellent book from the British Film Institute, *The Cinema Book* (1985). Barry Norman's *Talking Pictures* (1987) provides a very readable general introduction to Hollywood and I can warmly recommend William Goldman's *Adventures in the Screen Trade* (1984) as one of the best books on the dynamics of how and why movies are made; it is an excellent read. The relationship between American society and American movies is covered by *The American Film Industry* (1985) edited by T. Balio, Keith Reader's *Cultures on Celluloid* (1981), Robert Sklar's *Movie-Made America* (1978) and *American Film and Society Since*

1945 (1984) by L. Quart and A. Anster. More theoretical analyses include V.F. Perkins' *Film as Film* (1972) and Peter Wollen's *Signs and Meanings in the Cinema* (1972). The contemporary debates can be followed in the many film journals: see *Screen, Sight and Sound, Film Comment* and *Film Quarterly*. General introductions to the western include Philip French's *Westerns* (1977) and two excellent books from Phil Hardy, *The Western* (1983) and *Encyclopedia of Western Movies* (1985). In *The War, the West and the Wilderness* (1979), Kevin Brownlow gives an introduction to the early westerns of Hollywood. A more intellectual analysis of the western can be found in Jim Kitses' *Horizons West* (1969) and in the explicitly structuralist reading by Will Wright, *Six Guns and Society* (1975). Wright is an influential writer on the western and for an assessment see the article, 'The American Western and American Society' by Christopher Fraying, in the edited book by P. Davies and B. Neve, *Cinema, Politics and Society in America* (1981). Amongst the many books on John Ford, have a look at Peter Bogdanovitch's *John Ford* (1968), Andrew Sinclair's *John Ford* (1979) and the more intimate and revealing book by his grandson, Dan Ford, *The Unquiet Man: The Life of John Ford* (1979).

There is, of course, no substitute for actually watching the movies. Useful guides are Leslie Halliwell's *Filmgoer's Companion* and his *Film Guide*. My copies are dated respectively 1979 and 1987 though there are more recent editions.

Landscape painting

In *Ways of Seeing* (1972), John Berger provides an interesting angle of vision. Kenneth Clark's *Landscape into Art* (1949) is a well-written introduction to the subject although it lacks any sensitivity to the social context of art production and consumption. John Barrell's *The Dark Side of the Landscape* (1980) and Micheal Rosenthal's *British Landscape Painting* (1982) are examples of a more radical perspective which is sensitive to questions of power and social conflict.

General introductions to painting in Australia include the books of Bernard Smith, *Australian Painting* (1971) and *European Vision and the South Pacific* (1986), and Robert Hughes, *The Art of Australia* (1970).

Individual artists and particular schools are covered in the following selection: John McPhee *The Art of John Glover* (1980); Candice Bruce *Eugen von Guérard** (1980); Jane Clark and Bridget Whitelaw *Golden Summers: Heidelberg and Beyond** (1985); Lou Klepac *Russell Drysdale* (1983); Patrick McCaughey *Fred Williams* (1980); Jennifer Isaacs *Australian Dreaming: 40,000 Years of Aboriginal History* (1980) and *Australia's Living Heritage* (1984).

* Exhibition catalogue

A painful fact of life is that one cannot please everyone. To my anonymous reviewer, I apologize for the lack of a concluding chapter. I hope that this guide, introduction and conclusion combined, fills the gap. However, I have to inform the reviewer that at some time or another everything, including this book, just ends.

Bibliography

Aitkin, D. (1973) 'The Australian Country Party', in Mayer, H. and Nelson, H. (eds) *Australian Politics: A Third Reader*, Cheshire Publishing, Melbourne.

Allen, C. (1975) *Plain Tales from the Raj*, André Deutsch/BBC, London.

Allen, C. (1979) *Tales from the Dark Continent*, André Deutsch/BBC, London.

Astbury, L. (1985) *City Bushmen: The Heidelberg School and the Rural Mythology*, Oxford University Press, Melbourne.

Baldwin, J. (1962) *Another Country*, Penguin, Harmondsworth.

Bell, C. and Bell, R. (1972) *City Fathers: The Early History of Town Planning in Britain*, Penguin, Harmondsworth.

Bennett, J.D. (1975) *Frederick Jackson Turner*, Twayne Publishers, Boston.

Billington, R.A. (1973) *Frederick Jackson Turner: Historian, Scholar, Teacher*, Oxford University Press, New York.

Blow, S. (1987) *Broken Blood: The Rise and Fall of the Tennant Family*, Faber, London.

Bogdanovitch, P. (1968) *John Ford*, University of California Press, Berkeley and Los Angeles.

Boyd, R. (1980 2nd rev. ed.) *The Australian Ugliness*, Penguin, Harmondsworth.

Bridgeman, H.A. (1902) 'The suburbanite', *The Independent* 54: 862–4.

Brown, D. (1970) *Bury My Heart at Wounded Knee*, Chatto & Windus, London.

Burchfield, R. (1985) *The English Language*, Oxford University Press, Oxford.

Canberra Times (1985) 'The greatest Australian paintings', *Canberra Times, Good Weekend Magazine*, 8 September.

Cannon, M. (1973) *Life in the Country*, Thomas Nelson, West Melbourne.

Carpenter, R.M. (1983) *The Eloquence of Frederick Jackson Turner*, Huntingdon Library, San Marino, California.

Carrington, C.E. (1956) *The Life of Rudyard Kipling*, Macmillan, London.

Carson, R. (1962) *Silent Spring*, Houghton Mifflin, Boston.

Coleman, B.I. (ed.) (1973) *The Idea of the City in Nineteenth Century Britain*, Routledge & Kegan Paul, London.

Columbia University (1896) *Dedicating the New Site, Morningside Heights*, Saturday, 2 May, New York.

Cook, J. (1955) *The Journals of Captain James Cook*, vol. 1, edited by J.C. Beaglehole, Hakluyt Society, Cambridge.

Corrigan, P. (1985) Untitled, in Johnson, C. (ed.) *The City in Conflict*, Law Book Co., Sydney.

Crowley, F.K. (1973) *Modern Australia in Documents: Vol. 1 1901–1939*, Wren, Melbourne.

Daiches, D. (1981) *Robert Burns*, Spurbooks, Edinburgh.

Dampier, W.A. (1927) *A New Voyage Round the World*, edited by N.M. Penzer.

Davidson, J. (ed.) (1986) *The Sydney-Melbourne Book*, George Allen & Unwin, North Sydney.
Dijksterhuis, E.J. (1969) *The Mechanization of the World Picture*, Oxford University Press, Oxford.
Dixon, M. (1983) *The Real Matilda*, Penguin, Ringwood, Victoria.
Drabble, M. (1979) *A Writer's Britain: Landscape in Literature*, Thames & Hudson, London.
Essien-Udom, E.U. (1966) *Black Nationalism*, Penguin, Harmondsworth.
Facey, A.B. (1981) *A Fortunate Life*, Penguin, Ringwood, Victoria.
Fedden, R. and Joekes, R. (1973) *The National Trust Guide*, Jonathan Cape, London.
Ford, D. (1979) *The Unquiet Man: The Life of John Ford*, William Kimber, London.
Freestone, R. (1984) 'The Australian Garden City', unpublished Ph.D. thesis, Macquarie University.
Friedland, R. (1982) *Power and Crisis in the City*, Macmillan, London.
Galbraith, K. (1977) *The Age of Uncertainty*, André Deutsch/BBC, London.
Gans, M. (1962) *The Urban Villagers*, Free Press of Glencoe, New York.
Girouard, M. (1985) *Cities and People*, Yale University Press, New Haven and London.
Goldman, W. (1984) *Adventures in the Screen Trade*, Macdonald, London.
Goldschmidt, W. (1978) *As You Sow: Three Studies in the Social Consequences of Agriculture*, Allanheld, Osmun, Montclair, NJ.
Graber, L.M. (1976) *Wilderness as Sacred Space*, Monograph Series of Association of American Geographers, no.8, Washington DC.
Grant, M. (1979) *Latin Literature: An Anthology*, Penguin, Harmondsworth.
Hall, S., Cricher, C., Jefferson, T., Clarke, J. and Roberts, R. (1978) *Policing the Crisis: Mugging, the State and Law and Order*, Macmillan, London and Basingstoke.
Hammond, J.L. and Hammond, B. (1948, first pub. 1911) *The Village Labourer*, Longman, Green & Co., London.
Heizer, R.F. and Elsasser, A.B. (1980) *The Natural World of the California Indians*, University of California Press, Berkeley and Los Angeles.
Hine, R.V. (1984) *The American West*, Little, Brown & Co., Boston.
Hofstadter, R. (1955) *The Age of Reform*, Random, New York.
Hofstadter, R. (1970) *The Progressive Historians: Turner, Beard, Parrington*, Vintage Books, New York.
Hopkins, H. (1986) *The Long Affray: The Poaching Wars in Britain 1760–1914*, Secker & Warburg, London.
Hughes, R. (1970 rev. ed.) *The Art of Australia*, Penguin, Harmondsworth.
Huizinga, J. (1954, first pub. in English 1924) *The Waning of the Middle Ages*, Doubleday, New York.
Jacobs, W.R. (1968) *The Historical World of Frederick Jackson Turner*, Yale, University Press, New Haven.
James, H. (1893) *Essays on London and Elsewhere*, London.
Johnstone, P.H. (1937) 'In praise of husbandry', *Agricultural History*, 11: 80–95.
Kagan, P. (1975) *New World Utopias*, Penguin, New York.
Katz, W.L. (1971) *The Black West*, Doubleday, New York.
Kemeny, J. (1983) *The Great Australian Nightmare*, Georgian House, Melbourne.
Keneally, T. (1983) *Outback*, Hodder & Stoughton, London.
Kirk, W (1963) 'Problems of geography', *Geography* 48: 357–71.
Kitses, J. (1969) *Horizons West*, Thames & Hudson, London.
Klare, M.T. (1969) 'The architecture of imperial America', *Science and Society* 33: 257–84.

Klepac, L. (1983) *Russell Drysdale*, Bay Books, Sydney.

Kolodny, A. (1975) *The Lay of the Land*, University of North Carolina Press, Chapel Hill.

Kolodny, A. (1984) *The Land Before Her: Fantasy and Experiences of the American Frontier 1630–1800*, University of North Carolina Press, Chapel Hill.

Lane, B.M. (1968) *Architecture and Politics in Germany, 1918–1945*, Harvard University Press, Cambridge, Mass.

Lansbury, C. (1970) *Arcady in Australia*, Melbourne University Press, Melbourne.

Lovejoy, A. and Boas, A. (1935) *Primitivism and Related Ideas in Antiquity*, Johns Hopkins Press, Baltimore.

Lubove, R. (1962) *The Progessives and the Slums: Tenement House Reform in New York City 1890–1917*, University of Pittsburg Press, Pittsburg, California.

Lubove, R. (1969) *Twentieth Century Pittsburg: Government, Business and Environmental Change*, John Wiley, New York.

McPhee, J. (1980) *The Art of John Glover*, Macmillan, South Melbourne.

Mainwaring, E.W. (1925) *Italian Landscape in Eighteenth Century England*, Oxford University Press, New York.

Marsh, G.P. (1965) *Man and Nature*, edited by D. Lowenthal, Harvard University Press, Cambridge, Mass.

Martin, C. (1978) *Keepers of the Game*, University of California Press, Berkeley and Los Angeles.

Marx, K. and Engels, F. (1968) *Selected Works*, Progress Publishers, Moscow.

Marx, L. (1964) *The Machine in the Garden: Technology and the Pastoral Ideal in America*, Oxford University Press, New York.

Massey, D. and Catalano, A. (1978) *Capital and Land: Landownership and Capital in Great Britain*, Edward Arnold, London.

Meek, D.E. (1987) ' "The Land Question Answered from the Bible": the land issue and the development of a Highland theology of liberation', *Scottish Geographical Magazine* 103: 84–89.

Merchant, C. (1980) *The Death of Nature*, Wildwood, London.

Mitchell, L.C. (1981) *Witnesses to a Vanishing America*, Princeton University Press, Princeton, NJ.

Moseley, M.J. (1984) 'Conflict and change in the countryside', in Short, J.R. and Kirby, A. (eds) *The Human Geography of Contemporary Britain*, Macmillan, Basingstoke.

Mumford, L. (1961) *The City in History*, Secker & Warburg, London.

Myers, S.L. (1982) *Western Women and the Frontier Experience 1800–1915*, University of New Mexico Press, Albuquerque.

Nairn, T. (1977) *The Break-up of Britain*, New Left Books, London.

Nash, G.B. (1979) *The Urban Crucible: Social Change, Political Consciousness and the Origin of the American Revolution*, Harvard University Press, Cambridge, Mass.

Nash, R. (1982) *Wilderness and the American Mind*, Yale University Press, New Haven.

Newby, H. (1979) *Green and Pleasant Land? Social Change in Rural England*, Hutchinson, London.

Nicholson, M.H. (1959) *Mountain Gloom and Mountain Glory: The Development of the Aesthetics of the Infinite*, Cornell University Press, Ithaca.

Noble, D.W. (1965) *Historians Against History: The Frontier Thesis and the National Covenant in American Historical Writing Since 1830*, University of Minnesota Press, Minneapolis.

Onslow, S.M. (ed.) (1973) *The Macarthurs of Camden*, Rigby, Sydney.

Park, R.E. (1952) *Human Communities: The City and Human Ecology*, Glencoe Press, Illinois.

Pearson, G. (1975) *The Deviant Imagination*, Macmillan, London and Basingstoke.
Pearson, G. (1983) *Hooligan: A History of Respectable Fears*, Macmillan, London and Basingstoke.
Pegrum, R. (1983) *The Bush Capital: How Australia chose Canberra as its federal city*, Hale & Iremonger, Sydney.
Perera, S. (1988) 'Love it, loathe it.',*The Guardian*, 26 October 1988.
Perrott, R. (1968) *The Aristocrats*, Weidenfeld & Nicholson, London.
Peterson, M.D. (ed.) (1975) *The Portable Thomas Jefferson*, Viking, New York.
Peterson, N. (1981) 'Art of the desert', in *Aboriginal Australia*, Australia Gallery Director's Council, Sydney.
Pocock, G.N. (undated) *Some English Diarists*, Dent, London.
Porter, K.W. (1971) *The Negro on the American Frontier*, Arno, New York.
Prynn, D. (1976) 'The Clarion Clubs, Rambling and Holiday Associations in Britain since the 1890s', *Journal of Contemporary History* 11: 65–77.
Raban, J. (1974) *Soft City*, Hamish Hamilton, London.
Reich, R. (1982) *The Next American Frontier*, Times Books, New York.
Reynolds, H. (1981) *The Other Side of the Frontier*, James Cook University of North Queensland.
Robson, L. (1985) *A Short History of Tasmania*, Oxford University Press, Melbourne.
Roddewig, R.J. (1978) *Green Bans: The Birth of Australian Environmental Politics*, Hale & Iremonger, Sydney.
Rothblatt, D., Sprague, J. and Garr, D. (1979) *The Suburban Environment and Women*, Praeger, New York.
Rude, G. (1972) *Europe in the Eighteenth Century*, Weidenfeld & Nicholson, London.
Ruskin, J. (1884) *St Mark's Rest: The History of Venice*, George Allen, Kent.
Said, E. (1978) *Orientalism*, Pantheon, New York.
Saloutos, T. and Hicks, J.D. (1951) *Agricultural Discontent in the Middle West, 1900–1939*, University of Wisconsin Press, Madison.
Sartre, J.P. (1964) *The Problem of Method*, Methuen, Andover.
Schlesinger, jun., A.M. (1965) *A Thousand Days: John F. Kennedy in the White House*, Houghton Mifflin, Boston.
Sharp, T. (1932) *Town and Countryside: Some Aspects of Urban and Regional Development*, Oxford University Press, Oxford.
Shoard, M. (1980) *The Theft of the Countryside*, Temple Smith, London.
Shoard, M. (1987) *This Land is Our Land: The Struggle for Britain's Countryside*, Paladin Grafton, London.
Short, J.R. (1989) *The Humane City: Cities As If People Really Mattered*, Basil Blackwell, Oxford.
Simmel, G. (1950) *The Sociology of George Simmel*, edited by K.M. Wolff, Free Press, New York.
Slotkin, R. (1973) *Regeneration Through Violence: The Mythology of the American Frontier, 1600–1800*, Wesleyan University Press, Middletown, Conn.
Slotkin, R. (1985) *The Fatal Environment: The Myth of the Frontier in the Age of Industrialization 1800–1890*, Atheneum, New York.
Smith, B. (1962) *Australian Painting*, Oxford University Press, Melbourne.
Smith, H.N. (1950) *Virgin Land: The American West as Symbol and Myth*, Harvard University Press, Cambridge, Mass.
Smith, N. (1986) 'Gentrification, the frontier and the restructuring of urban space', in Smith, N. and Williams, P. (eds) *Gentrification of the City*, Allen & Unwin, London.
Smith, P. (1984) *The Rise of Industrial America*, vol. 6, McGraw Hill, New York.

Stone, L. and Stone, J.C.F. (1984) *An Open Elite? England 1540–1880*, Clarendon Press, Oxford.

Streeton, H. (1971) *Ideas for Australian Cities*, Georgian House, Melbourne.

Strong, J. (1885) *Our Country: Its Possible Future and its Present Origins*, Baker & Taylor, New York.

Summers, A. (1975) *Damned Whores and God's Police: The Colonization of Women in Australia*, Penguin, Harmondsworth.

Thomas, K. (1983) *Man and the Natural World*, Allen Lane, London.

Thompson, E.P. (1971) 'The moral economy of the crowd in the eighteenth century', *Past and Present* 50: 76–136.

Thompson, F.M.L. (1963) *English Landed Society in the Nineteenth Century*, Routledge & Kegan Paul, London.

Tocqueville, Alexis de (1835) *Democracy in America*, 2 vols, New York.

Trudgill, S. (1983) *Sociolinguistics: An Introduction to Language and Society*, Penguin, Harmondsworth.

Tuan, Y.F. (1979) *Landscapes of Fear*, Basil Blackwell, Oxford.

Turner, F.J. (1963) *The Significance of the Frontier in American History*, edited by H.P. Simonson, Ungar Publishing, New York.

Tweeten, L. (1984) *Causes and Consequences of Structural Change in the Farming Industry*, National Planning Association, Washington, DC.

Venturi, R., Brown, D.S. and Izenour, S. (1972) *Learning from Las Vegas*, Harvard University Press, Cambridge, Mass.

Vogeler, I. (1981) *The Myth of the Family Farm: Agribusiness Dominance of US Agriculture*, Westview Press, Boulder, Colorado.

Wakstein, A.M. (ed.) (1970) *The Urbanization of America: An Historical Anthology*, Houghton Mifflin, Boston.

Ward, D. (1971) *Cities and Immigrants*, Oxford University Press, New York.

Ward, R. (1958) *The Australian Legend*, Oxford University Press, Melbourne.

Watson, S. and Helliwell, C. (1985) 'Home ownership: are women excluded?', *Australian Quarterly* 57: 21–31.

Webb, W.P. (1937) *Divided We Stand: The Crisis of a Frontierless Democracy*, Farrer & Rinehart, New York.

White, Jr, L. (1967) 'The historical roots of our ecological crisis', *Science* 155: 1203–7.

White, M. and White, L. (1962) *The Intellectual versus the City*, Harvard University and MIT Press, Cambridge, Mass.

White, R. (1981) *Inventing Australia*, George Allen & Unwin, North Sydney.

Williams, G.H. (1962) *Wilderness and Paradise in Christian Thought*, Harper & Brothers, New York.

Williams, R. (1973) *The Country and the City*, Chatto & Windus, London.

Williams, W.A. (1969) *The Roots of the Modern American Empire* Random House, New York.

Williams, W.A. (ed.) (1972) *From Colony to Empire*, John Wiley, London.

Wolfe, T. (1980) *The Right Stuff*, Jonathan Cape, London.

Index